PRAISE FOR

Building Co-operative Power!

"Within hours of being given *Building Co-operative Power* I was devouring its content. The book is beautifully written, attractively presented and describes the impactful journey of worker cooperatives throughout the Connecticut River Valley. The authors honestly detail a number of the issues such as decision making that ask ordinary people to think differently about power.

The book does a good job of highlighting what I call "clustering" which is the act of many co-ops purposefully cooperating together within a region. "Clustering" is at the heart of the success of cooperatives in Mondragon in Spain, Emilia Romagna in Italy and the early beginnings of the modern co-op movement in Rochdale, England.

What is most valuable about the book is that it uses stories about real worker co-operatives in today's America to make its case. And in doing so it is a welcome gift to the writing about co-operatives that are changing the world in which we live into the world we want to live in."

— *David J. Thompson*, President, Twin Pines Cooperative Foundation;
author *Weavers of Dreams: Founders of the Modern Cooperative Movement.*

"Creating a cooperative and community-sustaining economy means moving beyond isolated projects to larger ecosystems of support and collaboration designed to foster change at a municipal and regional level. *Building Co-operative Power* is an important contribution to this essential work. It begins with detailed accounts of the day-to-day process of building a sustainable culture of community in single democratic workplaces. It then goes further, tracing the inspiring ways in which these autonomous projects chose to come together to leverage their collective assets in order to build a new kind of regional economy. The authors rightly suggest that the models of worker, consumer, and producer co-ops remain largely invisible in the press and the academy. However, this goes double for the vital work of the new emerging regional cooperative institutions like the Valley Alliance of Worker Cooperatives. That makes this behind-the-scenes look into the organizing process they offer here a valuable and rare resource for organizers and communities engaged in the work of democratizing wealth."

— *Gar Alperovitz*, Professor of Political Economy at the University of Maryland and author of *What Then Must We Do? Democratizing Wealth and Building a Community Sustaining Economy From the Ground Up*

"*Building Co-operative Power* is an important and ambitious work. The movement in the Connecticut River Valley, as laid out beautifully in this book, is a model for regional cooperative thinking and planning, and should be an inspiration to people and activists around the world. In this book, the authors explore the cooperative organizing process from a multitude of levels and in ever-widening circles: locally, regionally, and in the larger world. They discuss the nuts and bolts of why cooperatives are of vital importance in creating a successful, humane world where our grandchildren can thrive. They explore the problems and triumphs of cooperatives, through unflinching, yet visionary eyes. They provide valuable historical contexts. In the course of their exploration, they visit a great variety of co-ops in the Connecticut River Valley region, and discuss their successes and problems unflinchingly. This type of on-the-ground regional thinking is a key to developing cooperative networks that are deep and sustainable. This book makes important contributions to our understanding of how to continue laying the groundwork for a constructive future based on the expansion of regional cooperative development. Building Co-operative Power is highly readable, and at the same time is an essential reference work for anyone interested in cooperatives and the cooperative movement."

— *John Curl*, professional woodworker and thirty-year member of
Heartwood Co-operative Workshop and author of
*For all the People: Uncovering the Hidden History of Cooperation,
Cooperative Movements and Communalism in America*

"A thoughtful, inspiring account of the nitty-gritty process of building a democratic economy from the bottom up. Read it and cooperate!"

— *Nancy Folbre*, Professor of Economics University of Massachusetts
and author of *Greed, Lust and Gender: A History of Economic Ideas*

"Building Cooperative Power is a must read for anyone who wants to take back the economy for people and the planet! It presents inspiring real life stories of worker-cooperatives and puts the faces on everyday heroes who are forging good lives in economically and ecologically responsible ways. It documents a quiet revolution that has been taking place in the Connecticut River Valley where for decades groups of people have experimented with a radically different business model. The diversity of cooperatives, the ingenuity of enterprise strategies, and the humane care for self, others and environments showcased in this book is impressive, instructive and visionary."

— *J.K. Gibson-Graham*, Institute for Culture and
Society, University of Western Sydney, author of
The End of Capitalism (as we knew it) and *A Postcapitalist Politics*

"I enjoyed reading the book for several reasons: the many good co-op examples, including examples of cooperation among co-ops; the emphasis on regional cooperation; the broader analysis of cooperation (and its invisibility) in our economy; but most of all for its enthusiasm and strategic thinking about building cooperative power in the future. I think the book has value as both an educational resource and as a very useful means to help people organize co-ops and co-op communities.

— *E. G. Nadeau*, Head of the Overseas Co-operative Development
Council and author of *The Cooperative Solution*
and co-author of *Cooperation Works!*

BUILDING CO-OPERATIVE POWER

Stories and Strategies from Worker-Cooperatives in the Connecticut River Valley

Janelle Cornwell
Michael Johnson & Adam Trott
with Julie Graham

Levellers Press

AMHERST, MASSACHUSETTS

Cover design: Design Action Collective

Photography courtesy of Rebekah Hanlon,
Derek Goodwin, Collective Copies
and Simple Diaper & Linen

Published by *Levellers Press*, Amherst, Massachusetts

Printed in the United States of America

ISBN 978-1-937146-46-7

Dedicated to Julie Graham

Contents

Acknowledgments

WE WOULD FIRST LIKE TO THANK CO-OPERATORS of the Connecticut River Valley and the greater area of Western New England. Without them the co-operative movement in our region and this book about it would not exist. We are most grateful to the Valley Alliance of Worker Co-operatives and its member representatives especially Libby Garofalo, Angie Gregory, Rebekah Hanlon, Alex Jarrett, Seth Mellen, Leah Mutz, Kim Pinkham, Phillipe Rigollaud, Charles Strader, Steve Strimer, Brian Van Slyke, Anasuya Weil, Ruthy Woodring and Randy Zucco, who welcomed us in meetings and social events as friends, participants and researchers. Great thanks to Margaret Atkinson, Erika Arthur, Javiera Benevente, George Brace, Jay Casssano, Erbin Crowell, Bruce Davidson, Jen Gallant, Bob Gardner, Mitch Gaslin, Dave Gerrat, Cory Greenberg, Jen Gutshall, Gail Hanes, Katcha Hahn d'Errico, Hugh Harwell, Louis Hasbrouck, Gayton Hebert, Mary Hoyer, Jonathan Leighton, Dick McLeester, Tim McNerne, Rachel McLean, Terry Mollner, Stephen Roy, Brian Sable, Anne Saint Jean, Caleb Wetmore, and last, but definitely not least, Suzette Snow-Cobb whose stories and work also inspired this book.

We are very grateful to the members and former members (some of whom are mentioned by name above) of Brattleboro Holistic Health Center, Collective Copies, Common Wealth Printing, Coop 108, GAIA Host Collective, Green Mountain Spinnery, Pedal People, PV Squared, Simple Diaper & Linen, TESA, and Valley Green Feast, for contributing profiles of their co-operatives.

Special thanks to the people who read early and late drafts of the manuscript and offered their wonderful feedback: Za Barron, Claire Brault, Olivia Geiger, Katherine Gibson, Cristina Grasseni, Olivia Geiger, Stephen Healy, Oona Morrow and Cordelia Sand from the Community Economies Collective; Erbin Crowell and Bonnie Hudspeth from the Neighboring Food Co-op Association; Cheyenna Weber from Solidarity NYC, as well as Gar Alperovitz, Steve Dubb, Nancy Folbre, Ana Margarida Esteves, E.G. Nadeau, and Clark Dougan from the University of Massachusetts Press for their time, thoughtful perspectives and encouragement.

We would like to extend our deepest gratitude to Alfie Graham, Sharon Livesey and again to Katherine Gibson for financing this project with Julie Graham's bequest. We are also very thankful to CHS for a generous Co-operative Education grant and to the Co-operative Foundation's grant for Research in Co-operatives. Funding from CHS and the Cooperative Foundation enabled us to complete this project. Special thanks to Jessica Gordon-Nembhard and Jim Johnson for their support and collaboration with the Ecological Democracy Institute of North America. We would like to thank the Department of Geosciences at the University of Massachusetts for funding an assistantship at the early stages of this research. We are also deeply thankful to the Ganas Community, which covered all of Michael's research expenses and the Sirius Community, which provided him with housing and support during the first year of his research.

We are grateful to Food For Thought Books for hosting a fundraiser in 2009, Levellers Press for contributing a republication of *No Bosses Here* as well as the generous supporters in the Valley who attended that event and whose pre-purchases of the book paid for interview transcriptions: Apple Ahearn, Erika Arthur, Joan Barberich, Bellingham Bay Builders, Tom Chans, Grace Cox, Lisa Depiano, Leslie Fraser, Mitch Gaslin, Julie Graham, Melisa Hoover, Mary Hoyer, Tim Huet, Adam Hurter, Amy Jackendoff, Ethan B. Jackson, Alex Jarrett, Sharon Livesey, Gabor Luuacs, Dick McLeester and Vision Works, Molly Merrett, Janel Nockleby, Phillipe Rigollaud, AnnaMarie Russo, Brian Sable, Suzette Snow-Cobb, Maggie Shar and the Franklin Community Co-operative. We are so thankful for their support. Lastly thanks to Steve Strimer who planted the seed in 2006 that grew into this book, and whose faith in it will bring it into being through Levellers Press.

We accept full blame for mistakes, opinions and misinformation published in this book, however, any value is credited to a truly collaborative effort involving the many people mentioned above and others who we are sadly but surely leaving out.

INTRODUCTION

Building Co-operative Power!

THIS BOOK IS FOR EVERYONE who currently is, formerly was, or hopes to become a member in a worker co-operative. It's for members of all kinds of co-operatives everywhere including food co-operatives, credit unions, energy and water co-ops and agricultural producer co-operatives. It is for anyone who is curious about worker and other kinds of co-operatives, for those who want to know more about co-ops in the Connecticut River Valley and anyone interested in creating an economy that puts people and the planet before profit.

In 280 action-provoking pages, we introduce the history and concept of worker co-operation. We relay the past and present stories of Valley worker co-operatives (in their own words) including cautionary tales and sagas of personal transformation. We offer brief practical essays on topics like co-op governance and managing conflict, and outline a vision of building a fully co-operative regional economy in the Connecticut River Valley of Western Massachusetts and Southern Vermont. Actually, we do a lot of other things too—you'll find those hidden treasures as you read along. At the end you'll also find a history of co-operation in New England contributed by John Curl.

Why write a book about worker co-operatives now?

Three reasons: First of all, we face global economic and eco-logical crises that threaten the survival of all creatures and eco-systems worldwide. The co-operative business model has something to offer to communities and workers wanting stability and sustainability in their economic lives. While not immune to the ills that plague the larger economy, co-operatives have been remarkably resilient in the face of economic downturns, and their commitment to putting people and planet before profit makes them more likely to be "green" than regular capitalist businesses. After the 2008 economic crisis, while media and poli-ticians didn't seem to notice, co-operatives and credit unions were among "the *only* businesses to weather the storm" because they function on an entirely different model.[1]

Second, there is now a vibrant global movement for eco-nomic autonomy, justice and self-determination. Waves of this movement have come together in the World Social Forum and its national and regional offshoots, the solidarity economy move-ment, the movement for re-localization and the recent Occupy movements that are all seeking and claiming spaces for new ways of meeting our economic needs. The worker co-operative movement is an active participant in the global push to build new economies. Mondragon Co-operative Corporation's 2009 collaboration with the United Steel Workers Union sparked new interest among traditionally skeptical lefties.[2] Michael Moore's 2009 *Capitalism: A Love Story* and Avi Lewis and Naomi Klein's 2004 documentary *The Take* that shared the harrowing story of worker takeovers in the wake of Argentina's economic crisis, in-spired popular interest. We too are inspired by the Argentina Autonomista movement, and more recently, the United Nations declaration of 2012 as the International Year of Co-operatives.

Finally, there's our local and personal rationale—this book is part of an organizing project of the Valley Alliance of Worker Co-operatives (VAWC). We are raising awareness about the value and viability of creating a truly co-operative economy in Southern Vermont and Western Massachusetts. That's an economy in which co-operative businesses flourish in every sector, and individuals and co-operatives can meet all needs co-operatively. In such an economy, we believe the spirit of co-operation, democracy and economic security will permeate every economic interaction, transforming our work and our lives.

Who are we?

The authors of this book include the late Julie Graham, a former professor at the University of Massachusetts, two researchers and one worker co-op member. Under the sponsorship of the Valley Alliance of Worker Co-operatives (VAWC), we conducted some fifty interviews and attended five years of monthly meetings, conferences and social gatherings between 2005 and 2011. We didn't interview *all* co-operators in the Valley and surely some co-operators may not share the experiences of the authors or our interviewees. However, we hope to represent common themes from our interviews and common experiences of co-operation based on what we learned during research with the Valley Alliance of Worker Co-operatives. That said, we are choosing to tell particular parts of the stories we've heard. As in any piece of writing or media, the views expressed here are strictly our own (the authors).

What is VAWC?

The Valley Alliance of Worker Co-operatives (VAWC) is a co-operative of worker co-operatives based in the Connecticut River Valley and surrounding hill towns in Massachusetts and Southern Vermont. Locals often call the Massachusetts portion the "Pioneer Valley," a brand name adopted in the 1930s to promote tourism, or (as we do in this book) just "The Valley" for short. VAWC members are all worker co-operatives but they vary greatly in the products and services they offer—from providing copy and design services, publishing, and farming to the production of body oils, massage therapy, education, diaper laundry and delivery, vegetable delivery and photovoltaic panel installation. The VAWC system of co-operative businesses (which is currently made up of twelve member co-ops) has increased revenue and employment over the last three years despite an economic downturn. At the time of this writing, VAWC co-operatives employed 70 worker-members and generated more than $7 million in collective annual revenue.

VAWC's mission is to "build a sustainable local economy by facilitating the growth, development and promotion of worker co-operatives." This involves:

- **Providing support for member co-ops** including maintaining and sharing information, providing technical and organizational assistance, offering joint marketing and promotional services, developing group benefits, improving access to financial resources, strengthening ties among worker co-operatives, and developing relationships with other segments of the co-operative and labor community;

- **Developing** new worker co-operatives, helping to convert traditional businesses into worker co-ops; offering mentoring and skill-sharing to start-up co-operatives;

- **Promoting worker co-operatives** in the region through education and developing community awareness of worker co-operatives as sources of meaningful employment and economic empowerment, providers of quality goods and services, and viable alternatives to conventionally-owned and managed businesses.

That's a lot to do in the spare time of worker co-operators with full-time jobs and families! That's why in 2009, with the help of a matching grant from the Co-operative Fund of New England, VAWC developed a dues structure to pay for staff. You'll find the full story of VAWC in Chapter 7.

> *The VAWC project is moving from a social club to WOW! It's getting serious...We need to touch more people, more families, more businesses and have them understand that you deserve to have a say in your business!*
> Phillipe Rigollaud, February 24, 2009

What's in this book?

In this book, we share personal stories of co-operators and some of the experience, strategies, struggles and successes of worker co-operatives in our region. We touch on the stories of former co-operatives and co-operators who share cautionary tales about "founder's syndrome," conflict, and the costs and benefits of governing by consensus versus majority rule. We also consider the bigger picture. We explore major obstacles to building coherent co-operative economies, along with practical solutions and exciting opportunities for building co-operative economies here in the Valley and beyond.

Part I focuses on the nitty gritty. In Chapter One we offer a bit of background, history, and a definition of co-operatives by sector to lay the groundwork and get us on the same page regarding basic terminology. Chapter Two explores the personal side of working co-operatively, with common themes from our interviews including the day-to-day experience of working without a boss. In Chapter Three, we address practical strategies for making cooperation in the workplace work—*despite* difficulties.

Building Co-operative Power is based on and inspired by some fifty interviews with current and former worker-members. So you'll find the words of those co-operators peppered throughout the book. You'll also encounter a cast of characters that includes existing and former Valley co-ops. Eleven co-operative businesses contributed co-authored profiles of their workplaces. In Part II, we present them, to the extent possible, in the collective voices of the co-operatives themselves. In chronological order of establishment, we meet Common Wealth Printing, Collective Copies, (PV)², Pedal People, Green Mountain Spinnery, GAIA Host Collective, Co-op 108, Valley Green Feast, Toolbox for Education and Social Action, Brattleborro Holistic Health Center and Simple Diaper & Linen.

In Part III, we step back to look at the bigger picture. We begin in Chapter Four with an exploration of what all co-operatives across sectors—worker, producer and consumer—and industries share in common and how that common identity makes co-operatives across sectors and industries radically different from "business as usual." Chapter Five shows how the impact and viability of co-operatives as well as "the co-operative difference" has been wiped off the map of our economic imaginations. We argue that the invisibility of co-operatives has been a major obstacle to building co-operative economies and we outline the consequences of that invisibility in Chapter Six. Chapter Seven returns to the story of VAWC. We describe how VAWC is facing obstacles and taking advantage of opportunities for worker co-operation and worker co-operative development while reaching out to co-operatives across sectors to build an integrated co-operative economy in our region. Chapter Eight outlines a VAWC-inspired vision for a fully co-operative economy and introduces the Valley Co-operative Business Association (VCBA). It shares the stories of two founding VCBA members and concludes with an invitation to co-operatives across sectors in our region and beyond to initiate relationships with other co-ops.

They say that victors write history. Well, this book is evidence of daily victories spun by generations of co-operators in our region. In recounting their stories, we hope to inspire the current and next generation of co-operators and to share some of the knowledge and lessons that co-operators have shared with us about struggles and celebrations along the way. We are inspired by VAWC and with them envision an economy where a person can live the whole of their economic day co-operatively.

Notes

[1] See Restakis, J. 2010. *Humanizing the Economy: Co-operatives in the age of capital.* Society Publishers Gabriola Island, p. 9.

[2] Mondragon, the U.S. Steelworkers Union and the Ohio Employee Ownership Center announced a Union Co-op model in 2012. See http://www.uswork.org/our_union/co-ops (accessed 8/23/12).

PART ONE

The Realities of Worker Co-operatives

I

Worker Co-operatives in Historical, Sector and Pioneer Valley Contexts

THE ORIGINS OF WORKER CO-OPERATIVES CAN BE TRACED to the early days of the industrial revolution when workers recognized that factory-based work was impoverishing and exhausting them while enriching and empowering owners and investors. Underlying the co-operative movement is a vision of workers' rights to control their own labor and to enjoy the fruits of that labor, the wealth, great or small, that they produce. In capitalist enterprises, that wealth belongs to individual capitalists or to the board of directors and shareholders of the enterprise. They return a portion of it to the workers in the form of a wage and (maybe) benefits and they decide how to distribute the rest of it, paying it out to shareholders as dividends, or to high-level employees as bonuses, or investing it in developing and expanding the business. In this way, the surplus produced by workers—that portion of the wealth they produce over and above what is returned to them as compensation—goes into expanding capitalism, fueling speculation, and supporting luxurious lifestyles among people who don't work for a wage.[1] This process, in which wealth is produced by some and appropriated and distributed by others, is known as "exploitation."

From the outset, the worker co-operative movement aimed to eliminate capitalist exploitation, but it wanted to do more than that. Early co-operators hoped to democratize all the activities of business, including day-to-day decision-making and the production process itself. Perhaps the most famous of the early co-operators were the Rochdale Pioneers of England, 28 weavers and other activists who established a consumer co-operative in 1844 to supply food and other necessities of life to struggling workers and who later founded a worker co-operative in 1850 called the Rochdale Co-operative Manufacturing Society. The Rochdale Pioneers envisioned a co-operative economy with consumer, producer and worker co-operatives supplying and supporting each other. Their early worker co-op, while initially very successful, was taken over by non-co-operating shareholders (investor-owners who were not workers) and converted into a capitalist business but their other co-operative endeavors continued to thrive. Future worker co-operatives learned a great lesson from the demutualization of that early worker co-operative,[2] but it also contributed to the skepticism toward workers' self-governance that led influential late-nineteenth century-thinkers to favor consumer co-operatives over worker co-ops.[3]

Worker Co-operation in the Pioneer Valley

The Pioneer Valley has a rich history of co-operation. Since Shays' Rebellion in 1786, people here have demonstrated an intolerance for exploitation. In the appendix you can find a brief history of co-operation in the Pioneer Valley by John Curl, author of *For All the People: Uncovering the Hidden History of Co-operation, Cooperative Movements and Communalism in America*. Curl traces the co-operative history of New England back to Indian settler co-operatives, the protective unions, the National Grange, and the Northampton Association of Education and Industry, a large radical worker co-operative formed in Florence, Massachusetts in the mid-1840s.

In 1842 members of the Northampton Association established a "utopian" community organized around a communally
owned and operated silk mill. Like the co-ops of the Rochdale
Pioneers, the co-operators of the Northampton Association of
Education and Industry had many facets and goals including the
abolition of slavery, communal living, and racial and gender
equality. They governed themselves democratically according to
one member-one vote and many of the members lived above the
silk factory that they operated as a worker co-operative. Although they disbanded in 1846, approximately 120 men and
women lived and worked together for four-and-a-half years,
practicing democratic self-rule and economic self-sufficiency,
while actively pursuing the abolition of slavery. Northampton,
Massachusetts was a central hub of abolitionist activities. African-American abolitionist speaker Sojourner Truth lived and
worked at the Northampton Association for a number of years
traveling to her speaking engagements along with Frederick
Douglass and others from that home base.[4]

> *"Life is with some a mere round of frivolous occupations...,*
> *with most a hard struggle for the bare means of subsistence.*
> *The former are exempted from productive labor while they*
> *enjoy its fruits. Upon the latter is imposed a task with un-*
> *reasonable severity and inadequate compensation."*
>
> From the preamble to the constitution of
> the Northampton Association, 1842

All three co-operative sectors—consumer, producer and
worker co-operative—have a long history in the Pioneer Valley
and Western New England more broadly. Curl notes that workers established the New England Association of Farmers, Mechanics and Other Workingmen, which is said to be responsible
for the development of some forty cross-sector co-operatives in
the region. The Grange and the Knights of Labor of the late
nineteenth century were influential in New England and across

the country, moving forward the progressive agenda of workers and actively promoting co-operatives in multiple sectors. To this day, there is a high concentration of producer, consumer and worker co-operatives in the Connecticut River Valley. Of an estimated four hundred worker co-operatives nationwide, fourteen are located in the Connecticut River Valley of Western Massachusetts and Southern Vermont.

Co-operative Boom

The 1960s and '70s were a fertile time for a variety of movements in the Valley including the feminist and civil rights movements, the peace/anti-war, anti-nuke, and 'back-to-the-earth' movements. Collectivist projects developed and blossomed including food and housing co-operatives, rock bands and community gardens. Several worker co-operatives were founded during this period. Pelham Auto started up during the '70s and is still operating as worker-owned business today. Squash Trucking, established in 1973, converted to conventional ownership. Others such as Common Wealth Printing, Good Things Collective, and, most recently, Food for Thought Books, began in the '70s and closed their doors after a number of years of operation.[5]

The legacy of this era enriches downtown Amherst and UMass to this day. A number of co-operatives initiated by students and UMass staff during the '70s are still thriving and expanding. For example, the People's Market—a student-run natural food store founded in 1973—is now just one of eight student-run businesses on campus functioning under the Center for Student Businesses.[6] UMass is the only university in the country to host such student-run businesses. Students who run these eight businesses as if they were worker co-operatives report graduating with a transformed sense of work, business and themselves thanks to their co-operative work experience. Another experiment from this era is the UMass Five College Credit Union that was initiated by university students and employees and founded in 1967. It began as a relatively small collaboration but has grown into a co-operative financial institution of substantial size. By 2011, the UMass Five Credit College Credit Union had 27,000 members and managed $350 million in assets.[7]

The Western Massachusetts section of the Connecticut River Valley has a high concentration of educational institutions. Called the "Five College Area," it is home to Amherst, Smith, Mount Holyoke and Hampshire Colleges as well as to the University of Massachusetts. There are important connections between worker co-operatives and the educational infrastructure of the Five College Area. For example, part of Collective Copies' start-up capital was raised by pre-selling photocopies to university clients like the Center for Popular Economics. Food for Thought Books also had a long history of providing text books and progressive reading for university classes.

It is partly due to these long-term relationships that faculty and worker co-ops in the Valley collaborated in 2009 to establish the UMass Co-operative Enterprise Collaborative (UMCEC). Undergraduates in this program take courses in co-operative economics and win internships with local co-operatives to earn the Certificate in Applied Research in Co-operative Enterprises. The Economics Department at UMass was already one of the few heterodox economics departments in the country but, as a result of this collaboration, it now has the *only* program in the country that offers a Certificate Program on co-operatives that was co-developed and is co-managed by co-ops and faculty.

Defining co-operative sectors

Worker co-operatives are just one among several types of co-operatives. It's important to have a picture of the whole co-operative business-world which, according to the International Co-operative Alliance (ICA), has one billion members and generates $1.6 trillion in revenue worldwide. The ICA defines all of them as autonomous associations "of persons united voluntarily to

meet their common economic, social, and cultural needs and aspirations through a jointly-owned and democratically-controlled
enterprise."[8] In *Cooperation Works!: How People Are Using Co-
operative Action to Rebuild Communities and Revitalize the
Economy* (1997), E. G. Nadeau and David J. Thompson offer a
punchier definition: "A co-operative is a business owned and
controlled by the people who use or perform its services."

We can define co-operatives more specifically by providing a
typology of different co-ops. There are three basic types or "sectors" of co-operatives: consumer, producer and worker, the latter
being our primary concern in this book. There is confusion in
the literature on co-operatives between the terms "type," "sector" and "industry." Some authors use these terms interchangeably. For the sake of simplicity and clarity, we use the term "sector" in this book to denote the kind of co-operative based upon
membership: consumer, producer, or worker.[9]

The three co-operative sectors are different from one another
according to which economic actors are the voting members
(consumers, workers, or producers). Yet, all three identify as
member-owned, democratically-controlled enterprises and share
a common Co-operative Identity and set of Principles and Values. We discuss the Co-operative Principles and Values below
and they surface as a recurring theme throughout this book.
However, before going into further detail about what co-operatives share across sectors, we want to outline how they differ
from one another.[10] We believe that these cross-sector differences
offer exciting opportunities for inter-cooperation rooted in the
strength of a common Co-operative Identity.

The basic co-operative categories are sometimes confused
with the types of industry in which they operate. For example,
we say credit unions are in the banking/credit/financial services
"industry," but they participate in the consumer co-op "sector."
In consumer co-operatives, consumer-members own the enterprise (consumer-members hold the vote).

Consumer co-operatives are also called "users" co-operatives (especially in Italy) in order to distinguish the sector based on membership from the narrower category of food co-operatives which is what tends to come to mind when people in Europe think of "consumer co-operatives." Users co-operatives are synonymous with how we are using the term "consumer co-operatives;" they include food co-operatives, credit unions, energy co-ops and the like.

Consumer co-operatives give members purchasing power, enabling them to save money by buying in bulk and to set policy about what is being sold (for instance, "Do we want to sell genetically modified agricultural products or at least label them as such?"). The consumers who make up the membership decide. In some cases, members of a consumer co-operative receive an annual patronage dividend; and sometimes members bring down the cost of consumer goods by volunteering their labor.

Typical examples of consumer co-operatives are food-buying clubs and co-op grocery stores, commonly known as food co-ops. The Park Slope Food Co-op (in Brooklyn, NY) is a great example with 16,000 members, as are the food co-operatives in the Valley including the Brattleboro Food Co-operative in Brattleboro, VT; and in Western MA, the Old Creamery Co-op in Cummington, the Leverett Co-op in Leverett, River Valley Market in Northampton and the Franklin Community Co-op with stores in Shelburne Falls and Greenfield MA. Food co-ops and buying clubs are popular all over the world, especially in parts of Europe; and in Japan, 22 million people are members of food co-operatives.[11] Also included under the rubric of consumer co-operatives are **housing co-ops**, whose members own and inhabit a dwelling. There are **utility co-operatives**, whose members jointly purchase or manage telephone services or electricity, and **mutual insurance co-operatives**, where consumers pool resources to protect themselves against risks of all kinds. A **credit union** is a not-for-profit, federally insured consumer co-operative that provides lending, saving and other financial services to its members, typically offering better interest rates and terms than commercial banks.

Producer co-operatives are businesses in which people in the same trade or industry (for instance, forest products, agriculture, or arts and crafts) jointly purchase supplies and share work and storage space, equipment, or services such as accounting and marketing. Agricultural producer co-operatives are prevalent worldwide providing everything from tea and coffee to grains and vegetables. The U.S. is no exception in this with producers joining to process and market everything from milk, to grapes, orange juice, flour, corn and cranberries. A producer co-op comprised of hundreds of dairy farmers, for example, may handle the transportation, processing and marketing of dairy products in a region. Cabot Creamery is an example of a dairy co-operative in the U.S. Comprised of more than 1200 farms in New England and upstate New York. Cabot processes and markets dairy products (most notably cheddar cheeses) that are sold throughout the Northeast. In the Pioneer Valley, we have the Greenfield Farmers' Co-op providing farm, pet, garden and home supplies and, Organic Valley and our Family Farms that process and market organic milk.

In a **worker co-operative**, membership is made up of the workers of the enterprise. Worker co-operatives bring co-operation to an activity that constitutes a large part of our lives— work itself. Like other co-operatives, worker co-ops put people rather than capital and profit at the center of their business. Worker-ownership and control is the distinguishing feature of a worker co-operative enterprise. Worker co-operatives are often called "producer" co-operatives, however, we consistently use the term "worker" here because many worker co-operatives operate in services as well as in production.

Worker-members democratically determine how work is conducted, how surplus is distributed, as well as how policy is set and day-to-day decisions are made. Worker co-operatives are special in that the source of worker livelihood and the products and services delivered are all created through a process of co-operation rather than through bosses or distant CEOs giving orders for others to follow.

Worker co-operatives empower workers to set the terms of their work environment, including how they will govern themselves, manage their finances and develop their business. Worldwide, they exist over the full range of industries from agriculture, construction and manufacturing to wholesale and retail trade. In the Valley, worker co-ops are active in auto repair, photocopying, production and marketing body oils, photovoltaic panel installation, publishing, waste removal, vegetable delivery, retail book sales, laundering, education and health care.

Some co-operative enterprises have "hybrid" structures so that membership is made up of more than one of these three stakeholder categories. For example, Fedco Seeds of Maine and Weaver Street Market in North Carolina have both consumer and worker-membership. The board elected to govern the co-operative has representatives from both the consumer and the worker side. Mondragon's Ersoki food co-operatives have also structured themselves as hybrids with 50/50 worker/consumer representation and a consumer president.

Together, consumer, producer and worker co-ops comprise a substantial portion of the world economy. According to the ICA, they provide 100 million jobs worldwide. That's twenty percent more than multinational corporations! They involve one billion people as members. All co-operatives share the one member-one vote governance structure, and while decision-making is often consensus-based in smaller co-operatives (especially small worker co-operatives), decisions are generally made by majority rule in larger ones. Co-ops distribute surplus to members, in the form of patronage, based on the amount transacted or hours worked, rather than on amount of equity invested—this is called "benefits proportional to use." Co-ops offer limited returns because members "buy into" or invest in co-ops to enable the co-op to produce or serve, rather than simply make profit. In the chapters that follow, we discuss and clarify the meaning of terms like "equity," "buy-in," "surplus" and "profit."

> *More than one billion people around the world belong to co-operatives, and at least 100 million are employed by co-ops. More often than you probably realize, co-ops play a vital part in your everyday life.*
> Valley Co-operative Business Association[12]

Since the mid-twentieth century in the U.S., consumer, producer and worker co-operatives have been relatively isolated from one another. This is called "sectoralization" and it is a great misfortune for the co-operative movement because it severely limits the potential of interconnection and co-operative capital investment. Resources get locked up in silos, rather than being invested and shared among co-operatives, flowing between areas of surplus, need and opportunity.

In the Pioneer Valley, however, a major effort is underway to reverse this trend, moving toward collaboration and recognizing the shared advantages of the co-operative model as a whole. Worker and food co-operatives in our region are following the examples set by the Basque region of Spain and the Emilia Romagna region of Northern Italy. For example, New England food co-ops have formed the Neighboring Food Co-op Association just as worker co-ops in our region have formed the Valley Alliance of Worker Co-operatives. These associations (which you can read about in greater detail in Chapters Seven and Eight) are pooling surpluses within their sectors for the purpose of development and education, and they are co-operating across sectors to develop more of what a clever marketing campaign calls "co-opportunities." They are discovering exciting possibilities for development and co-operative growth through inter-cooperation based on a shared co-operative identity.[13]

Worker Co-operatives Around the World

In the U.S. context, worker co-operatives represent the smallest of three co-operative sectors. The United States Federation of Worker Co-operatives (USFWC) estimates there are 400 worker co-ops in the U.S. employing from 3000 to 5000 worker-members, concentrated in service and retail industries and accounting for over $400 million in annual revenues. They may be small in size and few in number, but worker co-op associations and networks of internal and external mutuality are highly active in the co-operative movement.

Local and regional networks like the Network of Bay Area of Worker Co-operatives (NoBAWC), Worker-Owned and Run Co-operative Network (WORC'N) of Greater Boston, the New York City Network of Worker Co-operatives (NYC NoWC), the Madison Worker Co-operatives (MadWorC) and VAWC are among the most visible and active regional associations. At the national scale, the USFWC works to support the growth and development of worker co-operatives. Regional associations like VAWC and NoBAWC are federation partners of the USFWC. The USFWC is a member of the International Organization of Industrial, Artisanal and Service Producers' Co-operatives (CICOPA), which is the worker/producer sector organization of the International Co-operative Alliance (ICA) working to unite co-operatives worldwide.

The Mondragon Co-operative Corporation (MCC), one of the largest, most integrated and widely known cross-sector co-operative complexes in the world, is located in the Basque region of Spain. It grew out of a priest's school during the lean years of post-civil-war Spain. Don Jose Maria Arizmendarrieta educated his students in co-operative economic principles and practices. After they graduated in the 1950s, five of his students founded the first Mondragon co-operative called ULGOR, a small company making cooking stoves. To help finance ULGOR's growth as well as many more co-operative businesses that would follow in its footsteps, Don Jose Maria Arizmendarrietta encouraged the community to pool their small savings into a co-operative bank that would fund business development. The "People's Bank" (La Caja Laboral Popular) was founded in the 1950s and has financed rapid development of interconnected co-operative businesses in the region.[14] Mondragon grew into an international co-operative corporation that in 2009 had $22 billion in annual sales and employed more than 100,000 workers, 82 percent of whom are members.

The Emilia Romagna region of northern Italy is another area with a highly integrated co-operative economy. Two thirds of some 7500 co-operatives in the region are worker co-operatives.[15]

Emilia Romagna's co-operative complex is less centralized than Mondragon's. Relying on co-op identity and integration through inter-cooperation, Italian co-operatives associate and contribute surplus toward the development of new co-operatives. The political economic culture there differs greatly from the U.S.[16] Co-operatives are more "mainstream" in Italy, constituting the norm rather than the exception.

In both Emilia Romagna and the Basque region of Spain, a person can satisfy all of her daily needs—from housing to groceries, work, healthcare, education, or fitting a home with appliances—with goods and services provided by co-operatives. You can work in a worker co-operative, shop at a food co-operative and live in a housing co-operative. The lessons, models and social inventions coming from experiences in the co-operative complexes of northern Italy and the Basque region of Spain are playing an important role in U.S. co-operative movements. "Co-opreneurs" from California to Cleveland have taken lessons from the Mondragon and Emilia Romagna models and applied them to co-operative development in their unique contexts.

Co-operatives in Canada and Argentina are also thriving. In Canada, especially in Quebec, despite recent funding cuts to social programming and co-op development agencies, there has been a strong recognition of the "third sector" and "social economy," with research and government programs supporting and benefiting from co-operative development. In Argentina worker co-operatives are succeeding where capitalist enterprises failed. Since the economic crisis in 2001, many worker-occupied factories have become legitimate co-operatives employing more than 13,000 workers today.

Co-operative Principles and Values (the co-operative difference)

An enduring legacy of the Rochdale Pioneers of nineteenth century England, the Co-operative Principles and Values differentiate co-operatives from their capitalist and nonprofit counterparts. They infuse all aspects of co-operatives—from structure to decision-making—with a purpose that is fundamentally different from charity organizations and typical profit-driven businesses.

As last modified in 1995 and listed on the International Co-operative Alliance website, the international Co-operative Principles are:

1. *Voluntary membership, open to all*
2. *Democratic control by members*
3. *Economic participation of the membership (members share the co-operative's wealth)*
4. *Autonomy and independence (governed by members, independent of other organizations)*
5. *Education and training for all members (plus informing the public about co-operatives)*
6. *Co-operation with other co-operatives at all levels*
7. *Concern for community (co-operatives working for the sustainable development of their communities).*

These Principles provide a framework that co-operatives can use to put their values into practice. The internationally recognized Co-operative Values are:

- self-help
- self-responsibility
- democracy
- equality
- equity and
- solidarity

as well as the personal Co-operative Values of:

- honesty
- openness
- social responsibility and
- caring for others

According to scholars and practitioners like Novkovik, Webb, Crowell, and Trott and educators of Mondragon and Emilia Romagna, identifying with the Co-operative Principles and Values is key to success and co-operative led economic development. They serve as a guide for ethical decision-making and as parameters for co-operative management. Identifying with these values has empowered co-operative complexes like Mondragon and the co-operatives of northern Italy to grow and prosper. By recognizing their "co-operative difference" as embodied in the Co-operative Principles and Values, they have been able to inter-cooperate and marshal surplus toward development.

Despite the substantial size of the co-operative economy worldwide, it has largely been ignored by economics and business departments of colleges and universities.[17] We tend to think of the economy, especially in the United States, as strictly capitalist. Newspapers, television, advertising and fantasies of social mobility, as well as the lack of education about the diversity of economic models all lead to the generally held conclusion that the capitalist economy and its attendant consumer culture is the only path to economic prosperity. The size of the co-operative economy is overlooked, and the co-operative difference is often made invisible in both popular and academic spheres.[18] The invisibility of the co-operative difference has even affected co-operative enterprises themselves because managers are often trained in capitalist rather than co-operative management and accounting, which has all sorts of implications for how those co-operative businesses are being run.

Co-operative principles are devised and adopted by co-op members. They function as a statement of a shared vision and as guidelines for democratic decision-making. Do all co-ops operate according to their principles all the time? Of course not. Do they ever stray from them? Yes, of course. Worker co-operatives are real-life organizations made up of real people. But the Principles give them something to measure up to, something to return to, something to help shape their visions and decisions. In Mondragon, they use another principle called "equilibrio" or "balance" to help them negotiate difficult situations where principles need to be interpreted and possibly abridged. In order to enact their pay solidarity principle, for example, they usually adhere to a pay ratio of six to one. However, this practice has to be balanced against the realities of the labor market. When they are hiring an experienced manager from outside the co-operative complex, or hiring a doctor for their hospital, they may agree to pay seven or eight times what the lowest paid worker earns.[19] But that decision is an ethical one made with their principle of pay solidarity in mind, attempting to adhere to it wherever possible, and bringing it into balance with the need to get the best worker for the job.

Co-operation Among Co-operatives

When we look at regions with coherent co-operative economies, we see co-operative enterprises that identify strongly with
the Co-operative Principles and Values. In these regions co-operation is recognized as a viable economic alternative. There is a
dedication to innovation and education and co-operation among
co-operatives for everything from marshalling funds to sharing
services and development. Co-operation with other co-operatives at all levels, the sixth Co-operative Principle is one of our
favorite principles because inter-cooperation opens up exciting
opportunities for developing all sectors of the co-operative
economy today.

The co-operative movement is rooted in a vision of cross-sector inter-cooperation. In many places, however, that vision has
eroded due to a number of factors including political climate and
lack of education. Moving forward, we see this changing and
hope to contribute to that change because we see inter-cooperation as one of the most promising ways to build coherent co-operative economies that can satisfy needs without putting profit
before people!

Conclusion

In this chapter we provided a brief background and a snapshot of worker co-operatives in the Valley and beyond. We offered a definition and differentiation of co-operatives across sectors in order to make clear what we mean when we say "worker
co-operative" in the context of a shared co-operative identity
across sectors. This book's focus on worker co-operatives is inspired by our passion for democracy in the workplace. However,
we believe in the viability and power of economic democracy
across sectors. In subsequent chapters we share the stories that
have sparked our passion for democracy in the workplace and

offer some strategies for engaging the Co-operative Principles and Values through worker co-operation. We present challenges to worker co-operative development and demonstrate how the Valley Alliance of Worker Co-operative's development model is addressing those challenges. We conclude with a vision and invitation for strengthening co-operative economies in our region and beyond.

II

What's It Like to Be a
Worker Co-operator?

I've been at Pelham Auto for 25 years, half of my life. There are many things I love about being here. I like the role I have as service manager, the health insurance, my passion for automobiles, the job security, the amazing flexibility around time and balancing other life obligations. But the fact that it is a worker co-operative is one of the biggest things. I worked at Western Electric when I was a teenager. I worked in a giant factory on an assembly line putting circuit boards together in my early 20s and I tell you, it's a night and day difference.

Pelham Auto member

Working co-operatively has been a life-changing experience for many worker-members regardless of their co-op's industry or their position within it. We heard this and other common themes throughout interviews with worker-members.

There is a genuinely revolutionary dimension to the dynamics we are going to discuss here. So let's look at that dimension and then go through the common themes and experiences from our interviews.

Say you want a revolution?

Many Americans take pride in U.S. democracy despite its imperfections. Democracy is an important component of living in our "free" society but our ideas about democracy tend to be relatively thin. Our democratic exercises are usually limited to local and national elections in which we cast votes on ballots every two to four years. Few of us readily think about participatory democracy in local governments not to mention democracy in the workplace or in the market. As uninvolved as our democratic imaginations may be, most of us are thankful to live in a democratic country rather than one ruled by a fascist, autocratic or oligarchic regime. We get excited when a political region attempts to move from autocratic or oligarchic rule to a democracy. We celebrate revolutions of the people. We celebrate people's "liberation."

However, when we think about freedom and democracy in society, freedom and democracy in the workplace is often overlooked.

For us (the authors of this book and many co-operators), worker co-operation is a revolutionary business model that deserves a similar, if quieter celebration and perpetuation. Worker co-ops are practicing democracy rather than oligarchy on a smaller but no less important, personal scale: that of governance and ownership of an enterprise. Worker-members practice equality and democratic governance on a daily basis rather than being governed by owners and capital. Worker co-operatives confront us with the fact that typical job situations unnecessarily strip workers of authority over their own working bodies as well as the goods and services they produce. This is called *alienation*, and it pushes a big question up front:

How can we create a free and just society when we spend much of our waking lives being told what to do?

There are long and varied histories of political, philosophical and legal struggles over who owns and governs land and labor. Economist David Ellerman reminds us that in the not-too-distant American past, it was argued *in court* that a person should be allowed to voluntarily relinquish the ownership of his or her personhood in order to submit voluntarily to slavery.[20]

The abolitionist movement shot down the "logic" of voluntary slavery. However, we are left to wonder how far typical work situations are free of this logic.

Rather than selling oneself for a lifetime (which is called slavery and considered illegal in most countries) one must *rent* his/her labor time thus attempting to relinquish his/her personhood for the duration of the rental period. Ellerman uses the words "hire" and "rent" interchangeably to highlight the problematic nature of the employer/employee relationship. We may be lucky to rent our labor hours, as wage laborers, at a decent rate. However, even when the rental price is high, it comes at the expense of our self-governance. The historical connection of the labor contract with the past arguments supporting "voluntary" slavery is, at the very least, unsettling. For Ellerman there is no "very least" involved: the same mistaken logic applies and thus should invalidate the nearly ubiquitously accepted notion of "freedom of contract."

Worker-membership turns the relationship between labor and capital on its head. In a worker co-operative, rather than being hired by capital, labor hires capital. This makes worker co-operatives fundamentally different from their capitalist counterparts. It also makes being in a worker co-op member fundamentally different from being an employee.

So what's it like to be a worker-owner? Themes from our interviews

Worker co-ops offer opportunities for personal growth and self-realization because their members have a unique capacity for control in their economic lives. They break down the dichotomy people often experience when they leave their autonomy at the doorstep of their workplace and relinquish their ideas, values and opinions in the service of profit. Worker co-operators do not have bosses. Some worker co-ops hire or elect management, but members have a say in governance.

Worker-members say they are more secure than they were as employees and this encourages them to cultivate aspects of their "true selves." They don't have to feign disinterest or hide their opinions and feelings because they fear losing their jobs. Many co-operators appreciate the flexibility of work time, donations of surplus and the ability to live in line with their values and to pursue personal interests. Some members work in co-operatives because the pay is better than industry average; others suggest they could make more money elsewhere but prefer the freedom and responsibility of worker-membership. Let's look at these factors one by one.

> *We're trying to create a humane working environment for ourselves and model that for other people. Those are the things that keep me here…The value of not having to answer to a boss and not having my life dictated by someone who's not necessarily thinking in my best interest—that's invaluable to me.*
>
> Erika Arthur, Food For Thought Books

Working without a boss

A typical workplace sets up an antagonism between employer and employee that is absent from a worker co-operative.[21] In a worker co-operative, the owners are the workers and vice versa. They are working together, for each other, not for people they don't know in the corporate world. They still get frustrated and don't always get their way (just like they wouldn't at a regular workplace), but co-operators typically don't feel like someone is trying to control their lives.

For example, Pelham Auto members have specialized skills and understandings of their department or job (parts, service or bookkeeping for example) and varying levels of experience, but nobody has authority or formal power over their co-workers. The policy, for some forty years now, is to *ask* rather than to *tell* someone what to do. One member of Pelham Auto who works in the Parts Department, appreciates working on equal grounds with his co-workers. It's important to him to be a member of his co-operative because he has a say in his working life. He and his co-workers want their needs addressed and don't like the kind of working relationships in which someone has power over them.

Like many co-operatives with a collective culture, at Pelham Auto workers aren't beholden to a boss who may or may not know anything about the work process. As worker-owner Jonathan Leighton says, "You're responsible to yourself and your co-workers instead of a single owner, somebody who may be out doing something else."

> *I like working here because I have a say in my working life.*
>   Pelham Auto member

Worker co-operators never have to deal with someone "above" them making arbitrary decisions or telling them what to do. As Charles Uchu Strader from Gaia Host Collective notes:

"It gives me a lot of the joy and satisfaction to know that the other people I'm working with are actually working *with* me instead of trying to control me in any way." Working without a boss or single owner cultivates a feeling of *self-reliance with others* and that experience has empowered big changes in members' lives. These changes have taken the form of being able to live in line with their values, or develop professional skills and financial literacy, purchase a house, pursue a passion and/or stand up for what they believe in.

Flexibility

Unlike work in a typical capitalist enterprise worker-members haven't rented their time to an employer so they are not subject to a manager or to capital. They own, manage and make decisions about their work and work time together. With the support of their co-workers, members can leave in the middle of the day for a personal or family emergency, to get a check cashed, pick up the kids or meet the plumber if those needs come up.

Controlling their work time together empowers worker members to support each other so they can be more involved with things outside of work: their families, communities, hobbies, organizations and other relationships. Having a say in scheduling and time off also allows them to pursue personal interests, fulfill obligations or accomplish something that's important to them.

> *When my kids were younger, I used to run off and volunteer at the elementary school or get out early to coach a soccer team. I think we've been really flexible for that type of thing, like daycare, or if I needed an extra week, or something like that. Whether you just need to do it, or it's an obligation. I don't think you get that everywhere. It's a freedom you wouldn't have at every job out there in the world.*
> Pelham Auto member

Stephen Roy, founding member of Collective Copies, has more than twenty-five years of experience working co-operatively. He says there are times when worker-members put in more hours than they might if they were just employees. The most stressful times for him have been when the machines were broken, customers were at the counter and his partner was mad at him for working too much. Times like those have pushed him "to the brink" but for him and others, the benefits outweigh the stress. He values his job and sees Collective Copies as a legacy that will provide quality work to members long after he's retired.

Steve Strimer agrees with his co-worker that being a worker-member can be more stressful than being an employee but "it's definitely more liberating to be a member of a worker co-operative" than a wage laborer because you have "a say in what you do all day." It's more responsibility, he says, but it's worth it so many times over that he can no longer "imagine working that *other way* anymore."

Striking a balance between work and home life is a challenge for most working people. It has been a struggle for members of PV Squared, especially those who have children, to strike a balance between home and work life. However, founding worker-member Kim Pinkham believes that it's part of their jobs to take care of themselves and each other. She has encouraged fellow members to go home and take care of their relationships and she has learned where her own boundaries lie, when she can be a workaholic and when she needs to rest and restore.

> *I think it's part of our jobs to say, 'You, go home; preserve your relationship.' Because we're trying to be whole people. I have learned sort of where my boundaries are—that I can be a workaholic for a certain period of time, then I'm damaging myself in other areas and I would be more productive for the company, if I were less stressed.*
>
> Kim Pinkham (PV)[2]

Erika Arthur's experience as a member of Food For Thought Books was similar to Pinkham's in that she enjoyed the flexibility of her job and tended to draw clear boundaries between work and home life. She could have that freedom because the additional responsibility of ownership didn't rest upon her shoulders alone:

> Unlike if I owned a store by myself, I don't necessarily have to respond to every crisis by myself. If the door get's left unlocked, and the police find it open, I don't necessarily have to come all the way from Northampton to lock it. We all have the responsibility of being store owners. It's a lot and it's definitely nice to share.
>
> *Erika Arthur, Food For Thought Books*

Rebekah Hanlon compares her collective, Valley Green Feast, to a living creature that she and her co-workers are giving of themselves to grow and sustain. They put a lot of themselves into the collective but, she says, it's a balance, they also get a lot out so they don't feel like their "energy is leaving the cycle." When one member of Valley Green Feast gets stressed out or when something isn't working, they redistribute responsibilities. "There's a lot of support that goes on to try and keep us happy as workers."

Security

The cool thing about working co-operatively is that even and especially in a crisis, workers have a say in the direction of their businesses; they can represent their stakes in maintaining the security of their jobs. Co-operators are more secure than employees in a traditionally-held company because they have a full say in daily operations. It's important for members to be aware of the financial statements of the business because when the numbers are strong, their jobs are secure. If there is a dip in revenue, they can work together to make mid-course corrections and, if necessary, absorb losses together. This security is one reason out-

siders suggest worker co-operatives are less "flexible" than traditional firms. Co-ops can't respond as swiftly to changes in the
market as capitalist enterprise with its more stream-lined management structure and willingness to treat workers as expenses
on the income statement. They can't just "downsize" by laying
off workers.

In the event of a crisis, co-ops might opt for stategies such as
launching a new service or product line, members taking a leave of
absence, increasing advertising or marketing, or even lowering
pay. Members share the risks as well as the benefits of ownership.

> *All of our perspectives help us to get a bigger picture under-
> standing of challenges or decisions that we need to make.
> I've had good employment situations before but I have
> more ownership of what's happening here. You don't just
> show up and go home and not think about it. It's like your
> baby. You're nurturing it, you want it to succeed; you're
> more invested in it on an energetic level and more connected
> to the other people who you're working with because you're
> in this together. We all want this to succeed.*
> Libby Garofalo, Brattleboro Holistic Health Center

If they find themselves in a bind, rather than firing someone,
workers can come up with unexpected strategies. They don't get
as stuck as a traditional business might. Remember, the purposes
behind co-operative and capitalist firms are fundamentally different: a co-operative exists to meet the needs of its members
and, among those needs is the members' need for work!

Not only are workers sheltered from the perils of being
"downsized," together they can do more than they would be
able to on their own. Several members of Brattleboro Holistic
Health Care Center, one of VAWC's newest members, ran separate sole-proprietorships before going into business together co-
operatively. Working together they're able to have a main street
store front and reach more people, something they could not do
when they were working on their own.

> *I wouldn't be able to have a Main Street store front without doing it with a group of people and we're all in that situation. We can do bigger better things together than we could individually.*
> Libby Garofalo, Brattleboro Holistic Health Center

For many worker co-operators, this aspect of security extends beyond their immediate employment. They appreciate the fact that they're investing time and energy in a community enterprise that can live beyond their personal tenure with it. Members of Brattleboro Holistic Health Center, Collective Copies, Gaia Host Collective, PV Squared, and Valley Green Feast were particularly proud of their businesses as multi-generational community assets. Despite the stress of starting a new co-operative business, Leah Mutz is inspired by this vision of longevity and her voice echoes others we heard:

> That's another beautiful detail about this: the sense that it's totally different than a sole proprietorship or traditional LLC because we're building something that can have a life of many generations and it doesn't have to be our kids! We're building something that can last beyond our time with it. It's such a graceful and sustainable notion that membership may ebb and flow over the years but what we've built will continue and sustain.
> *Leah Mutz, Brattleboro Holistic Health Center*

Communication

It is rare to be asked to leave a worker co-op. This means that co-operators are more secure, but it also means that members are stuck with each other. Accountability and communication in the workplace become extremely important. They have to make things work together because when they have a conflict or trouble communicating at work, co-operators can't go to the boss and complain. They can't just fire someone who's difficult to work with and, because they like their jobs, they don't want to quit and find another one when there is conflict.

I feel like it's made me grow up because working in a collective you have to deal with human beings. You can't avoid them; you can't silently scorn; you have to talk. You have to work things out with your co-workers because they're not getting fired. So I'm much more capable of opening my mouth and saying, this isn't working for me; this is my work-place too.

Randy Zucco, Collective Copies

Worker-members say that learning how to communicate in their co-operatives is an ongoing process. No one we talked to claimed to be an expert, but most said they have learned a lot about sharing what is and is not working for them and hearing the perspectives of their co-members. Communication is important but it isn't always easy. Even longtime members say that giving and receiving feedback face-to-face can be tough!

I've always tried to be compassionate in my communication with people but when it comes to money sometimes I have these emotional reactions. So, being involved with this means I have to say, 'okay, what is an emotional reaction? And what is my need? How can I express my need honestly without adding all this other junk to it before I say it?' Because what I say is going to have an impact on everyone. So you have to state what your needs are and be honest but compassionate because we need to be on the same page.

Libby Garofalo, Brattleborro Holistic Health Center

When people aren't afraid of saying what's on their mind, honest dialogue begins. However, it's difficult to communicate when people have strong opinions and feelings about things. The challenge for worker-members is to listen to each other's feelings and opinions and to communicate honestly about their own. It's important to value and act on co-workers' input when dealing with important (and even trivial) decisions. This enables co-ops to make informed decisions that are based on the biggest asset of a co-operative—its members. It's always a work in progress.

It takes time to trust the decision-making process and to learn how to communicate ideas, opinions and needs openly and effectively. Rebekah Hanlon learned a lot about communication during her two-year experience at People's Market, a nearly forty-year-old student-run business with some twenty-four members at the University of Massachusetts. She brings that experience to Valley Green Feast, a two-year-old collective, but her own learning process continues.

> It's not all sunshine. You have rainy days. Even though there are only four of us, we're very different people and we believe in unique things according to our experiences and personalities. Sometimes I'm a little frustrated in a three-hour meeting because we're not all on the same page. It's just really important to take responsibility for bringing each other to the same page and being able to express frustration articulately instead of blankly expressing negativity. It's important to be able to say, 'I'm feeling this way and this is why' and take responsibility for how you feel about something. Otherwise it's not going to be received and nothing is going to happen.
>
> *Rebekah Hanlon, Valley Green Feast*

Worker-members across industries suggest that learning how to communicate effectively has been a big part of their co-operative growth. Many co-operatives practice tricks of the trade that help members communicate effectively and facilitate the decision-making process. We talk about some of these in Chapter Three.

> *You have to try to navigate the best solution, trying to take everybody's opinions into account. It can be rough but you know, people here tend to come through, and everybody has something to offer.*
>
> Pelham Auto member

Personal Values

Worker co-operatives invite co-operators to integrate personal values into their working lives.[22] They are encouraged to negotiate and practice them with others when making decisions about the business. This practice removes the alienation we might feel when having to leave our opinions and governing faculties outside the door of the workplace. For example, most of us value democracy and equality. Worker co-operators are able to put these values into practice at work through the principles of democratic member control, autonomy and independence in decisions made *every day*—not just once every two years at the voting polls.

From managing and distributing surplus (or profit)[23] to daily business operations, the myriad of decisions made by co-operatives are informed by their members' multiple spheres of interest. In our area several worker co-operatives have looked to the example of Mondragon co-operatives as a model for the appropriation and distribution of surplus. In Mondragon a typical division of company surplus might be seventy percent returned to worker-members, twenty percent returned to the business and ten percent to the community.[24] Even when such a breakdown is established, many decisions have yet to be made. For instance, the size of surplus produced is partly determined by factors like pay rates and benefits (such as health care) and the costs of other inputs. In traditionally organized firms, workers are excluded from making these decisions but in worker co-ops, members make them together.

Critics of worker co-operatives, like the Webbs and other Fabian Socialists of the late nineteenth century, thought that self-managing workers would drive up wages and, therefore, the price of goods beyond the capacity of consumers, to the ruin of business and community.[25] However, worker co-operatives of the Valley and beyond demonstrate that co-operative decisions are informed by values beyond the self interest of maximizing pay and dividend share. Members care about their communities, co-workers and the environment and those concerns are reflected in business decisions. They feel good about donating ten percent of surplus to their communities, being able to provide health care for themselves *and* their co-workers' families; and they feel good when they can make positive contributions or reduce the environmental impact of their enterprises. Some environmentally friendly inputs are more expensive than their more polluting or resource-intensive counterparts, yet many co-operatives choose to reduce surplus in the service of values beyond profit including environmental commitments.

Deciding on a rate of pay is one of many decisions members make together. So the pay structures of co-operative enterprises vary, reflecting differences in the needs and values of current and past members. For example, Gaia Host Collective founding member Charles Uchu Strader's perspective on compensation is that everyone's time should be valued equally "because it's all the same thing." As a worker-member he has the right and responsibility to represent his perspective to his co-members when his growing collective negotiates decisions regarding administrative tasks and the pay scales for new members.

Members of Equal Exchange—a fair-trade worker-owned coffee-roasting company that also imports tea, chocolate, olive oil, almonds, bananas and other products—have kept the mission of their co-operative central to their structure for more than twenty-five years. Former member Erbin Crowell recalls how members' concern for the mission of the co-operative often overshadowed interest in their own pay:

> We almost always had debates about how much we could afford to pay over market and how much more was going to go to our mission but all those years that I was at Equal Exchange, we never once had a debate about increasing the amount of money that came to ourselves.

Since his departure, Equal Exchange hasn't strayed from its commitment to fair trade vis-à-vis worker salary. With some 120 members conducting trade in the global market, this worker co-operative is of substantial size but they maintain a top-to-bottom pay ratio of four to one.[26] That's a far cry from the disparity between the average wage and CEO pay in the U.S., which measured 364 to one in 2007![27]

Members of Pedal People, a worker-owned human-powered delivery and hauling company in the Valley, put their values into practice in the services they provide as well as in their scheduling, pay, tax structure and surplus distribution. Delivering goods and removing trash and recycling by bicycle is physically demanding, so they feel good about earning a decent rate of pay for their work. However, as stated in their mission they,

> believe in the idea of low-income living as a counter to the work-consume-spend lifestyle common in America today. We also believe that by spending less time making a living, they can have more time to contribute to the community and live life at a human pace rather than a motorized pace.[28]

In accordance with their mission and the physical demands of the job, Pedal People's thirteen active workers, eleven of whom are members of the collective, work between one and three days per week. Some Pedal People shore up their expenses with outside work but many do not.[29] Founding member Alex Jarrett explains that "making and needing less money leaves more time to provide for needs in non-monetary ways like growing food rather than buying it and having time to develop new projects."

> People work really hard in Pedal People so however much money comes in, they're happy to have it distributed to them and it's distributed fairly. It's based on what you work during the year. If there's extra at the end of the year, it's divided up and paid as patronage dividends based on the amount of work that you did.   *Alex Jarrett, Pedal People*

The capital generated by the productive labor of delivering vegetables or recycling and removing trash must balance out administrative needs. Pedal People continue to offer a few services even though they don't bring in much money. For example, Jarrett says, they don't promote it because "it doesn't bring in any money," but they still provide grocery delivery for folks who can't get out and buy their own groceries. They have also decided to be members of VAWC, which requires a contribution of dues and surplus.

Co-operatives have a mission, but they also help individual members to live in line with personal values and responsibilities and to pursue unique interests that co-workers may or may not share. One person might have a passion for music while another cares strongly about animal rescue. A former Collective Copies member told us that with the support of her co-workers she was able to pursue interests that she might not otherwise have been able to pursue. Thanks to the flexibility of her schedule, as a full time worker-member at Collective Copies, she was able to volunteer at an aquarium. She also used her co-operative's equipment to do the typesetting for an auction booklet for animal rescue. Worker co-operators can use the means of production they own together for personal and community interest. Pelham Auto is another example: workers often carry on a project in the shop outside of work. Their love of cars is one reason many of them work there.

> *Everybody here has a passion for that [cars]. It waxes and wanes and comes and goes, but it's probably got to be the second biggest thing, or maybe it's the top thing for some people.*   Pelham Auto member

Co-operative members attempt to recognize and support co-workers on their unique paths. *They don't claim to be experts but they try.* For example, not all workers in a co-operative care strongly about co-operative movement building, but they support and validate their co-workers who are involved. Because they believe in the mission and in their co-workers, member co-ops have committed dues and surplus to movement building along with a myriad of other kinds of support and community involvement.

Rebekah Hanlon of Valley Green Feast is particularly enthusiastic about VAWC and the worker co-operative movement. She considers it her responsibility to bring that passion to her growing collective: "I'm bringing my*self* to the table. It's my responsibility to be articulate and bring my co-workers to the way I see it." Valley Green Feast's mission is "to support local farms and producers, to help their products reach consumers, and to make local, healthy, delicious food as accessible as possible to a wide range of consumers." Thanks partly to Rebekah's ability to articulate connections between her concern for inter-cooperation and her collective's mission, not only does Valley Green Feast provide local organic food to people of all incomes, they also deliver imported goods such as coffee, tea and oils from Equal Exchange and the products of fellow VAWC member co-operative, Co-op 108.

Negotiating diverse perspectives on quality of work, life, the environment, patriarchy, racism, group process, fair trade goods, and other opinions and interests can be challenging but it creates a well-rounded organization and movement. While most firms operate with the assumption that people should be told what to do and hire experts to decide upon the best course of action, *worker co-ops start from the premise that workers themselves can do what they need to do together.* As Rebekah Hanlon says, "We have a lot of freedom to do what we need to do!" Because they don't have to answer to someone in a hierarchical chain of command, they also have the power to live in line with their values during the daily grind of the work. A former member of Collective Copies offered the example of a customer who came in to get an obituary copied. She was able give away a dollar and ten cents worth of copies in order to acknowledge the customer's loss. It wasn't much, she said, but it was meaningful to the the customer, and she didn't have to ask her boss in order to do it.

Roads to Co-operation

The stories of how workers came to be members of their co-operatives vary considerably. Some members founded their co-operatives; some discovered their co-ops by answering newspaper ads; a few discovered worker-membership in school; and at least one of our interviewees traced his introduction to worker co-ops to rock-and-roll bands and communal households in the sixties. Regardless of how they found out about worker co-operation, it seems that for most co-operators, there was a notable transition from when work was "just a job" to the more fulfilling experience of worker-membership.

Randy learned from a newspaper ad that Collective Copies was hiring. He didn't know anything about worker-membership at the time; he thought the ad could be a hoax. Randy began to discover what it meant, however, when he went to the interview and was faced with *eleven* people interviewing him.

It takes time to trust the process of co-operation and to participate fully. For those members who came to established co-ops as apprentices and new members, there was already a system in place in which they would have to find their 'niche.' These days Randy is an active participant in managing his cooperative but it was three years before he felt like a full-fledged worker-owner at Collective Copies, comfortable enough to push for something or bring forth an agenda topic, to feel like what he had to say mattered and that he had the same kind of power as everybody else in the collective. He says when he arrived there were already people with agendas who were the leaders of the collective.

> *You know it can be overwhelming. There's already a dynamic; it's like entering a family that's already existed for seven years and then you show up. So it took probably three years for me to feel like I was really part of it.*
> Randy Zucco, Collective Copies

Rebekah Hanlon suggests that when there's a new hire, "There's a little bit of a process, where we're getting to know each other, oil our machine and be as efficient as possible." She discovered worker-membership at the University of Massachusetts where she worked in one of the student-run businesses. Rebekah was enamored with the process of working co-operatively but she didn't know that such work existed "out there" in the "real world." She learned about VAWC and other co-operatives in the Valley when Adam Trott came to speak in one of her classes as part of VAWC's educational mission. She remembers:

> I worked at the People's Market, a student business that operates like a worker co-op and I just couldn't believe there were people outside of the university working like this. It was fascinating to learn from Adam about all the different co-operatives like Pedal People, Food For Thought, Green Mountain Spinnery, (PV)², Collective Copies and Pelham Auto, where everybody is doing very different things but they're all kind of working the same way and things are getting done; places where you can really be yourself. So I kept in touch with Adam and learned more about VAWC. ...I came across a craigslist posting for a job opening at Valley Green Feast. I had marketing experience so I got an interview and it was wonderful. I've been working there ever since.

As described in their profile, founding members of PV Squared got the idea to start a worker co-operative from Franklin County Community Development Corporation and the Co-operative Development Institute's invitation to an organizing meeting on the radio in 2000. Over one hundred people showed up to the first organizing meeting for a worker-owned solar panel manufacturing project. By the time they figured out that the initial vision would require a prohibitive multi-million dollar investment, their working group was down to five. They decided to become installers rather than manufacturers. In other words, they started where they were and they take great pride in having invested countless hours of sweat equity to build a successful, rapidly growing co-op from the ground up. As founding members of VAWC, they participate in worker co-op development and educational speaking events.

> *The fact that we're a worker co-operative is an added layer of self-worth for me to find comfort in. I think there are a lot of people, especially younger people, who might feel hopeless or pessimistic about their prospects who could benefit from that kind of reinforcement and I wish there were more opportunities for that to happen.*
>
> Kim Pinkham, (PV)[2]

For Charles Uchu Strader, working co-operatively is the most natural way of working. He learned the hard way that for a co-operative business to persist, its bylaws and structure must embody its co-operative principles. Despite their initial intentions to operate co-operatively, his first business was structured as a partnership and it fell apart when two of the three partners wanted to grow and one wanted to leave. When Charles and a former co-op member founded Gaia Host Collective, they structured it this time as a co-operative with limited equity. As a co-operative, he says, they have the capacity for longevity, "a member doesn't own half or a third of the company. They have a limited equity so if they decide to retire there's a specific mechanism that we have to deal with that."

At the time of their interviews, Leah Mutz, Libby Garofalo and co-members of Brattleboro Holistic Health Care were forging their way through the first year of business after founding their collective in 2011. VAWC staff and its member co-ops helped with the process of incorporation, drawing up bylaws, and thinking through tax structures and workers' compensation laws but for the many decisions that need to be made, there is no *one* map.

> *You feel nervous when you're making choices because you*
> *don't want it to come back and bite you if it's the wrong*
> *thing. That's a struggle but also the lovely thing about it*
> *and the more I learn about co-operatives, I learn that there's*
> *not a wrong way to do it. You can tailor it very specifically*
> *to your situation.... None of us has an MBA. This is our*
> *business school immersion program so we're learning by*
> *doing.*
>   Libby Garofalo, Brattleboro Holistic Health Center

Conclusion

The many stories we heard during interviews with worker-members suggest that bringing themselves to the decision-making table and participating in the co-direction of their businesses has encouraged and enabled various kinds of personal growth. Worker co-operators are pursuing passions, living according to their values, and developing communication and other skills like financial literacy, bookkeeping, marketing and web design. They feel good about their jobs and making a positive contribution to the world. That is why many of the co-operators we talked with are working to expand the movement to provide others with similar stable, dignified work that doesn't put profit before all other values. Their motivations, values and personal experiences are unique, but they have faith in their individual and collective capacity to make it work *together*.

In the next chapter we share some tried-and-true methods that worker-members use to make working together *work*. In Part Two we share profiles of some of the worker co-ops in our region before broadening the perspective to explore what worker co-operatives share in common with co-operatives of other sectors in Part Three.

III

Democratic Participation in Action

BEFORE WE GO INTO THE MECHANICS AND DYNAMICS of collective decision-making, let's begin with an understanding of how difficult this can be. Underestimating the challenges involved can end a worker co-operative project at any time, early on, ten years down the road or even prevent it from getting launched. Long-time co-operator and historian, John Curl clues us in to this at the beginning of his history of the co-operative movement in the United States, *For All the People*:

> Co-operatives are visionary institutions that we can all create, wherever we are. All it takes is three or more people in a mutual relationship. Of course, that's not as easy as it may sound, as you probably know if you've ever tried to share a kitchen, a bathroom, or bed with another person. Human relationships are rife with problems and so, of course, are co-operatives. But the answer is not to reject life, but to embrace it, to work with it, and create constructive relationships and communities *in spite of all the obstacles*.[30]

This chapter is about embracing worker co-operation "in spite of all the obstacles" with effective practices of democratic decision-making. An important theme coming out of our research and interviews, though at times hard to hear, was the value of the challenges co-operators faced and how they dealt with them. We might agree that there is no one right way to form or operate a co-op, but it seems, some ways are better than others. We share cautionary tales in the spirit of informing current and future co-operators of what others have done so that they may make better decisions for themselves and their co-ops.

Dick McLeester's Cautionary Tale

Dick McLeester founded Food for Thought Books, a worker collective in downtown Amherst, Massachusetts that closed its doors in 2014 after 38 years in business.[31] He moved to the Valley in his youth in the mid-'70s and found a world teeming with political energy for change. In 1975 he decided to start a book store because he was in love with the power of books to inform people. Dick was also attracted to the idea of co-operation. So the project he started was "open to anybody to participate in running it."

> It started from nothing working very small…with a lot of sweat equity and good people, people who were looking for a meaningful project…. The number of people involved would fluctuate a lot but there were times when we'd have meetings of between twenty-five and fifty people.

It had a clear purpose—"to educate the community about the kinds of changes we need to have"—and a strategy:

> The idea was that we don't have to be just a bookstore; we can be whatever we want. We can be a vehicle for educating ourselves first and then bring whatever we know or think might be important to the various communities.

The name they eventually chose for the venture was very fitting: Food for Thought.[32]

The venture grew into a store of substantial revenues that also sold books at numerous conferences in the area and some that were far and wide. During the first ten years Dick served, effectively, as the general manager. However, one day in that tenth year everything changed for him. Here's his version of what happened along with his interpretation:

What took me away was partly internal process and partly that it was time for me to do something else. We had agreed upon a procedure in which every six months we would be evaluated by the members of the collective. One of my evaluations came up and I was presented with four typewritten pages of all the things I could change or leave. And I kind of looked at that and thought *wow people have been sitting on their criticisms of me for awhile*, and what it amounted to was that, as the founder, I was still doing too much. I was still doing all the ordering and I needed to get better at delegating responsibility. Basically I looked at that and thought I've got three months and I agree I need to change a lot of these things and I'll take a shot at it. I tried talking to a few of the people. I sat down with them, but basically they said *whatever you try to do is going to be too little too late*. Several other people were looking at the situation saying it sounds a lot like a common game collectives play called "kill the leader."

We were in a financial crisis mode when my evaluation came up and I think that was an overarching factor. They felt something big has to change and we may not survive no matter what we do and some people felt we should get rid of the leader. I can't pinpoint exactly how much of it was conscious or unconscious...and part of it was for me realizing I was feeling a little antsy just working with one store. I had wanted to develop networks between progressive booksellers and do more as a national network. I started to realize maybe this was not the time for me to try to fight it out; and others were saying to me that there had been battles somewhat like this at other collectives and it had gotten really messy; some group members had gone to the courts and locked down other collective members, so...

So I think part of it was lack of good communication and part of it was a feeling that, well, we're supposed to be a collective but it seems like this guy has more power than the rest of us. And in retrospect maybe it is natural that other people would have built up some resentments because maybe we hadn't talked clearly enough that we could be a collective and there could still be different levels of skill and maybe even different levels of pay. At that time I think we were all still at similar level of pay. There may have just been some levels of naivete around what it means to be a collective.

For our purposes here there are two things to note in Dick's account. First, that many factors were at play in his being ousted, but there was no shared process for resolving the issues involved. Second, that this highly un-democratic move was the direct result of the people involved not being able to talk out the problems they were having. It takes a long time to build up a four-page list of complaints as well as the amount of resentment that leads to the ultimatum to change now or leave, especially for someone who was the founder of the entire project, and who had led it to the level of success it now enjoyed.

We will never know what would have happened if the issues involved had been continually worked on as soon as they became significant. It seems that the members weren't able to see how essential it was to have processes that would encourage and support people taking responsibility for their own experience *and* that issues were addressed in a timely, effective way.[33]

Cory Greenberg, former worker-member of Good Things Collective (which closed in the late 1980s) echoed this sentiment:

> It's really important in any democratic organization that it's open and that even if one person has the time and experience, others should be taking leadership roles as well because it makes things more solid.... A particular danger is one person having a lot of time, energy and a strong personality taking control of the process.

The "kill the leader" dynamic is widespread, well beyond the co-operative world. It results from members of a group not being able to take full responsibility for their share of collectively managing their project and addressing the problems they were experiencing with the group. The longer a burning issue is postponed, the more the resentment can build until it becomes an irreversible tide. At that point, one of two scenarios will likely take place: the group will dissolve by a steady erosion of interest and commitment, or "kill the leader" will kick in as the only solution the resentful members can see.

Our discussion of the mechanics and dynamics of democratic problem-solving processes and decision-making is intended for future co-operators to avoid these kinds of outcomes.

Conflict is inevitable

> *It's really like a family. You have to work through your differences not to split up.*
>
> Randy Zucco, Collective Copies

Worker co-operatives are great but no one who's ever worked in one would suggest they are "utopia." Co-operatives offer abundant support, but members will likely encounter interpersonal problems at some point. Co-operators often describe their co-ops in familial terms—for better and worse. Randy Zucco compares Collective Copies to the experience of being part of a family—with plenty of internal strife:

> I think the biggest misconception about co-operatives is that there are no problems; if you work in a co-op, it's all set—life is great for you. The way I like to describe it is that working in a cooperative is like being part of like a thirteen person family, uncles, cousins, aunts, all together at the Thanksgiving table, and some of them you don't really want to see because you treated them badly last Christmas!

Conflict often arises due to miscommunication. We think we're saying one thing but something entirely different is being heard. Sometimes people have remarkably different perceptions of a single situation or issue. We can't avoid conflict but how we handle it is an important aspect of co-operation. As a former member of Collective Copies told us, how a group deals with this dynamic affects your life in every way. Most co-operatives have had or will go through extremely difficult times. Such circumstances might lead to fantasies of working in a "regular" job:

Whenever you have a group, there is a dynamic and how you deal with that dynamic affects your life in every way. There have been times at the collective that have been horrible, outrageous things have been said and done... in a regular work environment, either it would have been the boss saying it and nothing would have happened or someone might have been confronted or not...I don't know what would have happened. But you start to feel like if you were in a regular place, something would be done, right? You have this fantasy, and maybe it would.

Former member, Collective Copies

Conflicts can be dramatic when two or more parties are at an impasse. Conflicts between two people may seem simple (because they involve only two people) but they can affect the whole collective. So, it's the responsibility of the whole membership to address it. Disagreements about the direction of the co-operative can be intense and take a lot of time and energy to work through.

> *When people see a person in the co-op as a problem, it's polarizing. I think polarization was probably the worst aspect of what happened in Good Things Collective because it paralyzed things and misdirected people's energies. Instead of trying to solve problems, we were busy rejecting and reacting to the other side.*
>
> Cory Greenberg, Good Things Collective

A more common kind of conflict is rooted in day-to-day activities: things like people not finishing jobs, leaving things out, or not following through with something. Conflict is a constant and inevitable part of working together no matter the size of the group. The great thing about worker co-operatives is that members have the right, even the obligation, to approach each other and address things that are not working for them on the basis of equality. Of course, that is a challenging responsibility. Learning to communicate through disagreement, annoyance and conflict is an ongoing challenge and opportunity.

In what follows we offer a few methods for decision-making and communication. Our suggestions come from interviews with co-operators, participant observation during meetings as well as pointers from the book *No Bosses Here*. Using these kinds of tools will not prevent conflict, however, using them thoughtfully may help your co-operative communicate and execute decisions more effectively.

Decisions, Decisions, Decisions

The first thing a co-operative or collective needs to decide is *how* they will make decisions.

Why is it that *how a co-op makes decisions* is so important?

Decision-making structures are important because decision-making at meetings is when co-operators inform each other and improve their co-op, its services or products, and their membership. It's a powerful time when members come together on equal footing with a shared interest, and literally create and re-create the co-op by making changes and addressing needs. It's a time for co-operators to use their personal power co-operatively; to see and understand their own tendencies to use power to dominate; or to choose not to use their power out of fear of asserting themselves. People's feelings about decision-making structures and their experiences in those structures vary. From the get-go those differences of opinions will pose challenges but the uniqueness of perspective is one of the beautiful things about co-ops and, ultimately, a great reason to hone decision-making skills and continually learn how to work together.

> *Try to structure the decision-making so it doesn't have to be emotional. There's a place for emotion but not in the decision-making process.*
>
> Cory Greenberg, Good Things Collective

Co-operatives and collectives[34] practice two basic forms of democratic decision-making: ***majority rule and consensus***. Just as it sounds, majority rule is when the outcome of a decision is based on the opinion of the numerical majority. In contrast, full consensus decisions require agreement from all members. But groups can choose to modify these options to fit their needs and culture. Choosing a decision-making structure—consensus or majority rule—will have a great impact on the future of your co-operative so it's a good idea to really think through what will work best for you and your enterprise. Things to take into consideration when deciding on a decision-making structure are the size of your co-op, its goals, and how members communicate their perspectives while respecting those of their co-workers.

There are benefits and drawbacks to both majority and consensus. Both work best when accompanied by a willingness to work through problems together. When you're choosing a decision-making structure, it's also important to keep in mind the following basic tenets for effective decision-making:

- shared authority
- transparency
- individual responsibility to speak and hear
- clarity of commitment and
- valuing minority opinion

Shared authority – Authority in a worker co-operative is the permission to act for the sake of the co-operative. This authority resides in the whole membership. The group decides how to distribute this authority in order for the co-op to do its work. In making decisions together some members may specialize in the topic at hand. This doesn't mean they should be making decisions other members don't understand or support. Rather, their special knowledge is a resource for the whole membership to use to make good decisions. It is important to be aware of and to address both the development of informal hierarchies as well as formal hierarchies. Statements and policies like "I'll just do what Jane does because she's been here longer," or "Department managers make final decisions regarding hiring" are evidence of entrenched hierarchies that can erode the Co-operative Principle of Democratic Member Participation.

Transparency – Every member should be given access to the same comprehensive information with ample time to review it before being expected to make a decision. Some may choose not to read it; some may trust the work of a committee and feel they need not know everything. Ultimately, all members have a right to all information regarding their business. Transparency helps involve those who wouldn't otherwise be involved and establishes trust within a committee and the whole membership. When someone understands what others are doing and why, they are more likely to contribute to it and ask valuable penetrating questions about it. Further, when people appreciate and feel welcomed into the process, they are more likely to support the results.

Individual responsibility to speak and hear – A co-operative needs ground rules that guarantee every member has the right to speak in its open decision-making processes. Speaking involves

- asking clarifying questions to better understand the issue,
- voicing one's reactions and objections in order to hear responses from others, and
- making proposals to help the co-op achieve its purpose.

The right to speak is a serious responsibility. It isn't an invitation for one or more members to monopolize the group's time or talk on and on with an axe to grind. Rather, it is a way to establish a dialogue, a space for all to speak and to hear each other so that each member can develop their own **informed opinion** about the matter at hand. The right to participate in the co-op's decision-making carries with it the responsibility that members be honest about their feelings and open to the feelings and criticisms of others. Fear of honest communication can lead to subtle agreements to avoid talking about certain issues. That can end up hurting and ultimately bring a co-operative to its end.

Clarity of commitment – Most co-ops and collectives have mission statements that declare their purpose. It is helpful for members to understand their jobs in this context. A successful worker co-operative requires commitment to the specific purpose and mission of the co-op as well as to the Cooperative Principles and Values. Some co-ops supply temporary work to people with indefinite plans regarding their commitment to the job. A non-committed approach can serve a purpose, such as educating people about co-ops or introducing fresh energy to the co-operative. However, employing non-member labor that isn't meeting a temporary or seasonal need often leaves essential tasks on the shoulders of a committed few and burns out veteran workers.

Valuing minority opinion – There may be one person or group that has a different opinion or feeling than the rest of the group. It is important to treat this as a strength of the group that needs to be understood and utilized as much as possible, and not expect people to give up their position. Many decisions are improved with friendly amendments or creative solutions that incorporate the minority instead of moving along without it.

> *...it's a lot to learn about how to function within this group of people who came from very different backgrounds... the co-operative needs to develop from the different voices that are here, how this co-operative works and whose co-operative it is.*
>
> Gail Hanes, Green Mountain Spinnery

Democratic Decisions

Majority Rule

Majority rule decision-making is a structure that binds the group to the opinion of the numerical majority. Often called "democratic" by co-operators, under strict majority rule, when more than fifty percent of the group agrees to a decision, it is carried out by the entire group. Co-ops often modify this structure so that a greater majority must agree before a decision is carried through. Decisions having to do with by-laws, hiring or other long-term items usually require two-thirds majority even by those co-ops that typically practice simple majority rule.

The good thing about majority rule is that it's fast. It is up to the minority opinion to garner support to make a change in their co-op's direction. A drawback of majority rule is that the minority can feel disenfranchised and the co-op looses momentum when it tries to move forward with just under half of its members opposed to a decision they are expected to carry out. Power blocs can form where people are always against each other, and transparency and information systems can be compromised.

Louis Hasbrouck, co-founder of Pelham Auto, suggests that a simple majority doesn't work very well in collective organizations:

> In democracy, a simple majority or perhaps a little bit more than a simple majority can carry an idea forward. I don't think in a collective that a simple majority or in a very nearly even split in a group can carry the collective forward. I think there needs to be the consensus that even if you disagree, you're still going to work forward.

This seemed to be the case for Common Wealth Printing. Bob Gardner told us that democratic voting (majority rule) may have weakened Common Wealth Printing because the minority would often feel unheeded and even resist carrying through decisions made by the majority.

> *I've grown to believe in the general value of the consensus model—that's a challenge. We can look at Common Wealth; that was a straight democratic model. We had votes that went six to five and we went ahead with the motions.*
>
> Steve Strimer, former member of Common Wealth Printing
>
> *When people really believed in the democratic process, once we agreed on something to carry it through, it would work well. But when you sort of decide and a third of the group was dissenting to some extent and they weren't going to carry through on a certain decision, then it was difficult.*
>
> Bob Gardner, former member of Common Wealth Printing

Consensus

What Consensus Is

Consensus is a method for reaching effective decisions that are grounded in solidarity. All the workers take responsibility for coming to a shared decision in which everyone involved is at least comfortable with the decision, and feels able to implement it without resentment. Reaching consensus means that each member *actively* agrees that the decision is either good for the co-op and achieving its purpose, or that it is at least not harmful. "Arriving" at consensus can be a real piece of work. However, one of the big payoffs is that it can infuse decision making with the best information and wisdom the group has to offer. Another benefit is that consensus can contribute significantly to the over-all solidarity of the membership whatever the outcome. Each member sees her/himself as part of the whole group making the decision together. Therefore, there is no resentment.

Consensus is a tool. When it is used well, all the members feel heard and heeded and believe the co-op is moving forward and improving. Consensus relies on persuasion and/or the ability to come up with a proposal that is exciting to everybody. It takes time to use consensus successfully and, like any tool, it can fail to do the job even when it is used well and it can backfire if not maintained and used correctly. Consensus takes time. Even if, in the end, no decision is made, hearing everyone's ideas and opinions on an issue is an important part of the decision-making process and a step in the right direction towards the best available option.

What Consensus Is Not

Consensus is *not* a process whereby you can give long speeches or get into a back-and-forth with someone who has an opposing viewpoint and ignore others. It is *not* a process for pressuring people into saying something they don't want to. It is *not* necessary for everyone to feel a decision is the absolute best thing right away. It is *not* easy.

One difficult thing about consensus is that decision-making can be slow. It can be particularly difficult for those who bring agenda items to the group because they risk having their ideas rejected by their co-workers, which can leave a lot of feelings exposed. It's challenging, says Steve Strimer, to convince every person in your collective that your idea is a good one, but the benefit is that your proposals have to be "air tight" and that's good for the business.

> You don't just go in there with a casual thing and your clique of a majority group that will go with whatever you think. You don't just blow by the objections of the minority. You're forced to make a proposal that's so well thought out and so well documented that you think it can carry the day. But then when it doesn't—what does that do to you? You know, it's hard when you can see it so clearly and some people can't for whatever obstinate purpose. They have a right to their obstinacy. So that's a challenge. That's a constant challenge.
>
> *Steve Strimer, Collective Copies*

Worker-members who practice consensus-based decision-making in their co-operatives often say that it is both the worst and the best part of working co-operatively. While consensus can be painfully slow and personally challenging, it makes you accountable in a way that is different from majority rule. It takes time and research to come up with a proposal that might persuade your co-workers to take the course of action you believe is the best for the co-op and its members.

> My general worst thing about collectives, if they're consensus based—and you'll probably hear this often—is that progress can be slow. That's painful sometimes. One of the most challenging parts about being in a collective is that I can have an idea that I think is the greatest thing in the world, you know, and everybody should understand this [he's laughing] and agree with me [laughing harder]. And I can put it on the agenda, bring a great proposal and it can be shot down overwhelmingly! That's been one of the hardest things for me—one of the biggest learning experiences in my collective life.
>
> *Randy Zucco, Collective Copies*

A decision made by consensus is extremely powerful. In contrast to the majority rules, which can end up being seriously divisive (because the minority may dissent vigorously), consensus means everyone believes a decision is the best way to move forward at the time. Some consensus-based decisions are hard won but having your entire group behind a decision (especially one that was difficult) gives that decision far greater traction than a simple majority might have garnered.

> The best thing for me about collective worker-ownership is when, it's not every day, it's not all the time; but something happens in the collective where you feel like everybody rises to the occasion. Maybe it's a crisis; maybe it's a great new opportunity and you call a special meeting and everybody shows up and everybody has an opinion. It's an amazing feeling when everybody there cares about this project or cares about an agenda item. It's amazing to see everybody have a voice and everybody participate. I think that for me is the greatest thing.
>
> *Randy Zucco, Collective Copies*

The Art of Making Consensus Work

Most of us weren't trained in school on how run a business together cooperatively. So, co-operators suggest there are some important things to keep in mind that might not occur to someone intuitively. Each group decides for themselves what works best for them but it helps to follow a basic framework for decision-making. VAWC provides a basic framework for decision-making in its Owner's Manual for Member Co-operatives. Below we present some important thing to keep in mind.

> *There needs to be some safety in the circle so you can say what you need to say. I think we're very good at knowing that we all have emotional reactions and if that happens, you say, "Okay that was an emotional reaction. What's at the heart of that? Let's work forward and cut the drama out of that," because sometimes honesty and drama can go together.*
>
> Libby Garofalo, Brattleboro Holistic Health Center

It's important for the group to first **agree on the issue or problem**. This sounds simple but sometimes discussions can drag on because people are talking about different problems. Once the issue is agreed upon, it's important to give each person a moment without comment or interruption to state their feelings or ideas about it. Some co-operators call this a "circle" or "circling up."

It may sound cursory but we can't overstate the value of open ears. Being an active listener can take discipline. It's difficult to resist the urge to interrupt someone who is speaking when the desire to say something yourself is burning, to resist that and to actually hear what they are saying. Facilitation and keeping "stack" (see below) can help the listening process, but it is also an individual responsibility to actively hear what is being said. Another example of taking that responsibility is to listen for agreement and hesitations. If it seems that agreement is nearing, a good practice is to state what seems to be agreed in the form of a question. For example: "Do we all agree that we'll meet next Tuesday?" And then listen and actively look at the responses people are giving.

> *Learning how to communicate is the hugest thing. Learning how to get your point across without bringing too much emotion into it, and learning how to listen. That exchange is really important. I think you can learn a lot from people if you're listening.*
>
> Rebekah Hanlon, Valley Green Feast

Two tried and true methods for testing people's opinions are the "**straw poll**" and "**thumbs.**" A straw poll is a non-binding decision where everyone is asked to vote or show support for a certain idea without it being the actual decision. It is helpful to see at a glance how supported an idea or motion may be and whether or not to give it more meeting time.

Pedal People and Valley Green Feast use a process in which members are asked to use their thumb to show how supportive they are of a decision. If someone is fully supportive, it's thumbs up (12:00 if the thumb was a hand on an imaginary clock); if they are mostly supportive, they point the thumb somewhere around 9:00 on the imaginary clock; and thumbs down if they are against the decision. Like a straw poll, everyone can see at a glance how much support a motion or idea has and where more conversation is necessary.

> *We do thumbs up, thumbs down or in the middle so if somebody's standing aside with thumbs in the middle, we give them the space to speak about it if they want to. If they don't then that's fine, they've just kind of said, "I'm standing aside from this, I'm not going to block it but maybe I'm not totally on the same page." But if they do want the space to talk about it then it's everybody else's job to contribute to making that person feel good about it.*
>
> Rebekah Hanlon, Valley Green Feast

Some co-operatives and collectives employ a modified version of consensus-based decision-making. For example, Collective Copies and the Brattleboro Holistic Health Center allow majority rule to kick in if a decision needs to be made on an issue that has been brought three times to the group with no resolution.

> *At Collective Copies, one person voting no means that the proposal is squashed and that has huge implications for the collective. There are ways to get around that, which I'm glad our founders put in there. If the same question comes up three times, then there is—deeply embedded in our bylaws—a way to bring it to a vote so that one person can't block important changes. I'm glad that's there and that's what keeps us referring to ourselves as "consensus seeking" because we don't operate by consensus only.*
>
> Steve Strimer, Collective Copies

A good thing to avoid in making any decision is to agree to something you don't fully understand or don't really want. Nodding without knowing why can feel like the right thing to do at times but it often leads to confusion and not pro-actively supporting the decision. It is good to trust your co-workers and their judgment but it is equally important to actively participate in the decisions that affect you and your job. The health of the co-op requires that its members be educated regarding the topics at hand. It can be tough to find time or energy to research and read a proposal, but it is a necessary and important part of participation. It's also important to respect everyone's work: say "Yes" to a decision unless you have a good reason to say "No."

Never Assume. Experienced co-operators try not to make assumptions about what their co-workers are thinking. It's especially important to avoid assumptions in the decision-making process. Rather than assuming silence means agreement, it's a good idea to insist on a response from people. If there is no agreement, ask those who disagree to state their objections.

The Art of Making Meetings Useful

> We feel very torn when we spend time having meetings and we're not actually getting the work done that we need to get done. So that's been one of the challenges. We've done some work together this spring to try and balance that a little better. But just yesterday when we were meeting one person stood up and said, "I've got work to do, I've got to get out of here, okay!"
>
> Gail Hanes, Green Mountain Spinnery

Among other operations of a co-operative enterprise, decisions require meetings but it can be difficult (especially for new co-operatives) to find a balance between meetings and production. When meetings are run efficiently, people tend to feel like they've produced something, even if it was only a necessary decision. However, disorganized meetings tend to leave people feeling like they've wasted their time. The efficiency of meetings improves with experience and with the use of tools such as good facilitation, an agenda, note-taking and timing.

Preparation

It's important to provide materials, prepare the space itself, create an agenda (and have it approved in advance!), and appoint a facilitator, timer and note-taker. Make sure everyone is comfortable, that there are plenty of chairs and that everyone can hear. Copies of the agenda, paper, pencils, pens, an easel and markers should also be available for the meeting.

Hunger can be very distracting. Being aware of people's comfort could mean having a meal or food available before a meeting. When they are not held at local food co-ops where member reps can grab snacks before the meeting, VAWC meeting hosts usually provide a meal or some snacks. For Valley Green Feast, making sure members attending the bi-monthly meeting are well fed is as important as having a facilitator, note-taker and time keeper. They're able to use the food from their business "to nourish their meetings" which usually begin with a big potluck.

Running the Meeting

One thing we love about VAWC meetings is they **start on time.** Beginning on time is important for two reasons: you don't want to punish members who arrive on time and you want to be able to end on time.

> *I've been to a lot of meetings during my research and the only one I look forward to is VAWC. The worker-members of VAWC know how to hold an effective meeting. They have food, an agenda and a facilitator; everybody's opinions are heard and we always get out on time!*
>
> Janelle Cornwell, Co-op Researcher

Before diving into the agenda, you may want to have a "check-in." Give everyone a minute or two to say how they're doing so people can be aware of any outside tensions that may be affecting someone during the meeting. However, beware: people will talk about themselves for a long time if a timekeeper isn't keeping them in line with time limits. Review, add to and/or correct the agenda, prioritize items and get approval for the order in which they will be discussed. Assign someone to keep track of time and someone to take minutes. Minutes help with follow-through and filling in members who were absent. Minutes should include a list of those present, a record of every decision that was made, any responsibilities that were taken on (and by whom) and any announcements that were made. Use short items to break up intense or difficult decision-making. A group may agree on a brief extension of the meeting time, but this should not be a regular practice. As a reward for hard work— **end on time.**

Agendas

There is a lot of power in setting the agenda and deciding the order in which topics are discussed. Co-ops offer members unique access to setting and prioritizing the agenda so that they can work through issues and opportunities together. Make sure the agenda is set ahead of the meeting. Many groups post a sheet of paper on the wall during the week so people can write-in issues as they come to mind. Some co-ops, like Valley Green Feast, use an electronic application like Google Docs to get members' input on the agenda before the meeting. However you decide to assemble it, everyone in a meeting should have a copy of the agenda or be able to see the agenda posted. Set time limits for each item and separate quickly accomplished topics and announcements from longer discussions. Also, prioritize agenda items and make sure the group accepts the topics and the order in which they will be discussed.

Facilitation

The effectiveness of a meeting can be all about facilitation. Facilitation is a learned skill that can make the difference between discussions being informed, open, accessible, well-prepared, relevant, productive and implementable or unintelligible, inappropriate, irrelevant, boring and lacking follow-through. A well-facilitated meeting leaves members feeling productive and useful rather than resenting wasted time or being led by someone who can't be trusted to follow through on commitments. Good facilitation supports effective communication and focused energy. It doesn't prevent frustrating blocks but it can improve what is learned from them and avoid repetition, uneven contributions (like one member dominating the conversation) and misuse of everyone's time.

It is the facilitator's job to try to be neutral, to draw out the feelings of a group and connect them to the task at hand. The facilitator should go through agenda items one by one, ask for proposals, identify issues, re-state ideas, keep the conversation on topic, point out interpersonal problems, keep looking for minor points of agreement and state them and check for consensus. When decisions get blocked, conversations go off topic, two people start arguing or speaking out of turn, or when people get exhausted, the facilitator can redirect energy to make best use of the time of the group. Facilitating large meetings can be difficult but it is especially important for meetings of large groups. You may want to break the meeting into smaller groups so that everyone is comfortable participating.

> *We don't need heavy facilitation in Valley Green Feast meetings. I think it's helpful that we're such a small group. At the People's Market there were 24 of us so facilitation was very important. You had to be on and very aware of the stack and what was going on with all of that.*
>
> Rebekah Hanlon, Valley Green Feast member
> and former member People's Market

In an efficient meeting, when members of the group would like to speak, they raise their hand just long enough for the facilitator to acknowledge them and place their name on a list. The "**stack**" is the list of people who would like to speak. Taking "stack" is a good practice because it facilitates listening and speaking. People are prevented from talking over each other, or waiting impatiently with their hand up for their turn to speak.

At the same time, "stack" can occasionally disrupt a discussion's coherent flow. Making sure everyone gets to have their say can turn into a series of disconnected statements and actually prevent the group from having a meaningful discussion. Like everything else we are discussing here, there is no set of "right things" to do. These tools are useful, but participants and facilitators have to be reading the live and changing situation of a discussion to use them well.

The Really Tough Decisions:
Hiring, Firing and Leaving

There are several kinds of major decisions that can challenge workers' solidarity. Hiring and firing are at the top of the list. The potential for much stress is there. Although leavings—a current member deciding to quit the co-op or just choosing to move on to another venture—are in a different class than firing, they can be emotionally painful as well. We don't want to overload the metaphor, but all three of these events can be compared to some degree to family life (marriage, divorce, separation, moving on, etc.) There are ways in which co-operatives become like a family, including all the ups and downs. Members play vital roles in each other's lives, deep caring can develop, and, although members may not live together, they often grow strong connections earning their livelihoods together forty hours a week, year after year.

So bringing someone into the "family," saying "goodbye," or deciding to end a relationship can strike deep emotional chords. Below we discuss these matters mostly in their practical terms, but keep in mind the strong emotional features they involve.

Hiring a new co-operator is a long-term, large-impact decision. The hiring process often changes over the life of a co-op reflecting the formality of the organization. It may start with an informal conversation among friends or colleagues with no job description. Later on, hiring may become formalized through developing clear expectations about skills and experience, or other qualifications. Defining a position on affirmative action and Equal Opportunity Employment might become a priority.

Hiring and growth can be exciting and fun. Anne St. Jean's discovery of Collective Copies was a significant turning point in her life, and it was *fun* for the committee that found her at Staples (an American office supply chain) and invited her for an interview.

Some questions to consider when contemplating hiring are: What skills are you looking for in a co-worker? What skills does the co-op or collective need? How do you value previous co-operative experience? How do you value diversity in the workplace regarding race, age, gender, sexuality, ability, education, class, etc? What tacit political or social values are expected by the group? How much work is expected from this person?

The difficulty of being democratic in our relationships is another factor that cuts through the practical dimensions of hiring and firing. Democracy in face-to-face groups demands that the members assume a lot of responsibility for learning, paying attention, being emotionally honest, appreciating the skills and talents of others in spite of competitive feelings, seeking positive solutions when one tends to get very irritable or threatened in the face of certain dynamics. These qualities are of premium value in dealing with hiring and firing and leavings.

Co-operatives generally prefer to hire someone who is a good fit for the co-operative process—someone who communicates well and works with the group. When communication skills are viewed with priority, it may be necessary to "train up" a new hire. However, when technical skills are prioritized, it may be necessary develop those communication skills. PV Squared has often prioritized technical skills and licenses over co-operative experience. Several of their new hires have thus had to gain the essential skills of co-operative communication on the job.

It's a good idea to have your priorities and needs worked out before you put the word out or advertise. While it is difficult to predict when you'll need to hire someone (since democracy takes time) it is helpful to have hiring practices and priorities discussed before you need someone. There's nothing like an unsure and long hiring process to dissuade someone from taking the job. Your hiring process will be smoother, and the pool of candidates stronger, if general priorities are worked out before you begin.

Trial Period/Apprenticeship

Once a person is chosen for the job, co-ops generally use a paid trial period or apprenticeship. This can be an effective way of evaluating a candidate, but it is only useful if you are ready as a group to evaluate honestly and have the ability to say no. Most collectives require a unanimous decision to hire and saying no to someone who most people want can be difficult. It is worth the pain and time to wait for someone that everybody supports.

The varying skill sets, compensations, sizes and unique missions of co-ops means that trial periods also differ among co-ops. Some have multi-year apprenticeships; some require learning certain skills (like hauling recycling and trash by bicycle during the winter); and some involve political education about what it means to be in a co-operative or an active part of a movement. Whatever the circumstances of the trial, it should be used effectively. Apprentices should be challenged and trained adequately; they should be shown the responsibilities of co-ownership and encouraged to try out some of them. It's a good idea to see if a new hire is open to criticism, has the ability to offer constructive criticism, follow through on what they say they will do, and if they are open to being wrong about something and learning from inevitable mistakes.

*Here are a few examples of how
the apprenticeship period can work.*

At Collective Copies a new hire begins with a period of apprenticeship that continues month to month for six to twelve months. An apprentice gets two weeks of one-on-one training with a member on machines, customer service and co-operative process. During this time as a non-member, s/he may participate in meetings but not vote. As a worker, s/he *does* earn a wage, get medical coverage and earn a share of the surplus. Both parties, the apprentice and the collective, must agree to continue the apprenticeship each month. At each monthly meeting the apprentice is asked to step out of the room so the conversation can be frank and open without fear of hurt feelings. Members share their impressions, each submits one "plus" and one "minus" about the apprentice to a member whose job it is to relay the feelings of the group to the apprentice privately. After six months, if either party is still unsure, the apprenticeship can be extended to twelve months. At twelve months the apprenticeship must end in a "Yes, great, you're a member!" or a "No thanks, we aren't offering you membership." If the apprentice accepts the invitation they become a member. If they don't accept, the hiring process is renewed and the apprentice has the opportunity to continue working for up to eight weeks in order to maintain an income before being asked to leave permanently.

In order to become a member of Pedal People, a person applies to join. They often do several trainings in which the prospective apprentice rides around with members. If members get the sense that the person would be a good fit for the collective and that person thinks they would like to do it, the membership must decide unanimously to approve them as an apprentice. They have an apprenticeship period of nine months. Since the job requires bicycling through the snow and rain, three of the nine months of the apprenticeship period must be winter months, "so they know what they're getting into."

> During the apprenticeship period they have to participate in meetings… They get paid pretty much the same. Most of our work is actually by the job—only the administrative work is paid hourly. So, it could take them longer to do a job because they're beginning, that's fine. They get paid the same as long as they finish the job. After the nine months then we all have to unanimously approve them again to be a full member.
>
> *Alex Jarrett, Pedal People*

Here's what a founding member of PV Squared had to say about inviting new members to her co-operative:

PV Squared is different than a lot of worker co-ops that I know of in that we have a relatively long, I guess you could call it a dating period, before we get married. There are worker co-ops that have longer time but we are generally inviting people on board after they've worked for us for about three years. Part of the reason that we have a long trial period, or working period is just because we're in a specialized industry; we ask for people to integrate into a pretty tight team and they need to have certain skill sets, a certain sort of adaptability—the ability to be able to do more than one thing in the company. If a person doesn't fit solidly into the team, it makes it difficult for us to accomplish what we're trying to do on a daily basis. So we're very cautious...

I'm risk averse to the point of almost immobility sometimes...we're all quite cautious and I think that has resulted in this long time frame. There's a construction company out on Martha's Vineyard called South Mountain Company and they have a five-year apprenticeship before you're even eligible to be invited. In our co-op, you're eligible after a year but generally we've waited to about three years.

Kim Pinkham, (PV)[2]

Growth may indicate success but it can be a trying time for worker co-operatives. Some worker co-ops find it useful to look to the examples of other, especially older, well established co-operatives when making decisions about hiring, trial periods and membership. Pedal People, Food For Thought, PV Squared and Brattleboro Holistic Health Center have all brought questions about hiring to VAWC member meetings. Ultimately, like any decision a co-operative makes, the membership decides what will work best for them and their co-operative.

Buy-Ins

In line with the Principles of Member Democratic Control and Member Economic Participation, most worker co-operatives have a "buy-in" for membership. The buy-in, sometimes called a "share," provides clarity of commitment. The cost of buy-ins varies depending upon the value a co-operative seeks to represent in the commitment. A buy-in is usually set high enough to demonstrate this commitment but low enough to maintain open access in terms of affordability for new members. The price of a buy-in could, but usually does not, reflect the actual value of a share of the company. For example, if all member shares together equaled the total value of the small company, one or more members leaving and taking the value of their share with them could cripple the company. That is one reason a member's financial investment is limited.

Charles Uchu Strader founded Gaia Host as a co-operative even though it began with only two members. Here he explains this decision and offers a cautionary tale about partnership "shares":

> If you just have a partnership and one person decides they want to sell out, they have a right to sell out to anybody they want and define the terms of it. But then as a co-operative, it is a longevity type of thing. A member doesn't own half or a third of the company; they have a limited equity so if they decide to retire there's a specific mechanism that we have to deal with that.
>
> I've been down the road before of also starting a business that was originally formed as a partnership with three people, with principles of co-operation in how those three people were operating but not a clear structure of how to add more people to the co-operative. It fell apart when we wanted to add more people...Mostly it's about our ideals...We have a long-term vision that this is something that we're building that will most likely go beyond us and we also want to grow it. We wanted to set it up so that other worker-owners could come on and we really don't want to ever hire employees. We want anybody that's hired to have that potential to become a worker-owner. We want to have this co-operative democracy and have a business that lasts and provides a framework for other people to get involved if that's what we decide to do. So we've limited our member share buy-ins to $2000 because there's a limited equity piece. A member share doesn't equal a certain percentage of the company.

In a worker co-op, non-members do not have voting power and cannot hold shares. In accordance with the fourth Principle, Autonomy and Independence, when members leave the co-operative they must sell their share back to the co-operative. For example, the buy-in at Collective Copies is $250; when a member leaves, they no longer have a vote and they take that $250 investment with them. This prevents non-worker-members from having an influence over decision-making.

In order to uphold the Co-operative Values of equality and equity, and prevent problems due to an unequal distribution of power based on investment, it's a good idea to keep the value (some co-ops count "sweat equity" investments) of member shares the same for all members. In accordance with the Principle of Democratic Member Control, voting power is equal. Each member of a worker co-operative should always have only one vote.

Practicing Equality and Equity through the Principle of Democratic Member Control

> Unlike capitalist firms, in which shareholder votes are weighted, not counted, both primary co-operatives and at all other levels the co-operative movement adopts the rule 'one member, one vote.'
>
> Stefano Zamagni, Cooperative Enterprise Facing the Challenge of Globalization (2010)

In Mondragon, after a trial period, workers pay a membership fee of 13,400 Euros (approximately $16,478 at the 2013 exchange rate), which they can borrow from the co-operative bank. Membership provides them with the right to vote in the General Assembly and elect representatives in the corporation. Membership in one of the Mondragon co-operatives essentially means life-long employment. If one of the co-operatives fails (which is rare), has trouble or one's job becomes redundant, the worker will receive training and/or if necessary, placement in another position in the same or another Mondragon co-operative.

Some co-ops have a very low buy-in. Collective Copies' $250 buy-in can be paid incrementally. The thinking behind this is to keep the pool of applicants as large as possible and not discriminate against those who don't have more funding available. PV Squared, on the other hand, has a relatively high buy-in, reflecting the capital intensive nature of their business as well as the sweat-equity invested by the founders. Their buy-in of $8,000 is a tangible sign of commitment to the co-op and a chance to capitalize the business and build assets. Brattleboro Holistic Health Center has a buy-in of $1000 which can be paid incrementally and, as mentioned earlier, the member share at Gaia Host Collective is $2000. When making decisions about buy-ins, new co-operatives may find it useful to look to established co-operatives as examples. However, like all decisions in a worker co-operative operating in accordance with the Principle of Autonomy and Independence, these decisions must ultimately be made by the members of the co-operative themselves.

Firing

Firing in a worker co-operative is rare but it does happen. There is a lot to learn when a firing is necessary for, it was the group that hired them, right? A co-operative should examine any move to fire a member and take the opportunity to learn from mistakes that could be avoided in the future. There is a lot to learn about why people leave or are fired from their co-operatives at the level of the co-operative firm, regional associations and the broader movement.

> *You don't throw people out the door very easily in those situations and rightly so, the ideal is to struggle.*
> Bob Gardner, former member Common Wealth Printing

Firing is possibly the most difficult issue in a co-op. Regardless of whether it is due to lack of skills, lack of follow through, or a lack of ability to communicate with the group or for any other reason, it is difficult to ask or tell someone to leave. It helps to have an active accountability process so people aren't surprised and are given chances to have support in changing something or improving their skills. It's best to avoid allowing problems to build up over long periods. In the long run, active accountability processes like regular "check-ins" might prevent someone from leaving or being fired. That four-page list of criticisms delivered to McLeester, for example, was a little too much a little too late. Honest communication in a safe setting is dynamic and difficult to establish but it has a tenfold return when difficult decisions like firing or quitting arise. Patterns of bitterness, active or passive aggression, power struggles, hurt feelings and distance from the group get in the way of effective co-operation. Much of this is unnecessary and can be avoided through honest communication.

When the decision to fire someone has to be made, it is important that the guidelines are clear. Like hiring, firing is usually a unanimous decision within a collective or department, with the obvious caveat that the person being fired can't block their own firing. Someone, the facilitator or another person, may be specifically chosen to deliver the bad news.

It takes time to learn the dynamic of a co-op as a new member and sometimes intergenerational dynamics can be challenging and problematic. We've heard cautionary tales of "founder's syndrome" in which founding worker-owners accidentally keep power to themselves by hoarding knowledge or creating more formal barriers to membership. As Dick McLeester warns, this kind of unintended hierarchy is something to look out for. He departed Food For Thought Books under such circumstances because his fellow collective members thought, as the founder, he was still doing too much.

Conclusion

Capitalist and co-operative businesses have fundamentally different problems to work through. Because there is no common goal, a capitalist business has the problem of coordination, a problem of management. In a co-operative business, however, members share a common goal so the problem is of co-operation, *how to achieve that goal together*.[35] In this chapter we laid out some basic tools that help co-operatives navigate the problems of co-operative enterprise: the structures of decision-making, frameworks for meetings and maintaining spaces for open and honest communication, as well as hiring, trial periods, buy-ins and firing. We are thankful to Dick McLeester for offering his story as a cautionary tale. We share this and other tales from fomer co-op members not in order to criticize but with the hope that others will read and learn from their bravery and willingness to share their stories.

We have suggested that conflict is an inevitable challenge that co-operators must rise to on the basis of equality rather than hierarchy. Working things through, being honest and trying to understand others are primary sources of co-operative strength but we aren't born knowing how to do this together. Much of our lives are lived with people telling each other what to do—forcing us to either rebel or acquiesce. So it's important to beware that co-operation is a life-long learning process—a journey rather than a destination. The more we approach the challenges of co-operating this way, the more we can seek out and share our experience and wisdom with each other.

Part One Notes

Chapter I

[1] There are "good" alternative capitalist businesses and generous capitalist business owners. The problem is the enterprise model, not necessarily the people using it.

[2] They learned that worker-members should retain democratic control rather than give it away to non-working investors.

[3] For more on historical skepticism of the left towards worker co-operatives, see Gibson-Graham, J.K. 2006. *A Postcapitalist Politics*. University of Minnesota Press, Minneapolis (pp. 106-111).

[4] See Clark, C. 1995. *The Communitarian Moment, The Radical Challenge of the Northampton Association*. Cornell University Press, Ithaca.

[5] See Profile of Common Wealth Printing (pp 81-89) of this book.

[6] For more information about the People's Market and the Center for Student Businesses see http://www.umass.edu/rso/peoples/ and http://www.umass.edu/rso/csb.

[7] For more on UMass Five College Credit Union, see Chapters Six and Eight of this book and https://www.umassfive.coop/.

[8] See http://www.ica.co-op/co-op/principles.html.

[9] In the case of hybrid structures and some financial co-operatives, credit unions and insurance societies, members can be both producers and consumers of the services.

[10] This common identity, rooted in Co-operative Values and Principles, means that co-operatives have more in common across sector and industry with each other than they do with their capitalist and nonprofit counterparts. We discuss this common identity at length in Chapter Four.

[11] For more information on food co-operatives and buying clubs in Japan, SEIKATSU in particular see: http://www.seikatsuclub.co-op/english/.

[12] See http://vcba2012.co-op/; and www.ica.co-op.

[13] We share more of this story in Chapter Eight.

[14] See MacLeod, G. 1998. *From Mondragon to America: Experiments in community economic development*. Cape Brenton Press Sydney, Nova Scotia.

[15] See Logue, J. 2006 "Economics, Cooperation and Employee Ownership: The Emilia Romaga Model." http://dept.kent.edu/oeoc/oeoclibrary/emiliaromagnalong.htm; and Restakis, J. 2010. *Humanizing the Economy: Co-operatives in the Age of Capital*. Society Publishers Gabriola Island.

[16] There has been a range of debates, both internal to the movement and outside it, about hiring and labor practices.

[17] See Chapter Five of this book for more details on the ignorance of educational institutions in the US, Canada, and Europe.

[18] See Chapters Four and Five of this book for further details.

[19] Compare this 6:1 average difference to the 364:1 average wage gap between CEOs and workers in the US in 2007. Before the economic crisis of 2008, the average private equity and hedge fund manager's pay was 16,000 times higher than the average full time worker. See Sahadi, J. 2007. "CEO pay: 364 times more than workers." *CNN Money.* http://money.cnn.com/2007/08/28/news/economy/ceo_pay_workers/index.htm(accessed 10/19/13)

Chapter II

[20] Ellerman, D. 2005. 'Translatio versus Concessio: Retrieving the Debate about Contract of Alienation with an Application to Today's Employment Contract." *Politics and Society*, Vol. 33 #3, (pp 449–480).

[21] In a typical profit-driven firm, it is in the worker's interest to earn the most pay for the least amount of work while it is in the employer's interest to maximize productivity and minimize the cost of labor (pay as little as possible in order to increase profits). Some worker co-ops have a two-tiered structure that allows workers to stay on as employees, however, because of the antagonism of that relationship it is not recommended. Experienced worker co-operators suggest that having permanent employees can be problematic because it could set up a dynamic of inequality. See Ruggeri's (2014) fourth report on the recovered businesses in Argentina.

[22] These values are related but somewhat separate from the Co-operative Principles and Values discussed in Chapters One and Four.

[23] Profit is often called "surplus" in the co-operative context because it is the "extra" value created in the labor process that remains after paying for the costs of production including labor and other inputs.

[24] In *From Mondragon to America*, (1997), 31, MacLeod suggested that for Mondragon co-operatives "a typical division of profits might be" 10% to the Social-Cultural Fund; 20% to the company reserve fund; and 70% to the worker-members. We believe these numbers have changed as Mondragon co-operatives have evolved over the years but their influence is still visible in the practices of co-operatives like Collective Copies and PV Squared.

[25] See Gibson-Graham, J.K. 2006. *A Postcapitalist Politics.* of Minnesota Press, Minneapolis (pp 101-126).

[26] See Equal Exchange, http://www.equalexchange.coop/worker-owned (accessed 6/26/12).

[27] See: http://money.cnn.com/2007/08/28/news/economy/ceo_pay_workers/index.htm, (accessed 3/4/2012)

[28] Pedal People's full mission statement is available: http://www.pedalpeople.com/index.php?page=34.

[29] For an interesting discussion about time, work and quality of life see Gibson-Graham, J.K., Cameron, J., and Healy, S. 2013. *Take Back the Economy; Anytime, Anyplace.* Minnesota Press, Minneapolis.

Chapter III

[30] Curl, J. 2009. *For All the People: Uncovering the hidden history of cooperation, cooperative movements and communalism in America.* PM Press, Oakland CA. (Intro, p. v).

[31] This story comes from our interview with Dick in 2010 at his sole-proprietor store in Greenfield, MA. All quotes are from that interview. If our interest was in finding out all that happened in this event, we could not rely on Dick's story alone. We are sharing his story because it illustrates common dynamics that happen across the field of cooperative endeavors.

[32] For more information on Food For Thought Books see: http://www.foodforthoughtbooks.com/.

[33] Eleanor Ostrom won a Nobel Prize for her work on co-operative economies. She suggested that addressing issues in a timely and effective way is one of eight essential design principles for successful long-term collective action. See: Ostrom, E. 2000. "Collective Action and the Evolution of Social Norms."*The Journal of Economic Perspectives.* Vol 14, #3 137-158.

[34] Co-operatives organize themselves in a range of structural forms: hierarchy; a management team and a labor force; democratic or participatory management or collective. The collective structure is characterized by consensus decision-making, shared expertise, administrative, managerial, production, service and other skills. While some collectives have a division of labor with members specializing in certain skills or tasks, there is no formal hierarchy and, usually, a conscious attempt to avoid informal hierarchies. There is a collective culture in co-operatives of the Connecticut River Valley. VAWC practices flat, consensus-based decision making.

[35] For more on the difference between co-operative and capitalist models of business see Zagmani, S. and Zagmani, V. 2010. *Cooperative Enterprise: Facing the Challenge of Globalization.* Edward Elgar Publishing, Inc. Cheltenham, UK.

PART TWO

Worker Co-op Profiles

Introduction to
Co-op Profiles

In the preceding chapters, we outlined a history of co-operation in the Valley and defined three co-operative sectors based on membership. We shared stories from our interviews about what it's like to be a worker-member and some tried and true tools for co-operative governance and decision-making. In this section we present profiles of eleven co-operative businesses, written and contributed by the worker co-operatives themselves.

The first is Common Wealth Printing. We can learn a lot from Common Wealth's story as it is told here by Bob Gardner. The first lesson we take from the story is that starting a co-operative business is difficult but it *is* possible! This story also tells us that co-operatives, like any "regular" business, are not immune to technological change. They must keep up and evolve with the times. The challenge of technological innovation was the downfall of many printing businesses in the '90s, capitalist and co-operative alike.

Gardner's story also reminds us of the importance of valuing customers. He thought Common Wealth suffered because they took their customer-base for granted. Gardner and his former co-member Steve Strimer suggest that Common Wealth's decision-making structure, an elected board practicing majority rule, challenged strength of democratic decisions and the general cohesiveness of the co-op. The minority would sometimes feel alienated by decisions made by the majority and neglect to follow through with or, worse, resist decisions made by the board. Gardner also points to the traditional mindset of workers doing the minimum outside the gaze of the boss which led to reduced productivity and caused internal tension.

As great as it was to have the power to enact policies in accordance with their values, at Common Wealth some of the values of members seemed at odds. Members struggled to create structures and policies that reflected and balanced all of their needs and values. For example, the decision to provide family wage and leave-time challenged their value of equality because not everyone in the co-operative had or could have a family. Gardner also believed they compromised their principles and values in their interactions with non-member stakeholders.

Gardner questioned the logic of Common Wealth's union membership because they didn't negotiate the kind of adversarial relationships faced by typical employees. However, many worker co-operatives decide to be union members for a variety of reasons including solidarity with other workers. Common Wealth's union, United Electrical Local 264, helped form another worker co-operative which would thrive for many years. Their story is up next in this section.

Collective Copies is the third longest-standing worker co-operative in the Valley, a founding member of VAWC and major character of our book. Collective Copies grew out of a worker strike in 1982 and has since grown from five to eleven worker-members with two collectively-owned buildings. Pioneer Valley PhotoVoltaics, also known as PV Squared, installs alternative energy systems and is one of the fastest growing worker co-operatives in the Valley since it began in 2003. Their story offers cautionary tales about the difficulty of starting a business as well as shining a light on major growth and success. They are also a founding member of VAWC.

Following PV Squared is the story of Pedal People. They are probably the most visible worker co-operators in Northampton, Massachusetts, where they have been providing human-power trash, compost, recycling and delivery services since 2005. They too are a founding member of VAWC. Next up is Green Mountain Spinnery which has been around since the '80s but officially converted to a worker co-operative in 2006. Like Food For Thought, they agree in principle with VAWC's mission but have not (yet) decided to be members. In these pages, you'll also find the stories of the GAIA Host Collective, an eight-year-old webhosting co-operative, and founding member of VAWC; Co-op 108, a worker co-op making delightfully fragrant body oils since 2008 and member of VAWC since 2010. Lastly, though certainly not least are VAWC's four newest members: Valley Green Feast, providers of organic food delivery services in the Pioneer Valley and worker co-operative since 2010; the Brattleboro Holistic Health Center, a worker co-operative founded in 2011 that provides holistic therapies out of their center in downtown Brattleboro Vermont; TESA, the Toolbox for Education and Social Action founded in 2011, which is an emerging worker-owned, next-generation publisher of participatory resources for social change causes; and Simple Diaper and Linen, a green diaper launderer and delivery service that is protecting babies' bottoms and the future they inherit.

Common Wealth Printing

Contributed by Bob Gardner

Origins

Common Wealth Printing began legally in 1982, but the roots were set in a small artisan press that established itself in Haydenville, Massachusetts in 1978. Aldebaran Press was the brainchild of Steve Strimer, Martha Yoder and two other Valley acolytes, who formed the press as a partnership. Strimer and Yoder had experience in the fields of printing, and graphic design (Strimer at the *Daily Hampshire Gazette*, and Yoder at the *Valley Advocate*), and recruited several other friends to launch a small press. They purchased a small house in the village of Haydenville, on Route 9 west towards the Berkshires, and quickly moved towards building a barn facility to house the printing business.

The business grew, and found its niche in those first few years. When two of the original members left in 1979, and they were faced with the need for workers to get the print orders out, employees were hired, including me in 1980. I began work in printing in Holyoke in 1977 at Marcus Printing as a small press operator. When I left Marcus in 1980, I was looking for something closer to home (I was living in Williamsburg, and commuting to Holyoke), and began working part-time for Aldebaran and another small commercial print shop (the Printing Press, now defunct).

In the early 1980s, there were numerous co-ops in business, including Pelham Auto, Good Things Collective, ARC garage, Squash Trucking, Food for Thought and assorted food co-ops dating from the '60s. We made a decision sometime in 1981 to reorganize Aldebaran, sell off the house and barn, pay off the old owners (and all related debt) and re-establish as a worker co-op, with a new name and new location. Bylaws were drafted, using the bylaws of Good Things Collective (a retail clothing co-op) as a template based on the model by-laws of the Industrial Cooperative Association. The transition occurred in April of 1982, and Common Wealth Printing worker co-operative came into being, opening its doors at 47 East Street, Hadley. East Street was approximately half-way between Amherst and Northampton, the two largest towns in the county and primary sources for print work, as well as being cultural centers for happenings mid-Valley. As I remember it, there was very limited capital to pull off setting up shop, to buy equipment or put up office walls. In addition, we decided that membership fees should be limited, in order not to discourage those without means from joining as co-op members. We found ourselves then, and throughout our existence, short on the financial means to grow except by sweat equity (which is, of course, what we did). So that is one clear lesson I learned: always try to determine your capital needs, and ideally start with

Bob Gardner and Steve Strimer ca. 1984 at Common Wealth Printing's Hadley, Massachusetts shop

the capital necessary, if at all possible. Starting a business is very hard and starting one with little capital, and without business training, and without the financial support of local banks, or other sources of financing, is harder still.

Printing Environment in the 1980's

Offset printing in the 1970s and '80s was a multi-step process of typesetting, design and layout, producing negatives of the layout, stripping and masking the negatives, offset plate production for printing, the printing itself on offset presses, and finish bindery work. It was faster than printing modes that came before it, but still costly, time consuming and requiring of skilled labor and considerable investment in equipment. What we did not know when we began is that great technological innovations were about to enter the market, requiring radical adjustment. The first was the introduction of personal and office computers, which rapidly replaced having typesetting jobbed out to print companies, or type houses. In addition, new, powerful software tools came on the market, such as Photoshop and Pagemaker, which could and did replace much of the work of design professionals for everyday items such as brochures, letterhead and newsletters that were bread and butter not only for Common Wealth Printing, but every print shop and design house around. We were attempting to enter a field well established, with Newell Printing in Amherst, Hadley Printing and Marcus Printing in Holyoke, Gazette Printing in Easthampton, and some chain print operations catering to the quick printing market.

Early Years

In the first couple years of our existence, Common Wealth Printing grew from the three founding members to more than ten. We evolved from everyone doing most jobs, to having "departments" or specialties. We also grew our business base and volume three or four-fold. Throughout this time, we were acquiring new machinery and expanding the range of jobs we accepted.

1958, ATF Chief 20 printing press at Common Wealth, formerly owned by the New England Free Press of Boston   Photo by Karen Couture

Internally, we were also trying to figure out how to run a collectively-managed business, while producing quality work. It was not easy. In writing the structure of the co-op into bylaws, we decided that having all-member meetings to collectively make all decisions would be counterproductive. Some of us had participated in the early "anti-nuke" movement, and had seen the interminable meetings that seemed to block resolution of problems. To avoid such blocks, we built in a trigger where a managing board of directors was established when the Common Wealth reached seven members. Our experience with this approach was mixed. It did limit the number of members devoting time to decision-making, and streamlined the process (in that you had to convince a smaller number of people to move in any direction). However it also created "alienation" and a disconnection between the decision-makers and those not involved in making board decisions. Resistance and oppositions developed in many cases where decisions were not popular with non-board members. This is not to say that similar resistance doesn't arise in even the most "horizontally" structure organization, but it certainly heightened the trend at Common Wealth.

Effective power sharing and interpersonal relations are critical factors in any democratic organization. The development and maintenance of strong core values, and good relations between long-term members are the key factors of success for any business, cooperatively owned or not. Some of the essential core values transcend all businesses or services such as the philosophy of "serving the public," and not the other way around. That in fact was a particularly hard lesson for Common Wealth. Some values are universal to all co-operatives: To serve the public well, an organization must treat its members well; workers treated fairly will be more likely to provide good service and products.

I guess I would say such high ideals sound good on paper but in the real world, it is much easier said than done. People coming into a co-op have been trained and subconsciously conditioned into a whole other mode. A new, excited co-op member brings their past work, family, school experiences with them. As Frances Moore Lappe says—we live in a "thin" democracy; that

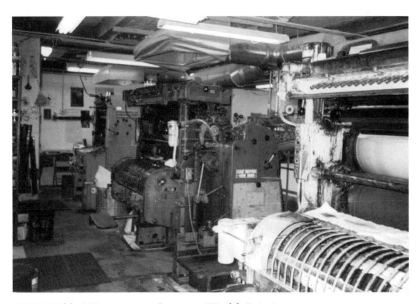

1958 Meihle 29" presses at Common Wealth Printing.

is we generally don't participate in legitimate decision-making in America, it just means that we get a vote every two or four years to let others make the big decisions. In the rest of our lives, we are told what to do, especially in our work lives. So, what happens when this newly empowered person suddenly has rights to influence major decisions? Well, I think many have found that self-interest is the driving force for new co-op members. Lets say for example that a co-operative has struggled to establish a long term vacation policy, where all members receive two weeks of paid vacation, and those with ten years of service receive three weeks of service. The rationale is that those who sacrificed and bore challenges and difficulties of the early years, and still have the lion's share of responsibility and stress, deserve some extra compensation. A new member is very likely to quickly take up the stance that this is in fact unfair and unjust and all members should receive the same vacation compensation. While the argument is portrayed as egalitarian, it is really naked self-interest at play. I now have the power, I will get what's mine. The other dynamic is the traditional mindset of the alienated worker: I will do what I am told, and no more; if the bosses are not around, I will "sloth off;" if left to my own devises, I will eat the whole pie, etc.

Organization of Production

Early on, we established supervisors for each production department, in order to get the work out, to coordinate between departments, and to train and direct new members. How this worked from section to section depended on the supervisor, and the people involved. It certainly was not the relationship of traditional business. Supervisors could not discipline or fire people, and were expected to treat people as co-equals. As the business grew, we developed a weekly production meeting, which organized the scheduling and production needs of jobs in the shop. During a brief period, we also had a production coordinator to do essentially what the weekly production meeting would do. So, throughout its history, Common Wealth experimented with a range of structures from hierarchical to flat, striving for what would make us successful and productive.

Community Involvement

We conceived Common Wealth Printing as more than a model of co-operation, and our aims were more than to build a better place to work. We wanted to make an impact and contribution to local movements and culture. From the beginning, we offered discounts to local community groups. When local opposition grew against U.S. wars and anti-insurgencies campaigns, we were actively involved. Co-op members individually participated in Central America focused solidarity groups, and some of us traveled to Nicaragua during the Sandinista period to work on brigades and/or building projects. We also lent support to the Sanctuary Movement, where refugees from repressive regimes were provided protection and support. We were immersed in the gay liberation movement (at least individually), and certainly in our willingness to hire and welcome openly gay community members. During the 1970's, and 1980's Northampton and environs became a "mecca" for feminist and gay activists. Common

Common Wealth Printing helped organize the Progressive Printers Network which held it first national convention at Orange Blossom Press in Cleveland, Ohio in the summer of 1988.

Wealth at times found itself both embracing community change on this front and at other junctures, internally struggling with gay-straight relations. Some of this dynamic played out on policy issues, such as maternity/paternity leave (this was well before the current boom in gay couples and individuals having children). Policies supporting families and parents could be seen as either progressive/pro-worker, or as a heterosexual bias.

Competitiveness & Co-operation

Being competitive in a capitalist environment does not always conflict with being co-operative and democratic, but it certainly did at times. On wage scales and benefits, we struggled to pay living wages, somewhat in excess of our competitors, and certainly in excess of where we were as a business. It was difficult to justify increases when we were losing money, or just breaking even, and we battled over wages early on. Ideally, an operation would begin raising wages when it built up reserves and was on sound financial footing. But those of us with families didn't feel we could wait. It was a tough business environment, and many of the other commercial presses around had good track records, strong customer bases, and on average, decent reputations for quality. However, in order to address the particular financial needs of members with kids, we approved a family wage differential even if this violated the traditional concept of pay based on merit or pay being a reflection of what you contribute to the whole.

Another component of this dialectic (competition vs. co-operative) was our work for liberal/left/progressive groups and individuals. We certainly were the only game in town if you wanted printing or design work by a worker owned, unionized shop. At times we took this constituency for granted and didn't deliver for them as well, or as respectfully as was due. Taking good care of repeat customers, especially ones that came to our door out of support for worker-ownership and unionization, was actually critical and indispensable for long-term financial success. Another critical external dynamic was our relationship with suppliers. In our drive to generate enough income to be viable, we induced a "bidding war" between paper company suppliers, pitting one against the other to lower the major supply cost on jobs. This allowed us to be more competitive on bids, and increased our return when we did win a contract. But was this a fair and equitable to these suppliers? Did this force them to bring the hammer down on someone else? I think we may have gone too far on this road, but it is a tough balancing act: surviving in a capitalist sea, while holding on to your "co-operatista" principles. I think co-ops need to examine their co-operative principals and how they are applied to everyone that has dealing with the group. All are stakeholders, not just the worker-owners.

United Electrical Local 264 & Common Wealth

As mentioned, we were a union shop. All members were enrolled upon becoming full worker-owners. But being a union member at a shop where the members were ownership, and management was elected by the owners confounded me. The typical adversarial relationships were missing, and there was no bargaining for a new contract. A few exceptions arose when "apprentices" in there probationary period (first six months), were let go, and looked in the direction of the union for support. Nothing came of this, as apprentices were not members. At times, the sole interaction with the union consisted of paying dues, and receiving the right to place a union bug on printed product. At other times, we had a fully involved union steward, and during one period, a co-op member (Diane Brawn) actually became union president.

Collective Copies

The Strike

Collective Copies started with eight or nine workers at the Amherst location of Gnomon Copies in the early '80s. Workers were dissatisfied with the way the business was run and concerned about job security and health issues; so the group decided to unionize and worked with United Electrical Local 264 to accomplish it. Efforts to negotiate had hardly gotten underway when the Amherst store was acquired by new owners as part of a move by Gnomon to franchise the shops. Negotiations continued with the new owners for a couple of months but by the end of August 1982, they'd gotten no where.

Fall was coming and since that was the busiest time of year for the shop, the workers agreed they might finally gain some leverage if they went on strike. The strike lasted from September into December. The workers had to manage on a fraction of their pay and bear up under frigid conditions on the picket line but they gained broad support from the wider community of Amherst. A rally was held each Wednesday and small crowds turned out to walk

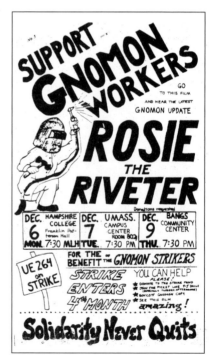

In 2013, Collective Copies worker-members celebrated thirty years of cooperation in Amherst, Massachusetts.

the picket line and hear UMass Labor Studies professor, Tom Juravich, play his guitar.

In mid-December, just two weeks after reaching an agreement and returning to work, the workers suddenly found themselves without jobs. Gnomon never had a lease on the Amherst location and, tired of all the disruption, the owner of the property served them with an eviction notice. A few of the workers moved on to other things but six or seven of the group, already accustomed to running Gnomon's business, decided to run their own. They were friends, they trusted one another and they wanted to operate the business as a worker-owned collective. They set about raising money: Some community members just gave outright donations. Businesses that had been Gnomon customers were offered a prepaid copy plan—so if they advanced $1000, they'd get $1,100 worth of copies when the shop opened. The Center for Popular Economics was one customer who contributed a substantial advance in this way.

The new company was conceived from the beginning as a workers' collective and based its bylaws largely on those of other collectives around at the time, including Common Wealth Printing. The collective members secured a space in the center of downtown Amherst. It was small and on the second floor, but it was affordable. They purchased an old copier, leased a new one and opened their doors in February 1983 with two machines and six founding staff. Community members and local business alike did their copying at the new shop and the area's colleges brought in a large share of the sales in course materials. The shop was tiny, stuffy and hot, and the staff did everything from stapling to ringing sales to totaling receipts by hand. They paid themselves only about $5.50 or $6.00 an hour – but they paid *themselves*. The shop prospered.

> *Everything was done by hand including adding up the slips at the end of the day. It was primitive. We had one window unit air conditioner and it was the second floor with a flat tar roof so in the summer it got to be about 100 degrees up there, particularly at the end of the day when the bricks started radiating all the heat. So it had significant drawbacks but you know, we were working for ourselves. We managed to prosper.*
>
> Stephen Roy, founding worker-member

At the end of their five-year lease, the shop was evicted and relocated to another second floor location across the street. The space was larger, lighter and *air-conditioned*. The business continued to grow and paid its worker/owners above-average compensation. Most years, collective members could look forward to a pretty good distribution of surplus.

Over the next several years, the shop relocated three times until opening at its present prominent location on Amherst's Town Common. It was shortly after settling in this spot that the shop acquired its first computer; it was a very basic PC with a faulty power switch that functioned only with a paper clip wedged into it. Three years later, Collective brought in its first color copier.

Over the last ten years, the shop has become entirely digital with four full computer stations, a central hub and RIPs [raster image processors] to a host of digital copier/printers. Where business was once almost exclusively based on placing an original on the copy glass to produce (what are now) fairly poor copies, now it depends primarily on electronic files delivered via internet or email. The digital and internet revolution has enabled Collective Copies to expand its reach to businesses and organizations around the country. Fewer customers spend time at the counter and some may never set foot in the physical shop. Yet somehow it remains a place where people feel connected and where community organizers are likely to bump into one another and carry on business over the self-serve copiers.

In 2000, the Collective made a big leap with the purchase of our first building to house a second store. The proposal first

Collective Copies, Amherst, MA   *Collective Copies, Florence, MA*

came out of the "Rule the World" committee, a tongue-in-cheek and unofficial committee of collective members with big ideas and visions of changing the world by example. This was a difficult decision, more difficult for some collective members than others. It was going to require loans, expenses to properly equip the shop and hire staff and the ongoing expense of a mortgage. With workers' earnings tied to profits (in the form of profit-share disbursements), some collective members were resistant. All were cautious. The proposal was defeated the first time it came up. And the second. One collective member felt strongly enough to go back and run all the numbers again, including re-search into population concentration, businesses located within a given radius, even testimonials from potential customers. This did the trick. With some misgivings and two abstentions, the collective went ahead. The shop in Florence, while tiny, offers all the same services and grew at a stunning rate – and by general agreement, made the difference in keeping the business profitable during some leaner years in Amherst as the market for "course packets" dried up.

> *For close to ten years I worked at Staples Office Supply in Hadley. I managed the copy center there and one afternoon two women came to the counter. They had a bunch of office supplies and I was ringing them in and one of them said, "Hi, my name is...We have a copy shop in the center of Amherst called Collective Copies and we've been in business for seventeen years. Right now we're looking to expand and add more members to our collective. Just by watching you we can see that you know the copy business. Would you be interested in coming in for an interview?" And I said you're from where? Co—what? Collective Copies?*
>
> Ann St. Jean, Collective Copies worker-member

Over the years, the number of staff had grown only slightly, mostly replacing workers as they moved on. The Florence shop changed that and made clear that the collective staff would have to expand. Aside from the challenges associated with hiring two or three new people at a go, there was the question of how the collective would function with staff working at a physical distance from one another and with different operating issues. What emerged was a two-tiered approach: the collective would remain a single collective with major decisions affecting the whole (pricing, equipment purchases, benefits, etc.) discussed and decided at regular full staff meetings once a month, but each shop would have a good deal of autonomy in daily operations and on-the-floor decisions. The character of the two stores reflects each of the communities. The underlying values and philosophy are unchanged, but the Florence shop also celebrates and promotes that community's unique history.

Collective Copies' retail center sells the products of worker co-operatives in their stores and online. In the photo below, taken inside the Florence shop, you can see coffee and chocolates, body oils, nut butters, seeds, canning equipment and greeting cards—all products of worker co-operatives.

Photo by Rebekah Hanlon

In 2007, the collective met once again to consider a proposal for expansion based on the successful Florence model. This decision was rockier and faced greater opposition. The numbers weren't as compelling and workers were feeling more pinched with regard to surplus. It's important to remember that collective members hold no equity in the company; each benefits from a profitable year and, if they stick around long enough, from decisions that bear fruit down the road. But there is no mechanism for compensating workers who sacrifice surplus during any given year to invest in the future of the business or to purchase property whose value may or may not increase. These are issues that remain and may well need to be addressed in the future, as they are of increasing concern to workers who are aging toward retirement (over half of the current staff is close to or over 60).

> *The way it looks now is that you know, if there's still a Collective Copies after all of us are dead or retired or gone, the buildings will still belong to Collective Copies. So it is a little bit of a legacy.*
> Stephen Roy, Collective Copies Founding worker-member

In spite of the success of the Florence expansion, downturns in the copy industry and academic course packets (a staple of Collective Copies' product mix) challenged the collective to maintain overall sales volume and profitability. By mid-year 2010, it was apparent that steps needed to be taken to stem what could be a first losing year. An often-heard criticism of cooperatives is their inability to be as nimble as traditional businesses when facing slowdowns. A "normal" business might lay people off or cut back on benefits, but cooperatives must deal with the input of a fully enfranchised workforce. The experience of Collective Copies in this period challenges this so-called advantage of the traditional business model. Collective Copies had timely business reports (important) and the ability to call special meetings and was therefore able to quickly craft an austerity plan that everyone signed onto and which sought to accomodate individual preferences on where to make sacrifices. By reacting in time and stepping up promotion the program was a success and by year's end the company was able to declare a patronage dividend. The reality of many small "Mom and Pop" operations finds the owners themselves taking the hit from their own reserves and equity, to keep and shield valued workers during a slump. The owners of a worker co-op can share the pain more equally and band together to arrive at equitable solutions through a transparent decision-making process.

The workers of Collective Copies made a commitment thirty years ago to work together and wed their fortunes. They have had the help and support of their communities, their customers and other co-ops, but on some level, they are on their own and making it up as they go along. Health coverage for same-sex partners, parental leave and benefits, staffing, extended sick-leaves – these are a few of the issues for which the collective created policy when suddenly confronted with a need for them. If the collective model has a single defining virtue, it is this amazing adaptability.

I get emotional because I love everyone there. To celebrate great things that happened in my co-workers' lives: weddings, births; accomplishments because of Collective Copies—owning your own home, [her voice is shaky] going on fantastic vacations, taking a leave of absence because they want to finish that children's book that they've been wanting to do for years. Seeing someone like Steve Strimer who had this dream for the past few years about making us a self publishing center... To see my co-workers accomplish these things makes me feel great [dabbing tears with a handkerchief]...We've all shared the sorrow of loosing relatives and rallied around and supported each other in a way that you just wouldn't feel if you were in a corporate office or cubicle office somewhere or a Staples kind of a thing, as much as you do here. The hugs are abundant.

Ann St. Jean, Collective Copies worker-member

PV Squared

Photo by Ogion Fulford

Pioneer Valley PhotoVoltaics Cooperative (PV Squared) grew out of a grand idea hatched by two friends, Donald and Richard, in the Spring of 2000 during a walk in the woods. Richard had been a solar energy designer and installer for twenty years, a rare veteran of the solar boom of the 1970s and bust of the 1980s. Don was involved in many aspects of the local community and was a fervent supporter of renewable energy. The two were discussing the decline of manufacturing jobs in Franklin county, leaving empty buildings and infrastructure to go to waste; and how difficult it was to find quality solar equipment that was made in the USA rather than Asia or Europe. They thought "why can't we start a solar panel manufacturing or assembly plant right here in Franklin County?" They also came up with what would become the company name at that time.

Don was friendly with Lynn, who was then the Executive Director of the Cooperative Development Institute (CDI). He brought the idea to her. Lynn thought the idea could work, and would provide needed jobs in the area. The company was conceived as a worker-owned cooperative right from the start. At the start, of course, it was envisioned as a 150-200 person cooperative, making hundreds or thousands of solar panels each year. CDI took on PV Squared on as a development project and assigned staff to shepherd the initial interest group through the fact-finding stage.

In the Fall of 2000, Don, Lynn and Richard, along with Don's wife Judy and a few others had fleshed out the idea enough to look for more people interested in making the company happen. Don went on local radio to publicize an open interest meeting. He expected fifteen or twenty people to come to the meeting, and was shocked when almost one hundred people attended. Among this crowd were future founding worker owners Philippe, Matt, and Kim, each of whom joined some of the volunteer organizing committees that were set up to envision or organize parts of the future company.

The extended group met monthly, and eventually the contact list topped 150 people. Each person had their own reasons for being involved in the project, but most expected to work for the plant once it was up and running. Almost none of the people on the list had manufacturing experience, or even exposure. No one recognized this as a problem; instead, long discussions were held about how to train workers in efficiency measures.

The group explored several avenues of opening a plant. None of the original group or the extended group had any experience or applicable background to allow us to innovate a new process for panel assembly, so we intended to use existing processes. We investigated a company who offered a turn-key solar assembly plant operation, including machinery, management training and technical support for around $20 million. Most other options we explored had a similar price tag. This was daunting; it was unlikely our group could come up with that kind of start-up capital. In the summer of 2001, CDI was able to obtain a grant that allowed us to have a feasibility study done on the prospects for PV Squared as it was initially conceived. The study came back with a result that surprised most of the extended group: an assembly plant would not succeed; there was not enough local demand for product; the start-up costs were too high, and the solar industry in the US at that time could not support even a severely scaled-down assembly or manufacturing operation. A sort of afterthought in the report suggested a small installation company could be started on a shoestring budget, installing ready manufactured components on homes and businesses, and could expect to do pretty well over time.

This was uncomfortable information to come to grips with for the large group of interested people who had gathered around the idea of PV Squared. The hopes most of us had, to have a job and a role in building the company, would not be possible for almost everyone involved.

The group maintained its large email list to give out information, but drastically revised its business plan to reflect the new direction outlined by the feasibility study. The company would be a small solar installation outfit with a minimal crew, a marketing and sales role, a general manager and an office management/bookkeeping role. There was some talk of other types of positions, but these were determined to be either unnecessary or not warranted in the start-up phase.

The larger interest group had distilled out to a governing board of nine, plus a few more seriously interested people. At the center of this group, as president of the Board and the public face of PV Squared to the community at large, was Don, who had the original idea. PV Squared was generally regarded as 'Don's Company' to most people in our area. It was taken as a given that Don would be a worker-owner and would lead the company when it opened.

Matt and Philippe had started to work for Richard's solar installation company during the planning years, and each had a little more than a year in the field under their belts at this point. I had been working as office manager and bookkeeper for a small children's educational theater company during this time, and had become secretary of the Board for PV Squared in the fall of 2001.

In December of 2001, the smaller group (Board plus a few) met for a day-long retreat. The agenda included finalizing an offer for Richard's solar business and a plan to raise capital for the purchase. During the course of the retreat, in a radical change of direction, the plan to buy the existing solar business was abandoned and a real picture of what would need to happen to get the doors open began to emerge. The cost of start-up without purchasing another company was manageable and could be taken from each beginning worker-owner's capital investment. The withdrawal of the buy-out offer caused a falling-out between Richard and the rest of PV Squared, a situation which pained us all; especially Don, since he and Richard had been good friends.

The company legally incorporated in May of 2002. Further planning and discussion continued for almost another year, along with the actual hiring and buy-in of the first four worker-owners: Don for sales and marketing; Philippe and Matt as the first crew members, system designers, and all things technical; and Kim as office manager, bookkeeper and general administrator. During this time, with assistance from CDI, PV Squared obtained one of the first solar incentive "cluster" grants funded by the Massachusetts Renewable Energy Trust, as part of its Small Solar Initiative. This funding ensured a supply of customers via an installer-specific grant, as well as a sum of money applicable to start-up costs, which allowed the initial worker-owners to avoid taking on loans to start the company. This grant proved to be a large factor in our early survival.

From the first, the PV Squared interest group had been advised and assisted by CDI, most especially by its executive director, Lynn. Following her advice in the spring of 2003, PV Squared embarked on a search for a general manager to help the company get on its feet as the doors opened. We hired a consultant to help with the search, and after interviewing several good possibilities, we settled on a candidate for that role, Bill. Bill brought considerable name recognition in the solar field, a long career at an area electric utility, and a wry wit to our team. He initially came on as a consultant, an arrangement we were comfortable with at the time. Also arising from this process came a relationship with a business systems and procedures consultant who brought real-life small company start-up experience to the table. PV Squared officially opened its doors for business on March 1, 2003, in a two-room office in the Venture Center at the Franklin County Community Development Corporation in Greenfield, MA.

Right from the start, PV Squared struggled to make sales. We spent time developing systems to handle inquiries. We attended festivals and fairs and events to promote the company. We got the word out and had calls from interested people coming in, but none of them turned into actual contracts. We brainstormed. We put out proposals. We took phone calls. Still no contracts. All the worker-owners were working for no pay at this time, so pressure to produce built with each passing day. At last, it became clear that Don did not have sufficient sales experience to generate enough work to keep the company afloat. Each person in the company had gone through at least a nominal hiring process, except for him. The group tried to work around the problem, but in the end it became clear that it was just not a good fit for the company. Don tendered his resignation from PV Squared and was bought out in early October 2003.

This event was a significant challenge for the remaining worker-owners. PV Squared made its first three sales later that month, although sales remained our most pressing problem for a few years thereafter. Don had been the face of PV Squared and now we were continuing without him. There were hard feelings in the community about the split; some people felt we had treated Don unfairly and harshly. We did our best to rise above, and were never impolite in public despite some hard feelings we privately acknowledged. Don was a perfect gentleman in public concerning the separation, though we can only imagine his feelings on the subject. While it's true that Don didn't stay with the company very long once it had opened, we are convinced that the company would not have survived if Don had continued as the sole salesperson. All the same, the company would never have existed without Don and all the passion, enthusiasm, and hard work he put into bringing PV Squared into the world. For that we are grateful.

The company continued to struggle and build our reputation slowly. Bill came on as a full worker-owner in mid-2004. We tried different ideas for generating sales with modest success. In 2005, the company hired future worker-owner Jon as Project Manager and lead salesperson. This would be a turning point for us. Jon had managed projects for a large engineering firm in our area and brought expertise to a part of the business that previously had been accomplished by sweat and educated guesses. Sales improved immediately and efficiency improved in installations. Later in 2005 we opened a second office in New Britain, CT to take advantage of a new solar incentive program that the state had started. This new office got off the ground slowly, and went through many of the start-up growing pains that the Greenfield office had tackled in previous years.

Between 2005 and 2013, PV Squared has quadrupled in size, and it converted formally from a "home improvement" contractor to a licensed electrical contractor. This was an important step, as the regulatory climate in our state has evolved to make solar installation difficult for companies that are not electrical contractors. We have added four licensed electricians to our permanent staff as well as support staff and installation team members and have seen some changes in the worker-ownership pool: the addition of a worker-owner, Jon, in 2008, the departure of a worker-owner, Matt, in 2010 and new worker-owners, Ogion in January 2011, and Adam and Seth in 2012. We currently have seven worker-owners with two on track for membership next year. We are proud to say our reputation in the area is strong; we have been described as "the premier solar installer" in Western Massachusetts by at least one electrical inspector we have worked with. We pride ourselves on being the company that "does it right," in accordance with building and electrical codes and utility requirements, and that we act ethically toward our clients and everyone we work with.

During this time, PV Squared also has spent considerable time working to make policies and practices within the cooperative that reflect our values. It has not always been easy to reconcile our natural urge to keep control with our desire to share responsibility and reward in our business. We have grappled with tensions between worker-owners and employees during some of the difficult times, when the small founding group of worker-owners was viewed with as much skepticism as some traditional management structures. Clarifying the steps to ownership and having some employees successfully become worker-owners has done much to alleviate this tension. Additionally, we strive to provide generous benefits to our employees, while reserving some perks for worker-owners in order to make ownership attractive. We are very proud of the balance we have managed to achieve between the economic, social, and environmental aspects of what we do.

Our business today is strong and growing, but the years have not been exclusively kind. PV Squared closed its New Britain office in late 2010 after Connecticut defunded and canceled their solar incentive program, knocking the legs from under the solar industry in that state. We were able to move some staff to the Massachusetts office, but we did have to lay people off. The loss of that program was a serious blow to the renewable industry in Connecticut. PV Squared was only one of dozens of installers who relocated or closed their doors in 2010.

PV Squared's plans for the future include more and larger solar installations, and expansion of worker-ownership to a greater number of our staff. PV Squared is conservative compared to some worker-coops in that we have a relatively long "dating period" before we might extend an invitation to buy in. We make governance decisions mostly by consensus after gathering feedback from the staff at large, though there is a fallback voting procedure in our bylaws. To my knowledge we have never needed to invoke it.

We look forward to serving the renewable energy needs of the Pioneer Valley for decades to come while providing good jobs to our people and the opportunity to own their business.

Photo by Rebekah Hanlon

Editor's reflection

PV Squared's profile gives us a sense of the hard work that went into starting the business and again shows that while working co-operatively can be rewarding, it isn't always easy. There were a lot of feelings at stake with the leaving of one of the co-founders and surely, negotiating tensions between employees and worker-owners has brought up strong feelings. Despite these struggles they are growing rapidly and remain committed to their community. As founding members of VAWC, they're also growing the co-op economy—contributing to the development of four new co-ops in the last three years. Remember, this book is about embracing co-operation *in spite of all the obstacles.*

Pedal People

When we called the city to ask about hauling trash to the transfer center on bicycles, the person who answered the phone said,

"You want to do what?"

Photo by Derek Goodwin

Getting Started

Pedal People was founded in December, 2002 by Ruthy Woodring and Alex Jarrett. Both of us were interested in starting some sort of bicycle-based business. Ruthy had done messenger work in Chicago and had experience with Bikes At Work trailers (www.bikesatwork.com) to haul donated food back to the Catholic Worker house where she lived at the time. Alex had recently bought a trailer and was using it to transport his own recycling and anything else for which he'd previously borrowed a car.

The City of Northampton doesn't provide curbside pickup of trash and recycling. Instead people must either transport it themselves to a transfer center in town, or hire a trucking company to pick it up for them. We called up the city and asked if we could take other people's trash and recycling by bike to the transfer center. The transfer center is only for individuals bringing their own residential trash, not for commercial haulers. Initially when we called the city to ask about hauling trash to the transfer center on bicycles, the person who answered the phone said, "You want to do what?" We were told we'd have to take it out to the landfill, which is seven hilly miles away. We then spoke with Karen Bouquillon, Northampton Solid Waste Coordinator, and she said, "I think that's great, and the city needs more businesses like this." She gave us permission to take things to the transfer center and she sent us a free permit sticker for our bicycle trailer.

We announced we were starting this business at a Massbike meeting (a non-profit advocacy organization that promotes bicycling in Massachusetts), and two folks said they would sign up for service. We began a couple of weeks later, in early December. We knew we wanted to start in the winter because we weren't sure if we could do it in the snow, and we didn't want anyone asking us, "What do you do in the winter?" if we didn't know the answer.

The first winter was difficult. That year the bike path wasn't plowed so we had to travel on some hillier streets. Sometimes it was really hard and I (Alex) didn't know if this was a good idea. We didn't have the waterproof overshoes, face masks and mittens that we have now and cold extremities and overheating was a problem. It was really hard work at times! But it was a lot of fun to be out there defying people's expectations about what a bicycle with a trailer (and person!) can do.

One of my (Ruthy's) fears about starting this business was, "What if I want to go out of town? Am I going to have to stay in Northampton to haul people's trash for the rest of my life? I mean, who's going to want to ride a bike around in the winter time and haul trash?" At the time, I knew very few people here who rode all winter long, and I had never seen anyone here hauling a big trailer. What were the chances that someone would do both, at the same time, to sub for me when I wanted to go south to see my family? I didn't know.... At least there was Alex. We didn't both go out of town at the same time for a few years after we started Pedal People. The first winter, we had one "extreme sport" friend who subbed for us once or twice. But as our presence became more established in town, it began to seem like we actually had more people asking to work for us than we even had customers.

By the middle of the first summer, we had about eight customers. Alex and Ruthy were each working one day a week at this point, while we did other part-time jobs. We gave referral discounts to existing customers, and most of our new customers came through word of mouth, mostly from people in the bicycling community.

Our primary business is picking up residential trash, recycling and compost on a weekly, biweekly or monthly basis using bicycles and bicycle trailers. Since there is no curbside municipal trash and recycling services in Northampton, Pedal People fits into this system and competes directly with the trucking companies. We are the only service to offer to pick up food scraps (separated from the trash). We bring these scraps to a local farm where they get composted.

We also do general hauling and delivery, though this doesn't constitute much of our business. We've helped folks move across town several times, pedicabbed at weddings, escorted children home from school on bikes and picked-up and dropped-off cloth diapers for a diaper service. Occasionally we do human-powered yard work, such as raking and hauling leaves, cutting grass with reel mowers and scythes, or shoveling snow from sidewalks.

Photo by Derek Goodwin

The Downtown Trash Story

We signed a contract with the City of Northampton to pick up trash from the seventy or so public barrels downtown in June of 2007. This was an exciting development for us, and a huge commitment. We bring the trash to a nearby trash compactor and the city pays for its disposal. We built a special wide trailer to transport the trash bags. The barrels have to be emptied (or checked) seven days a week, 365 days a year.

But this potential contract actually came up two years earlier…

In 2005, Bill Letendre, head of the parking division for the city, approached us and said, "I want you to submit a bid for this contract." At that time there were five of us doing Pedal People, and we didn't know if we had the people-power to take it on. Nor did we know exactly how we would do it. We said, "We don't even know how to begin to bid on this, so why don't you let us do a trial run for a week?"

Bill said, "Sure," so we rigged up a special trailer just for hauling downtown trash. At the end of the week, we came up with some numbers for a bid, but we actually weren't even sure we could do it without exhausting ourselves.

Before we got a bid formalized, Bill said, "By the way, the City requires that all of its subcontractors have liability insurance." We didn't have liability insurance, and had no desire to get it—partly because of the cost, and partly because it seemed fallacious to base one's economic security on an insurance company. Our economic security is based more on our relationships with people in the community. So we had to come to consensus amongst ourselves whether we wanted to compromise our values and get liability insurance. Meanwhile, the deadline for submitting the bid came and went.

Bill said, "Maybe next year." I (Ruthy) was actually a little relieved because I didn't know if we could pull it off. Furthermore, we hadn't yet incorporated as a collective (though we were

Photo by Rebekah Hanlon

functioning like one), and our legal structure was in limbo. The looming potential of a contract with the City was a major motivating factor in deciding to hire a lawyer to help us get legalized as a collective, which happened in January of 2006.

In the summer of 2006 Bill said, "This contract is coming up for bid again; you should submit one." We said, "Okay, we'll see what we can do."

Fortunately, we already knew how much time it would likely take us, and what the math for the contract would be. So we just had to figure out the liability thing and if we had enough people to do it. We were estimating it could take us up to four hours a day. For us, with the part-time nature of our work, that would mean bringing in probably three or four new people. But how do you know who's a solid person to bring into the collective unless they're tried and true? Most of the current members of the collective already had about all the work they wanted. If we brought in a few new people, and they didn't work out, the other collective members would be scrambling to fulfill the contract, and we would exhaust ourselves.

Sometimes the structure of the collective is a little tricky, because everyone who's doing work is also a decision-making member, but our work is so part-time (four hours/week minimum), yet even doing four hours of work a week requires you to come to a meeting every other week. Most Pedal People do one to three four-hour shifts of riding/hauling per week. The work is so physically demanding, it's not like you can just work five days a week if you want to. So if someone is sick and needs a sub, it can be hard to find another Pedal Person with the time and energy to sub. It's not like a job where if someone doesn't show up, everyone else sort of covers. No, if you're sick, you'd better find someone to do your route, or all your customers will be calling.

So, because of the strenuousness of the job, to suddenly add seven more shifts per week to the Pedal People workload would be a big jump. Anyway, we figured we would go ahead with pursuing the city contract. And we decided that sacrificing our ideals and buying liability insurance would be offset by the goodness that would come from potentially being able to pick up our downtown's trash on bicycle. Besides, the city would be paying for it, built into the contract.

We called up a few local insurance companies to do the dirty, but much to Ruthy's surprise, they said, "We can't find a carrier who'll offer you insurance." I was confounded. They'll offer liability insurance to garbage companies using trucks. We must be really dangerous! It took months before we found an insurance company that offered us insurance. Meanwhile, the deadline for the downtown trash contract had passed again.

Bill said, "This contract is going to come up for bid again next summer. Get your ducks in a row."

Finally, in May of 2007, we had the insurance lined up, and we had grown enough that adding seven more four-hour shifts to our business wasn't as overwhelming. We had three or four new people who seemed solid and eager to come into Pedal People to take this on. We submitted the bid, and received the contract. We came in cheaper than the other trucking company that submitted a bid. I don't think any of the other trucking companies really wanted the contract because it's a pain to have to stop and get out of the truck every twenty or thirty yards for a garbage can, and to have to work during low-traffic hours at 3:00 or 4:00 in the morning or have to work around parked cars and pedestrians during regular hours.

We take the trash to a compactor right downtown, no more than four blocks from the farthest can, and the city contracts-out with a trucking company to empty the compactor. Since we work on bikes, we can do the trash shift any time of day without being as affected by the traffic. And for the more social pedal people, we can dilly-dally with the cans and talk to friends and inquisitive onlookers while we're working. For us, it's kind of like being on display as a professional athlete, and for the city, they love how it enhances their reputation as a "progressive" town with a people-friendly downtown. It seems to me that other downtowns could emulate what we're doing, but I haven't seen it happen yet (2009). Give it time.

Incorporation

In January of 2006 we incorporated as a Massachusetts co-operative corporation (Chapter 157A) with cooperative by-laws. We are not employees, but all "associates." We pay ourselves advances every month on our expected end-of-year patronage dividends, subtracting a percentage for expenses and contingencies.

Pedal People uses the non-employment model. This means that none of us are considered employees of the cooperative. Instead, we are paid entirely in patronage dividends. We receive advances on our expected year-end dividends on a monthly basis, and then receive the final dividend in the following year when we finish our accounting.

Over the years Alex has come to the conclusion that we should re-evaluate using the non-employment model. It has some advantages. Some of us are war tax resisters and since all of the tax responsibilities are passed through to the worker, the worker can make decisions about whether or not to pay taxes without impacting the rest of the cooperative. Additionally, we are able to pay ourselves more because we aren't required to pay into worker's compensation or unemployment insurance. Some in the cooperative community also believe that patronage dividends are not subject to self-employment tax (Social Security and Medicare tax). It is not certain if this would hold up if challenged.

There are disadvantages too. We can't easily pay ourselves sick days or vacation time, since we are only allowed to be paid for work actually performed. There are ways around this, but it's not easy. Benefits are also not an option. It's also not possible to hire anyone outside the collective for temporary work. Hiring subs would be a good way for us to try out new workers, and have them try us out, without beginning the apprenticeship process. Although this might seem counter to the one-member one-vote principle, I (Alex) think that as long as we set strict limits on the amount of work we could hire non-members to do, it would be helpful for all involved.

Associates

Currently we are twelve members. We have monthly meetings and decide things by consensus. All of the administrative work is split up amongst the twelve of us so that everyone both hauls trash and does administration. "Admin" can include anything from being secretary-of-the-day to turning the compost piles.

We pay ourselves by the job. The carrier gets roughly eighty-five percent of what the customer pays. The other fifteen percent goes for administrative costs. Each carrier (associate) is required to do an hour of admin work for every $160 earned. Some people do more admin work than that, and they get paid an hourly rate that is equivalent to the overall average of what we all make riding. Even though, riding, we pay ourselves by the job, we still keep track of how long it takes us, which helps us come up with the admin pay rate.

People can work as many or as few hours as they want, with the minimum being four hours per week. Most people find that two or three days of riding a week is all that is physically sustainable for them to do and still have energy for commuting by bike, farming, and the rest of their lives. Sometimes people will work up to twenty-five hours a week, but it's rare that someone can sustain that without burnout, injury, or getting pissy.

A couple of people have asked where Pedal People come from, and if there is a Hampshire College connection. We (founders Alex and Ruthy) are implants to Northampton, but neither of us went to any of the colleges in the area. Some pedal people have been to area colleges.

For the first seven years of Pedal People's existence, we grew through word of mouth. People would see us on the street, or hear about us through friends, or, in one case, online, and approach us to see if there was work for any more pedal people. Usually we would gradually get to know each other before the time would be right when we needed a person and they were available.

This fall, for the first time, we did a more formal hiring process where we put an ad in the local paper and on Craigslist. The ad was up for about eight days. We got forty-three applications for one or two positions.

I (Ruthy) think a lot of people would love to be doing something physical and that feels more productive than, say, lifting a weight that falls back down again in the same place. Judging by the applications and interviews, people are eager to do things that are outside and that incorporate all parts of the human body, and that are good for the earth we share. But there are a lot of challenges in figuring out how to create this work for ourselves. I've been a lucky one. Part luck, part commitment.

GAIA Host Collective is a co-operative that offers website, e-mail hosting, and domain registrations. Each worker-member owns one share of GAIA Host, which enables us to be part of our co-operative decision making process. We are committed to pursuing environmental sustainability, and support the social justice movement through non-profit and co-operative organizations.

GAIA Host is based in New England, but we work "virtually." Our main server systems are located in enterprise class data-centers in Boston, Southern New Hampshire and San Francisco. Through these servers we manage the computers that run all the websites and emails for different organizations that are our customers. We also provide technical support to clients having problems with their email systems or websites, and other difficulties or questions that arise. 2013 marks our ninth year of operation.

Who we are

We are a co-operative of worker-owners currently made up of four members and looking to expand in the future.

Charles Uchu Strader is a founding member of GAIA Host Collective. He has more than twelve years of experience managing web and email servers and developing websites on a variety of platforms including FreeBSD, Debian, Windows and application languages: PHP, Perl, Javascript, ASP, and Cold Fusion. Charles works hard to keep his computer work in line with his co-operative and environmental goals. Therefore he's involved with many community organizing activities. He is a facilitator and board member of the Eastern Conference for Workplace Democracy, President of the Board at Institute for Environmental Awareness and founding organizer of the Valley Alliance of Worker Co-operatives.

Benjamin Bradley has worked with computers and developing software applications for over twelve years. He earned a computer science degree at the University of Texas at Austin in 2002. Benjamin worked in the corporate world for a few years before joining the Gaia Host Collective in early 2007. His goal is to live intentionally and working with Gaia Host gives him the opportunity to support a company whose work lines up with his values. Benjamin is interested in facilitating cooperation and collaboration, moving towards global sustainability, and participating in the re-growth of community.

Matthew King been working in collectives for over twenty years now, mainly as a bookmonger and community organizer. His first collective was Left Bank Books Seattle, WA, where he worked from 1990 to 1999. Since then he has been working with Food For Thought Books in Amherst, Massachusetts. He has been doing web design since 1995 when he first put the Left Bank catalog online. Since then he has continued to help people get online via his not-for-profit web design project homemadejam.org. He is excited to be working with GAIA Host, which he joined in the summer of 2011.

Marshall Vaughan has worked in tech support for a dozen years. Half of these he spent working for small Internet Service Providers mucking with UNIX and Cisco IOS. The other half he spent up to his elbows in computer parts. He is a devoted board member of ATX Hackerspace where he acts as deputy curmudgeon. Working with Gaia Host since the summer of 2012, he hopes to demystify technology and support collective ownership of critical infrastructure.

The GAIA Host Collective story started with One Choice, a single-proprietor web-hosting business owned by Charles. One Choice was sold to the new Gaia Host entity formed in October 2004 by Charles in partnership with Mark Bucciareli. By purchasing an existing company, rather than starting everything from the ground up, GAIA Host was provided with an initial revenue stream and the hardware resources required to run the business.

Mark and Charles spent the first two years of the business growing the customer base and building the major hardware and organizational infrastructure of the business. In late 2006, Mark's professional priorities changed and he began phasing out of the business. During the same time period, Charles began discussions with Benjamin Bradley about coming on. Over the next two years, Charles and Benjamin spent their time expanding the offerings of the business, improving the internal infrastructure of the business, and forming strategic partnerships with values-aligned website designers/developers.

Incorporation / Legal Details

We chose to incorporate in the state of Massachusetts as an LLC Partnership, not as a co-operative corporation because it provided the following benefits: 1) we could get a little bit more creative with our organizing principles with an LLC; 2) in an LLC the owners don't also have to be "employees," which allows us to work on a pure profit-distribution model without "wages"; 3) simplicity of filing and creating the organization. Three members are required to create a co-operative and GAIA Host was started with only two and; 4) the simplicity of yearly financial reporting and tax-level issues.

The main detriment to this structure is that each member must pay self-employment taxes on their profit distribution, where a co-operative member may only have to pay self-employment taxes on their wages, and not on their profit distribution.

How we work together

GAIA Host has no central office. Members work from home or a location of their choice. We distribute "on-call" shifts so that technical support is available to customers 24 hours a day, but have no fixed work schedule outside of those times. Thus, each member is free to choose his own work location, and to a large extent, his own schedule. This provides great freedom for us as members but can make it difficult to work together. We have developed a set of **"best practices"** to make the most of this unique situation and mitigate potential problems.

• **Prioritizing.** As items come up for discussion, we factor them into an "urgency triage:"

1. Critical issue: contact another member via phone for immediate consultation.
3. Medium urgency: needs attention soon, but not a critical issue.
2. Low-impact issue: send an e-mail for gradual discussion.

• **Weekly meetings.** We meet virtually online (in a private chat room) to discuss pending technical issues, business planning, scheduling changes, and other matters of medium urgency. During Benjamin's "ramping up" phase, we had meetings twice a week, and once he got more comfortable with the day-to-day affairs of the business, reduced them to once a week.

• **E-mail tagging / hand-off system.** For items that need group attention, a special tag is added to the subject header. This allows us to filter messages into a different folder for special attention. This may be used for announcements/notifications or requests for input/review.

• **Personal check-ins.** We include personal check-ins during our weekly meetings, giving members time to verbalize personal stresses, in or outside of the business. We may also address "gut" feelings during the meeting, related to the business, customers, or other members. Because we have so little face-to-face contact, it is vitally important to deal with potentially disruptive situations, and not to let them simmer and turn into grudges. This helps GAIA Host maintain the very high level of trust we have in each other, and enables us to work relatively independently for months of the year.

• **Consensus Decision-making** . GAIA Host has committed to using the consensus process as our decision-making model. In this model, feedback is sought from all stake-holders before a decision is made, and any member may block a decision from going through. This process tends to be slower than a strict majority voting system, but initial buy-in is much higher, so decisions rarely have to be revisited. At GAIA Host, the consensus process has been relatively easy with only four members, although we have had an occasional "stand-aside" on a decision, where the members essentially agree to disagree.

• **Individual / Collective decision-making balance.** Most daily tasks are routine in one way or another. In general, anything that falls outside of this "previously seen problem" category is up to the member encountering the problem as to how they deal with it. Large financial purchases should be run by the Collective, as well as significant changes to the technical infrastructure.

• **Accountability tracker.** The goal of our accountability system is to maintain a high quality of work produced by Collective members. We report missed deadlines and personal commitments, as well as mistakes which significantly impact finances, time, or customer perception. Anyone may submit an accountability report for any member, including himself. This idea is still in early stages, but has worked well so far to raise our awareness about the listed issues.

Why we chose to be a worker co-operative

We share social ideals including co-operative democracy. Co-operative democracy gives us the recognition that "I own my own." It also gives us joy and satisfaction to know that our co-worker-members are working with us instead of trying to gain control over us or, perhaps worse, trying to control them. That's the beauty of being in a co-operative—we learn to value each other's time in radical ways, and this is a basis for being equal with each other.

We began with just two worker-owners but we set ourselves up as a worker co-op so that we would never have to hire employees. There isn't a huge differentiation of skill level within our type of business, so we don't see a reason for different rates of pay and we want anybody who comes to work with us to have the potential to become a worker-owner.

We want our business to last a long while and provide a framework for other people to get involved. We envision GAIA Host growing and persisting. Being a worker co-operative is very important to that vision of GAIA Host's longevity. The co-operative legal structure offers a reliable way to achieve longevity in ways that legal partnerships cannot. Under a partnership arrangement one person can decide they want to sell out, and then they can sell out to anybody they want and define the terms of it. But in a co-operative a member doesn't own a percentage of the company. Instead, they have a limited equity. This means if a member decided to leave or retire, they would follow a mechanism specific to worker co-operatives. And this mechanism is one that they either helped to develop, or accepted when they became a member.

Charles was down that road. He helped form a business as a partnership with three other people. Everyone felt good about the principles of co-operation and wanted to operate that way. Things worked well for a while, but there was no clear structure for adding more people. The partnership fell apart at the point when two people wanted to add more people, but the other partner didn't want it to get larger.

We appreciate being able to incorporate our values into our work. GAIA Host's social and environmental missions are driven by our own personal missions to be a part of the positive change and vision for a co-operative culture. To fulfill this mission right now we donate 25 percent of our server resources to non-profits and non-governmental organizations that align with our social and environmental missions. We promote and support the development of open-source software. We purchase services and products from locally-owned, worker-owned and/or unionized businesses whenever possible and whenever possible we accept alternative payment arrangements such as barter and local currency. We realize that computers have a high impact on the planet so we are constantly looking to find ways to reduce our impact. To this end, we match our expenses for grid purchased electricity and grant those funds to local renewable energy projects. We purchase our computers from used sources as much as possible. We minimize paper consumption and only use 100% recycled paper and make personal choices to reduce our impact with activities like biking, gardening and walking rather than driving and shopping.

> *I had heard of the Mondragon model, a terrific success story for worker-owned co-ops. Coming from a more corporate background, I was disillusioned with working in a tightly regimented structure over which I had no control, and from which I derived little benefit. Most of all, I was tired of putting my time and energy into an enterprise that provided me little more than a paycheck in terms of life satisfaction. For several years prior, I had been interested in how to empower workers. I believe that an employee-owner would be more interested in the success of the business, more creative with problem solving and have a higher quality of life.*
>
> Benjamin Bradley

I'm very passionate about cooperation. I think my passion comes from the fact that our dominant culture—especially in the U.S.—is one that's about power-over, and not about power-with which doesn't work for building a long term perspective. To me it's something that has gone through its cycles of success and failure because the powerful have all this ability to control things but can't do it successfully. I don't think people are happy with it. I wasn't happy with it. So the passion comes from seeing models where people are exceptionally happy in the co-operative realm. For me, it feels like returning to the roots of our humanity. I think it's pretty unnatural trying to have power over each other and power over the earth. So part of my passion comes out of just believing cooperation is a natural thing to do [laughing].

Charles Uchu Strader

Green Mountain Spinnery

Photo: Spinnery Staff 2006 by Marti Stone

Libby Mills, Claire Wilson, David Ritchie and Diana Wahle founded Green Mountain Spinnery in 1981 based on the principles of E.F. Schumacher's *Small is Beautiful: Economics as if People Mattered.* In addition to making quality yarn, their goal was to create a workplace committed to sustainability, the wise and responsible use of natural resources and the support of small-scale farms.

Creating a worker-owned business was a goal from the beginning. The four founders worked collaboratively, shared responsibilities of management and made decisions by consensus, often involving the entire staff. However, they were initially registered as a regular corporation. They wanted profits to stay with the workers but for many years the capital/labor-intensive nature of the business and start-up debt kept profit margin small and until 2003, ownership and much of the financial decision-making was held by the founders who hired staff committed to the product and mission.

In 2003, as founders Libby and Claire contemplated retirement, questions about the Spinnery's future surfaced: How would the Spinnery adapt to changing markets? How would it retain its unique vision? How could employees become more involved in the company?

David, the remaining founder, preferred not to be a sole proprietor. This led the founders and staff to further explore the possibilities of co-operative ownership. We sought guidance from the Co-operative Development Institute and the Vermont Employee Ownership Center to assist with a succession plan for converting the longstanding mill into a successful worker co-operative. It took time, but the Spinnery became a full worker co-operative in 2006.

The Spinnery was an established business, so it wasn't like we were starting from scratch, but there were still many new things we needed to clarify. The transition to a full worker co-operative took longer than anticipated. We needed help thinking through a business plan, personnel policies and incorporation. Most of all, we needed help in bringing the six new worker-owners from being "employees" into understanding how to be an "owner."

The Vermont Employee Ownership Center helped the Spinnery obtain a US Department of Agriculture grant designed to help keep farm product enhancement jobs in the state of Vermont. With the help of the grant we were able to hire Stacey Cordiero from the Co-operative Development Institute. It was seen as a positive sign that, Stacy's surname "Cordiero" means "shepherd" in Portuguese. She worked with the whole staff to think about worker-ownership and the steps we needed to take to get there. We developed a business plan and worked in committees to address personnel policies and other tasks. The transition encouraged us to step away from the production process that we were all passionate about and to pay attention to other needs of the business. Striking a balance between production and planning was and sometimes still is a struggle but has been well worth it in the long run.

Someone asked me why we chose to stay and keep the Spinnery going. You know, it's a good question. Everyone of the six of us who did the conversion to worker-owners had already worked here for some time. So, I think some of the reasons for all of us certainly had to do with keeping our jobs and working in the community where we live. And there's certainly a lot of pride in the product. What we make is of really high quality and lots of us love the product. Some people like working with the machines and we love handling this beautiful yarn. All of us want to be making something with pride. We want a place where there's a space for our voices and ideas, and we get that by continuing to build the Spinnery.

Gail Haines, GMS worker-member

The transition to worker-ownership encouraged long-term workers to step up and become more involved in the financials and it allowed Libby and Claire to step away from daily work while still participating as members of the Co-operative Board of Directors. Their participation provided continuity as well as peace of mind that the business would continue with new energy while remaining true to its founding vision. David is the one original owner who still works at the Spinnery. He serves as general manager and in that role he maintains a strong continuity between the founding, the present and the years in between. He is the main person in contact with customers wanting customized yarn, evaluating and buying the fleece.

Stacy Cordiero worked with us as consultant on this transition for two years. Maragret Atkinson, a staff member who became a co-op member, recounts the experience:

It was a challenging process. The workers had so much to learn about the company's finances and its budgeting and planning process. We revised our business plan and personnel policies and grew to understand just how much David, Claire, and Libby had taken on over the years. We also had to keep producing and selling yarns and doing all the daily work...

The Spinnery has provided a great workplace in many ways, but wages have never been very high so the question of an appropriate "buy-in" or share fee was on the table for some time during the transition. Stacey worked with the staff considering becoming worker-owners, to help us decide upon a reasonable "buy in" for membership. We got it down to the equivalent of buying a fairly inexpensive used car and figured out a way for each member to pay their share fee over the course of a couple of years.

There is always a balance of needing to do the "productive" workof making yarn and selling it so the business will succeed and making time to function well together as a cooperative so that we thrive as a business and as a group. We still need to meet and work on clarity about each of our job descriptions and to identify the overlaps and gaps. We find it useful to develop committees that meet for specific purposes.

In November of 2006, six staff members made the final commitment to co-operative ownership and a new chapter in our innovative history began. We had a big party to celebrate the conversion. Co-op member Laurie Gilbert says of the transition, "I feel more a part of the place; I know more about the operation of the business financially and have a say in our direction."

Weekly staff meetings provide a forum for co-operative management. Teams of owners and staff work together on marketing, finance, personnel, and new product development. Over the six years of the transition to a co-op some of the original members have left the business while new employees have come on board. Currently, the Spinnery has six worker-owners and six part-time employees. The entire staff meets once a month so that everybody knows what's going on and has a chance to voice their concerns and ideas. After an employee has been here long enough (usually about two years) we could invite them to become a member of the cooperative, but at this point, staff members are either satisfied with their current role as employees or they haven't been here long enough. Co-op membership for them is still a few years down the road.

Since our founding in 1981 our goals remain unchanged: to create yarns of the highest quality, to help sustain regional sheep farming, and to develop environmentally sound ways to process natural fibers. The knitting world, it seems, has come around to the things that the Spinnery has always cared about. People are interested in organic yarns and they are increasingly concerned with the social and environmental components of the production process. Our production process, business model and long-term social and environmental commitments line up with these values.

Social media has revolutionized the yarn business so a key part of marketing is to communicate our unique social and environmental values to an expanded community of socially concerned knitters and connect them with great products people have always expected from us. We have been producing high quality yarns for more than thirty years but, in the last six or seven years, the internet has connected us to this whole new market of younger people who are discovering the joy of creating something beautiful and useful with their hands and to more experienced knitters who are discovering new teaching, learning and exchange communities on the internet. We reach this community and market through our Green Mountain Spinnery website, an active blog, Ravelry and on Facebook.

About our work and our production process

Green Mountain Spinnery is essentially a spinning mill. We are a certified organic processor and all the yarn we sell, we make. There are two main components to our business. The first is custom spinning for farmers, finished goods producers and independent yarn companies and the second is the spinning yarn for the hand knitting/crochet and hand weaving market. The custom spinning begins when a farmer who raises animals brings their fleeces here. We spin it to their specifications and they market it as they choose. We also produce yarns for high-end artisan weaving companies and have done some work for clothing companies. The other side is the yarn we produce and sell under the

Lauren VonKrusenstiern feeds wool into the picking machine.
Photo by Rebekah Hanlon

Green Mountain Spinnery label. Yarn styles range from lace-weight to bulky and use fleeces from a diversity of sheep breeds. We select predominantly US-grown fibers for our raw materials and work closely with fiber producers to help them improve flock management and ensure the availability of high-quality fibers. We pay a fair price, buying as much local and New England-grown fiber as possible and have used tiny amounts of mohair from our neighbors in Quebec and Tencel from trees grown in South Africa. We have also blended wool with fibers as varied as hemp, silk, angora, llama and quiviut. We have published two books and are constantly developing new knitting and crochet patterns that work especially well with our yarns.

Transforming raw fleece into yarn involves scouring, picking, carding, spinning and finishing. Quality fibers are transformed through hands-on processing and production on vintage equipment. From a large sink with hot soapy water to our 1896 extractor acquired from the laundry room of the old Windham Hotel in Bellows Falls, Vermont, the fiber is placed in an industrial dryer before moving on for "picking."

The fluffed-up fibers are then moved to the 1916 Davis and Furber carding machine, added to the feedbox and conveyed to a

Ashlyn Bristle works the spinning frame at the mill in Putney Vermont.
Photo by Rebekah Hanlon

series of rotating drums that blend the fibers into a web and then layered into the second half of the carding machine for further blending before being separated into pencil roving and wound onto spools holding 24 continuous strands.

The spools are then carried to the 1947 Whitin Model E spinning frame, where 96 roving ends are threaded into the machine by hand. Bobbins of freshly spun yarn are placed in the steam box for two-three hours to set the twist. After steaming, some types of yarn move on to the plying machine—another 1940's era Whitin Frame, adapted to fit our small space.

In addition to processing fiber into yarn, we answer the phones, pack orders and complete invoices. Some of us also develop knitting patterns and work together to develop new products. We also have a tiny retail shop at the entrance to the mill. We welcome visitors and enjoy giving tours of our mill.

Our story is a great example of how an established business with a succession plan can transition successfully to worker-ownership. It took time and our learning process is ever-evolving but with help from the Vermont Employee Ownership Center and the Co-operative Development Institute we made the transition and are thriving in new ways. Today the Spinnery's yarn offerings have expanded from its first basic wool yarn in five colors to many fibers all sourced in the USA including blends of mohair, organic cotton, New England grown alpaca, in many colors—more than 100 different yarns in all!

Since the conversion to worker-ownership, Green Mountain Spinnery has paid off the preexisting debt on our books; we have grown to become the majority owner of the land where the mill is located and we have begun reaching a whole new market through the revolution of social media. Success is attributed to hard work and innovation of current worker-owners and staff as well as the forethought and participation of founding owners. We are also very thankful for the help of Stacy Cordiero, a USDA loan that funded her work and the Vermont Employee Ownership Center. We are always thinking about new opportunities and possibilities for expansion with a good balance between our mission and continued success.

Editor's note: We are grateful to Green Mountaing Spinner for allowing us to quote from their book, *99 Yarns and Counting*.

Ashley Bristle and David Ritchie.   *Photos by Rebekah Hanlon*

Co-op 108

Co-op 108 is a small worker co-operative based in Haydenville, Massachusetts. Our original five members were Anasuya, her daughter Mira, and daughter in-law Erica, Ken and Stephen. We worked together since 2004 on this effort. In the last 18 months, Ken, one of our original members left the co-op and two others, Khalila and Angie are in the initial trial period considering full membership.

We design, manufacture and distribute natural body products to stores throughout the Pioneer Valley including River Valley Market, Thornes Market, McCuskers, Whole Foods, Cornucopia, Collective Copies, Greenfield Market and several co-operative food markets and businesses in Vermont, Connecticut and recently New York. While most of Co-op 108's distribution efforts have been in the New England market, it is possible to buy products on line at http://coop108.com.

The main line of products is a series of geographically themed body oils (a moisturizing product used throughout most of the world) that are produced using PABA-free base oils designed to penetrate the skin and leave it silky smooth. We add high-quality essential oils to evoke the spirit of place—Corfu smells of citrus and thyme, India deliciously spicy and exotic, and France of lavender and geranium, while Isle of Mann, true to its name, contains some manly, woodsy top notes. Co-op 108 also manufactures a salve for post tattoo care, a hand salve, and lip balms. Our latest creations are a line of deluxe facial serums made with costly oils and essential oils.

Co-op 108 got its start, like every business, as an idea. That idea came to be shared amongst its five members. Three of us, Anasuya, Ken and Stephen were involved with the Rethinking

Economy Project—a multi-year, NSF-funded initiative directed by Julie Graham. The aim of this project was to enliven alternative approaches to regional economic development. The culmination of the project was a trip to the "Festival of Community Economies" hosted by the University of Cape Breton where several of us went to present preliminary findings of the project to a sympathetic audience. We were joined by scholars and activists throughout Canada and the United States who were committed to practice innovative forms of economic development. On the return trip home we were so inspired by what we had heard at the conference, we began to imagine different co-operative businesses that we might be part of.

Late that year Ken and Anasuya became involved in a series of meetings that eventually led to the formation of Pioneer Valley Photovoltaics. From that experience both Ken and Anasuya became familiar with how the incorporation procedure generally worked along with what kinds of things co-operatives included in their own bylaws. Erica had studied similar inspiring materials at Reed College and shared our enthusiasm for a more humane business model. Anasuya and Mira, at this time, were also involved with learning about herbal medicines and

Co-op 108 production process. Photo by Rebekah Hanlon

aromatherapy. After several meetings at different locations—the Conway Inn being one of our favorites—the co-op decided to begin experimenting with the manufacture of beeswax based lip balms. After several more meetings Co-op 108 decided that we needed a product that would distinguish us in the market place. Tattoo parlors were springing up like mushrooms all over the valley and so we decided to market a salve that could be used to protect and disinfect freshly inked tattoos. Natural oils have an advantage over petroleum based disinfectants because they don't cause the ink colors to fade. Blue chamomile essential oil was added as a superior disinfectant. Erica designed a tin that featured the well-inked back of one of our friends. Our attempts at marketing this first product were only moderately successful. Almost as soon as our product came to market it was met by competition from other brands as well as a shift amongst tattoo parlors away from the use of any post-tattoo skin care salves in favor of saran wrap or nothing.

We were undaunted by this early set back. Anasuya and Mira began to formulate essential oils that could be used to scent body oils made from jojoba, sweet almond and other oils. As our geographical theme emerged, Erica began designing labels that described the spirit of place that each oil was attempting to evoke. Using a small renovated workshop/studio behind Anasuya's house to store our supplies, she and Mira began to mix and bottle the oils. Marketing continues to be something we need to work on as a group but we have been quite successful in selling our product line to many of the higher-end markets and specialty stores throughout the Valley. In the last two years we have successfully directed our marketing efforts towards food co-ops in the New England region and new orders have come in from other stores that have either heard about our product or have an interest in marketing locally-made products.

Being an active and early member of the Valley Alliance of Worker Cooperatives (VAWC) has been helpful. Some of the other coops have carried our products as well as offered discounts in printing and we have received a lot of good marketing resources. Recently, with VAWC's help, the NFCA (Neighboring Food Co-op Association) printed an article featuring our Co-op in their newsletter and have also made it available for reprinting. We have used this in our efforts to market our products with existing customers and to encourage food co-ops to pursue inter-co-operation and become new customers, co-ops helping co-ops.

Being a member of VAWC has also been a continual source of inspiration to us when things have gotten tough. It's good to know that there are other people out there with the same ideals and pursuing the same democratic goals in the workplace.

For now, Co-op 108 continues to be a part-time exercise in co-operation. Erica and Stephen work in higher education while Mira and Anasuya completed a four-year intensive course in the study of Tibetan medicine two years ago and now divide their time between that and the co-op. In spite of our limited time, the business has doubled its sales in the last year and we hope to double again in the coming year. One significant hitch we encountered was that we incorporated too early and had to pay incorporation fees before we were making any profits. Book-keeping and accounting logistics continue to be an area in which we need to acquire experience and expertise but we are well on our way to becoming 'legitimate' and are all encouraged by last year's growth and the enthusiasm that has greeted our products.

Valley Green Feast

valley green feast

Photos by Rebekah Hanlon

What can one person do to change the food system?

That's the question Jessica Harwood, the creator of Valley Green Feast, asked while attending Smith College for graduate school. She had a passion for food and an interest in making good, healthy food more accessible. She explored the question in a "five-college" course offered at UMass. The class facilitated a project based on self-directed entrepreneurship and gave Jessica the opportunity to enter a business plan into a competition. Her project, then called "Feast," was a local food delivery service that had a mission to connect people with the local food system.

Jessica's goal for the project was to address the issues of food access in the Pioneer Valley and bridge the gaps between food deserts and fertile landscapes. She hoped to make it easier for consumers to purchase fresh, local, and organic food at competitive prices. Jessica thought that more people would source food locally if they didn't have to tackle obstacles like not having a car. She hoped the union of these interests would foster a lasting connection between consumers and local agriculture.

Jessica's fragile seedling the "Feast" grew into a successful sole-proprietorship with the help of a $2,000 dollar prize from the Executive Summary Competition at UMass. In addition to that start-up money, she also won a $500 Grinspoon Spirit award, a well-publicized achievement at Smith College. With this money, Jessica acquired an old box truck, converted it to run on vegetable oil, and started to form connections with local farmers and small businesses. Her vision came to life as the 'farmer's market at your door' matured into a reliable business called Valley Green Feast.

However, after about three years as a sole-proprietor, Jessica started to realize that she might not be able to give the business the attention it deserved by herself. She was offered a full-time job with the Student Conservation Association so Valley Green Feast needed to change and it had to happen relatively quickly. Jessica sought guidance from her friend Alex Jarrett, co-creator of the Pedal People and Adam Trott, Staff Developer of the Valley Alliance of Worker Co-operatives, to find the new energy that Valley Green Feast needed.

The idea of converting Valley Green Feast into a worker-owned co-operative was an appealing one but Jessica had little time to facilitate the transition. She turned her business over to a farm that she had made a relationship with during the first few years in business. However, the farm didn't have time to nurture the growth of the young business either. So Jessica stepped back in and, necessity breeding innovation, Valley Green Feast was put on a track to become a worker owned co-op once again. Alex and Adam met with Jessica regularly, shared experience and an open environment for recreation. Jessica had a lot of support but the transition was unique because she would not be a member of the newly formed co-operative. A group of trusted people who shared a passion for food access and business ownership needed to be gathered.

Jessica's agriculturally-minded friends Maggie Shar, Molly Merrett, Danya Teitelbaum, and Akesa Mafi stepped in to help bring Valley Green Feast back to life. The group took the project seriously, working together and separately sharing tasks that would facilitate re-growth. On top of the packing and delivering of food, tasks such as bookkeeping, purchasing, marketing, and customer relations were all kept within the collective. They guided Valley Green Feast by consensus and decided that it would have collective identity, practicing consensus moving forward.

After a year of reestablishing connections and customer relationships, two of the four worker-owners left to pursue other dreams. Akesa joined the Peace Corps and Danya established her own farm. So Valley Green Feast would be recreated again. Jessica, Molly and Maggie conducted VGF's first hiring process as an incorporated worker co-operative and took on Rebekah Hanlon, a recent UMass grad and co-op enthusiast and Kathryn Worley, a teacher and avid gardener.

During the first year as a worker co-op, Valley Green Feast underwent many changes including becoming an official member of the Valley Alliance of Worker Co-operatives. As VAWC's new co-op, Valley Green Feast benefited greatly from the connections and contacts. Unique relationships were formed and the opportunity for interco-operation strengthened their model. VAWC's support really made a difference in the development of VGF. It included shared marketing, help with bylaws, and the advice of experienced co-operators.

Since Valley Green Feast's conversion, the worker-owners have learned the importance of connecting to their agricultural and co-operative networks. By asking for help and building relationships, Valley Green Feast's customer base has doubled in two years. In the future they hope to strengthen these connections and diversify the business beyond home delivery. The unique strengths within Valley Green Feast lend themselves to developing new projects. Their work is empowering, inspiring and nourishing, just like the food they provide. They look forward to offering educational workshops and classes on co-ops their impact on the food system, catering, and deliveries of local food to schools.

TESA Overview

The Toolbox for Education and Social Action (TESA) is a worker-owned creator of participatory resources for social and economic change. We design materials such as board games and curricula and distribute these resources through our website (toolboxfored.org). We also provide support to individuals and organizations to develop and implement their own educational materials, programs, and digital resources. TESA was founded in 2010. Since that time, we've already helped develop two cooperative academies, helped launch a conference on immigrant rights and developed and published the wildly successful *Coopoly: The Game of Cooperatives*. We're collaborating with groups engaged in community organizing; and as of 2013, we're working to create a new game, based off our success with *Coopoly*, about activism and movement building. This game will be called *Rise!*

TESA is dedicated to the principles of democratic education (also called participatory or popular education). This pedagogical philosophy is a co-operative approach to education that views teachers and learners as equals—where everyone has something to teach and learn based on their unique backgrounds, skills, insights, and experiences. From a democratic education perspective, learning is a collaborative, interactive process that aims to engage directly with the relevant interests and needs of learners. TESA's philosophy is that democratic education is a fundamental pillar for building democratic economies, communities, and organizations. All of our work—from program development with partners to those materials we create on our own—is based on this pedagogical approach. While more social justice approaches to education are needed to build a more equitable society, many people are unfamiliar with these skills. Developing real democracy starts in the way we learn and act, that's why we are committed to building materials that help people put democratic education into practice.

Turning Social Justice Education into a Worker-Owned Cooperative

TESA was able to get started because of our personal relationships with like-minded organizations. We worked with partners like the Co-operative Development Institute, Equal Exchange, Green Worker Cooperatives, the National Cooperative Business Association and others. Through these relationships, we received advice, financial support, client relationships, our first programs and projects, and were introduced to even more networks of cooperators.

Photo courtesy of TESA

TESA's first team was comprised of recent college graduates and we weren't looking to take on more debt. So, we maintained side jobs and saved up funds to expand the scope of TESA's work. However, as a new business, we were faced with the immense cost of *Co-opoly*, which was our first and flagship product. We needed to move from the idea stage into product development and completion, and had decided to produce the game ethically and sustainably, using mostly other worker co-ops and materials exclusively from the United States. We were able to launch *Co-opoly* as a result of inter-cooperation among cooperatives. It is a testament to the sixth co-op principle. (More on this below.)

Co-opoly's success has allowed us to create a whole line of products that teach about cooperativism through democratic education. These products stand alone but can be brought together to form a curriculum. Appropriately for our commitment to democratic education, we are constantly expanding and changing the tools we offer, both in terms of subject matter, and the audience they are designed to serve. We are developing other resources for activists, teachers, and cooperators. Because our tools are so accessible, we can customize them for any context.

We're still a young co-op, but we're making democratic education a vital and powerful tool for a wide range of topics and causes from the cooperative movement to community organizing, activism, and people's history. TESA's vision is to create dynamic educational resources to build a more just and democratic world, and we try to embody this vision in our daily work through our enterprise structure as well as the products we create.

Co-opoly: Made Possible through Inter-Cooperation

One of the Cooperative Principles is "Cooperation among cooperatives." In the case of *Co-opoly*, production was realized through cooperatives supporting each other by doing business with one another when they can, through mutual aid, by giving advice, and advocating for one another.

Co-opoly would not have become a reality without engaging this principle. Cooperatives supported us throughout the entire process—from development to design, production, and distribution. In turn, *Co-opoly* has also contributed to the cooperative economy by focusing much of our production and sales on other co-ops. An example of this can be seen in the cyclical nature of *Co-opoly's* funding and production: over half of the money raised for *Co-opoly* came from cooperatives (including a generous grant from the Cooperative Foundation), and two-thirds of the money spent producing *Co-opoly* was paid to local worker-cooperatives.

While we were first creating and designing *Co-opoly*, we tested the game at co-ops and co-op events around the country. Worker-owners at Equal Exchange and staff at co-op development organizations gave us feedback and advice on what was working, what needed improvement, and how to successfully reflect the co-op movement in a game. The game was test-played by cooperators and co-op supporters in Madison, WI; Chicago, IL; Northampton, MA; Milwaukee, MN; Washington, DC; Baltimore, MD; and beyond. Without their support, Co-opoly would not be the powerful educational tool and fun game that it is today.

Co-ops and individual cooperators also came out to support the funding of *Co-opoly* via our crowd funding campaign. We designed *Co-opoly* as an ethically-produced board game, manufactured entirely within the United States and mostly by co-ops, but doing so was going to be a monumental cost. To our knowledge, no mass-produced board game had been manufactured in this way before. So in order to make Co-opoly a reality, we asked individuals, other co-ops, and organizations for contributions; and we offered a range of benefits and rewards to our supporters. We raised two-thirds of printing costs via crowdfunding. Benefits included our thanks in the game's instructions, paragraph descriptions of co-ops in the instructions, a card in the game about their co-ops, co-op logos on the back of the box, and free educational materials. Co-ops and co-op organizations from around the country helped us raise over $11,000. Individual cooperators and co-op supporters helped us raise another $9,000.

We wanted to ensure that Co-opoly's production and success would continue to contribute to the cooperative economy. That's why we turned to Collective Copies and Red Sun Press, two co-op printers in Massachusetts. Producing game cards, instructions, and other materials through them would be more expensive than production in China but we were dedicated to working with them. And, as it turned out, Collective Copies and Red Sun Press were equally committed. Neither of them had ever worked on a board game before, and they had a lot to learn and work out in order to make it happen. Yet, through diligent collaboration and communication, Collective Copies and Red Sun Press worked with us to ensure that the game's first pressing was a success.

In addition, co-ops from around the world have been huge advocates of Co-opoly. Co-ops and co-op supporters in thirty countries—from the UK to Argentina, Spain, the U.S., Malaysia, India, Chile, and beyond—have put the game to use in their communities. The game itself is fun and a great resource, but it's success is in large part owed to the enthusiasm of the co-op community.

We distributed nearly 1,000 copies of the game to community groups, schools, households, co-ops, co-op developers and activists. At the time of this writing (April 2013), we are on the second pressing, which was once again made possible by the support of individuals and organizations that believe in our work. This second pressing is double the size of the first, and we anticipate that it will help teach 12,000 to 20,000 people about the cooperative movement through a fun, engaging, and democratic process.

BRATTLEBORO HOLISTIC HEALTH CENTER

The Brattleboro Holistic Health Center (BHHC) in Brattleboro, Vermont is a transitioned worker-owned cooperative business that incorporated in 2011. The business, formerly known as Watercourse Way, was an acupuncture, massage, herb and tea shop that provided products and services six days a week. Watercourse Way went up for sale in November 2010 after eight successful years of operation in downtown Brattleboro.

The six founding members of Brattleboro Holistic Health Center consisted of an acupuncturist, a massage therapist, a counselor, a dance and yoga instructor, and two herbalists. We saw the purchase of Watercourse Way as an opportunity to continue to fill a community need that would have been left empty by its disappearance and to bring our complementary practices to a larger more collaborative venue. Four of the original members had a history of weekly meetings to support each other's businesses, two of the members had been running an herbal medicine and body care product line, and one of the members had already been practicing at Watercourse Way during the previous year, so a worker-owned cooperative seemed like a natural fit for the new venture.

We were able to purchase Watercourse Way and transition into the Brattleboro Holistic Health Center, a worker-owned cooperative, with the help of the Cooperative Fund of New England and the Valley Alliance of Worker Cooperatives. We offer acupuncture, massage, herbal medicine, and counseling as well as classes and workshops in the newly renovated Community Room. As of the publishing of this article, there are six worker-owners and two on member track.

BHHC's mission:

To provide quality goods and services focused on accessibility, affordability, sustainability, and a local cooperative economy.

To provide community education that promotes the understanding that each individual is a unique integrated being; emphasizes self-care, self-awareness and responsibility; and provides information and referrals for a wide variety of healthcare options.

To Create a cooperative work environment that supports the practitioners through self-determination, professional development, peer supervision, personal growth, and a livable wage.

Simple Diaper & Linen

About Our Business

Simple Diaper & Linen is a cooperatively-owned (and currently mama-operated) cloth and compostable diaper and commercial linen laundering service. Nestled in the mill buildings along the canals of Holyoke, Massachusetts, Simple Diaper & Linen benefits from the renewable green energy produced by the city's hydroelectric plant. Those savings are passed onto our clients through affordable diapering alternatives that reduce waste and improve comfort and health for children and the environment.

Our diaper services include rental and laundering of 100% organic cotton cloth diapers and wipes as well as a compostable diaper service that delivers 100% biodegradable plant-based diapers. Clients have a choice of cloth diapers, compostable diapers, or a hybrid of the two.

Biodegradable diapers are a new addition to the eco-friendly scene in the United States, though there is a common misconception that they will break down in landfills. That environment is not optimal for decomposition however, and backyard compost piles are often not maintained at a level of heat and volume to be able to fully process some sixty diapers used each week. So we collect the biodegradable diapers and bring them to a professional composting facility that uses the highest standards for pathogen removal and decomposition, breaking them down to topsoil in just three months. Their future life will rest in landscaping applications as opposed to clogging landfills for 250 years or more. We are the first diaper service in the Northeast to introduce this service. It's been extremely popular with our clients as a method of guilt-free diapering; they

can enjoy the convenience of disposable diapers without the negative environmental impacts.

Simple Diaper & Linen also provides commercial linen laundering to a variety of businesses, including massage therapists, acupuncturists, yoga studios, and bakeries. We also launder horse blankets for various barns and residential horse owners on a seasonal basis. Our laundering system is top of the line and includes hospital-grade germ fighting technology. We have an industrial-strength commercial-sized washing machine/extractor and dryer. We also utilize Ozone technology which uses electricity and oxygen to create ozone that is injected into all of our wash cycles. Ozone kills bacteria 3200 times faster than bleach and eliminates the need for high temperature washes and harsh chemicals. This shortens our laundering cycles which reduces our consumption of natural gas and water. Our final product is 100% chemical-free and pH balanced.

From sole proprietorship to a cooperative governance

Angie Gregory founded Mother Herb Diaper Service in 2009, after the birth of her second child. With a background in environmental lobbying and community organizing, she had a vision for a truly eco-conscious diaper service that connected families and helped foster responsibility for the planet. Her idealistic and entrepreneurial spirit was threaded into being a mother and thus an at-home diaper service took form. With the birth of her third child in 2011, and the continued development of the service, Angie looked to the cooperative business model as a way to strengthen and grow the business. She wanted to empower people working with her to co-develop the business as community resource in which everyone took pride. She wanted co-workers to have a vested interest in the success of the business as well as the creative liberty to shift and adapt the service to suit the needs of clients as time went on. The principles of the cooperative model were inspiring and they echoed the consideration that shaped the original platform of the diaper service: to support other co-operative and mother-run businesses, holding concern for the community, valuing education, training and information sharing as a way to build the cloth diaper movement and client base, as well as maintaining autonomy as a small local business.

Jessica Montagna joined as an official worker-owner in the late summer of 2011. Angie and Jessica announced the next chapter of Simple Diaper & Linen together at their new commercial space in Holyoke. The shift from sole-proprietorship into co-

Jessica Montagna and family

operative ownership added a lot to our conscientious business. We have shared responsibility and shared ownership as workers. Our business model is fair and democratic and we are proud to be a cooperative!

Photos courtesy of Simple Diaper and Linen

Angie Gregory and family

Our relationship with VAWC

We have the Valley Alliance of Worker Cooperatives (VAWC) to thank for helping us through the process of converting to a worker co-operative and the Cooperative Fund of New England (CFNE) for being our fiscal sponsor. Paths were marked and direction was set about a year before the official incorporation took place. During that time, VAWC staff provided Simple Diaper & Linen with technical assistance, invited us into the region's rich network, and offered us knowledge of other models upon which to base our intentions. They linked us to financing opportunities with lenders who understand the mission and direction of a cooperative, CFNE and the Cooperative Capital Fund. We obtained a matching grant to hire a co-operative business developer as a consultant who helped us with lending projections and business evaluations. Working with VAWC and CFNE facilitated the process of drafting bylaws and articles of incorporation and supported our goals for expansion.

Having access to the knowledge base of older co-ops' "how-to's" in governance, support, and history—through VAWC—has been key to Simple Diaper & Linen's foundation. We see the co-operative network as an important component to thriving as a

business. Conferences, monthly VAWC meetings, and co-operation among cooperatives support our business vision and the
movement to social and economic enrichment. These cooperative businesses truly display and embody the supportive spirit of
co-operative values. We are stronger because of it and we are
confident in our future enrichment as a part of the co-operative
movement.

Who we are

Jessica Montagna: After hopping around at various professions
including, childcare, social work, higher education and aca-
demia, I was ready to switch to work that satisfied the eco-conscious mother and social justice educator in me. In 2009 I gave
birth to my son Oliver and was among the first clients of Mother Herb Diaper Service. Since then my path crossed with Angie's
in a variety of ways and in 2010, I joined forces with Angie to
grow Mother Herb. The co-operative model was very attractive
to me because I believe that our economic system is broken and
driven by few to make large profits, while ignoring people who
are doing the hard work. The model in which many people own
and operate business collectively, in a sustainable and mutual
way, is an important model for the future of our economy. I am
proud to be a part of the growing co-operative movement in
western Massachusetts.

Angie Gregory: I settled in the valley six years ago after many
years of traveling the country. I live in Northampton with my
husband and three kids. I'm an avid gardener who studies and
incorporates herbal medicine into my family's lifestyle. I have
worked in community fostering projects like Grow Food
Northampton and I started Mother Herb Diaper Service as an
opportunity to create hand-crafted herbal products for moms
and babies as well as offer the community an alternative to
wasteful diapering.

PART THREE

The Co-operative Difference: Challenges and Opportunities

IV

The Co-operative Difference

CO-OPERATIVE ENTERPRISES VARY BY SECTOR based on membership. As we discussed in Chapter One, they can be classified based on consumer, producer, and worker membership and as the profiles of various worker co-ops in our region illustrate, they also differ by industry.[1] However, when we only see how co-operatives are different from one another we miss the bigger picture of co-operative economies as alternatives to business as usual and as viable models to raise standards of living, build shared expertise and root jobs and wealth in communities. In this chapter, we take cues from ongoing discussions within co-operative associations and among co-operative activists and co-opreneurs in the Valley to explore what co-operatives across sectors and industries have in common with each other and what makes them radically different from "regular" or "capitalist" businesses.

Early organizers of VAWC came together to share unique experiences of worker co-operation. Businesses like Pelham Auto, Collective Copies, PV Squared and Pedal People participate in very different industries—they provide very different goods or services—yet they share common problems and opportunities related to their organization as worker co-ops. With these shared

experiences as a common ground, they formed VAWC based on
their enterprises' identity as worker co-ops.

As the benefits of new opportunities of co-operation among
the VAWC worker co-ops became apparent, the question of inter-cooperation across sectors arose. What could a worker
owned auto repair shop possibly have in common with a consumer-owned grocery store? What does a worker co-operative
copy shop have in common with a credit union owned by its depositors? How could businesses that vary so greatly be similar to
each other in any significant way? VAWC member co-ops began
asking themselves these questions in 2009 and the pages of this
chapter are inspired by them.

What do all co-operatives have in common? How does a co-operative enterprise differ from a capitalist one?

Co-operatives across sectors, like "regular" or "capitalist"
businesses participate in formal production practices. They pay
workers for their labor and participate in markets. However, unlike capitalist businesses, they are organized as "autonomous associations of persons united voluntarily to meet their common
economic, social, and cultural needs and aspirations through a
jointly-owned and democratically-controlled enterprise."[2] This
means that all co-operative enterprises differ from capitalist enterprises, first and foremost because they are democratic **membership organizations** designed to fulfill the "economic, social,
and cultural needs and aspirations" of a specific group of people
who are in solidarity with each other. The various types of cooperatives may provide the same good or service as a capitalist enterprise but they do so in order to satisfy the needs of their
members rather than simply generate profit. So, their fundamental purpose is radically different from a capitalist enterprise.
Erbin Crowell, Executive Director of Neighboring Food Co-op
Association (NFCA) and a former worker co-operator sums this
up well:

The core purpose of a capitalist enterprise is the generation of profit and its guiding influence is capital. A co-op just flips that on its head. Its guiding principle is service and surplus or profit is the tool to meet that goal. Profit is not the end goal.[3]

We are going to explore core statements by the ICA on Co-operative Identity, Principles and Values that spell out deep differences between co-operative and capitalist enterprises. However, let's take a moment first to wonder why it is that such profound differences between cooperative and capitalist enterprises are hardly recognized in our society.

Stop for a moment and identify what comes into your mind when you hear the words "the economy." Do you picture a world of cooperation and care? A world of very diverse kinds of economic activities and organizations including gifts, barter exchange and co-operative enterprises or does one kind of enterprise—corporations of various sizes—come to mind? Do you remember any newspaper article or news report talking about anything other than our "capitalist economy?" Would you be surprised that co-operative members outnumber direct shareholders of capitalist corporations by nearly four to one?[4] Would it surprise you that in the U.S., 21 percent of the population are direct corporate shareholders compared to 40.2 percent of the population who are members of co-operatives? Did you know that the U.S. has the third largest population of co-operative members (120 million) following India (242 million) and China (with 160 million)?[5]

The assumption that we live in a strictly capitalist economy, "the economy," is a big distortion of reality. This distortion not only wipes co-operatives off the economic map, it also leads us to believe—or at least go along with—the idea that competitive individuals maximizing their self-interest will ultimately make the most efficient society. Again, Crowell puts this into perspective:

There's sort of an assumption that somehow the capitalist system, this invisible hand, will make the right decision and that people acting out of their own self-interest will make the right decisions. I think when it is all about profit maximization that is actually dead wrong. When folks in a cooperative environment are given the opportunity to have more control over their own destinies and those of the people around them, they make choices that make a good balance between their communities and themselves. It doesn't mean there won't be disputes. There might be outright fights, there could be splits at times but those are all the things that are hidden in a traditional enterprise. Those are just covered over by this veneer of power. What a cooperative can do at its best is get all the information out on the table so people can make good decisions together about what they want to do rather than hiding it and making decisions based on some other priorities such as profit.

Co-operatives are owned and democratically controlled by **member stakeholders of the enterprise** whose interest lies in the sustainability of the enterprise and the communities that fulfill their needs. While some stakeholders may not be members (for example, nonmembers who rely on the service provided or non-member suppliers), the members who use and rely on the enterprise are those who democratically control it. They tend to be risk averse and even somewhat conservative with resources in order to protect the co-op and its purpose for the members. For this, among other reasons, credit unions, housing and other consumer co-operatives, worker co-operatives and producer co-operatives fared better than traditional banks and privately owned businesses in past and recent economic crises.[6]

Credit Unions and the Co-operative Difference

The 2008 economic crisis and public bail-out of large scale, private, investor-led banks highlights the importance of co-operative business models as viable alternatives to crisis-ridden capitalist investment.[7] For example: while banks collapsed under the weight of too many loan defaults and had to be bailed out by the government, credit unions were largely unharmed and went on without public bailouts.[8] Credit unions are consumer co-operatives that are popular alternatives to traditional banks. They provide similar services but unlike banks, which are owned by shareholders and legally bound to maximize profit, credit unions are non-profit financial institutions owned by their members (stakeholders known as customers or depositors in the banking world). Because they are member-owned and nonprofit, not only do they tend to offer better rates and services to members, they also take fewer risks.

> Credit unions are more conservatively managed than other financial institutions; they return earnings back to their members instead of generatng profits for outside investors. Therefore, credit unions do not have the same incentive to take risks, enabling them to avoid the sub-prime meltdown.
> *Linda Eagle Ph.D, Edcomm Group Banker's Academy*[9]

Credit unions, like co-operatives across all sectors and industries, **subordinate capital to the interests of user-members** of the enterprise rather than risking capital to make greater wealth for a few. **This is the co-operative difference.** It means co-operatives eliminate the antagonistic relationship between users and owners that is institutionalized in capitalist models. For example, contrast the credit union to your typical bank. A bank's motive for holding a person's money is profit. The more money it can make off depositors' investments the closer the bank gets to fulfilling its purpose.[10] Strategies for maximizing profit might include predatory lending and fees for everything from checking and withdrawals to insufficient funds.[11] This sets up an antagonistic relationship that is fundamental to capitalist enterprises. In contrast, rather than profit, a credit union's primary motive is satisfying the needs of its membership. It generates a surplus (or "profit") in order to serve that motive. A return on investment may be one of those needs, but others include sound lending practices, free checking and financial education.

Food Co-operatives & the Co-operative Difference[12]

Like credit unions and banks, food co-ops and capitalist grocery stores are similar in appearance but fundamentally different
in structure, values and purpose. And since the days of the
Rochdale Pioneers, working people have organized food co-ops
as a way of accessing healthy food and strengthening their position in the marketplace.

Shareholders of a capitalist grocery store, who often live a
great distance from their store(s), have a vested interest in mini-
mizing their own costs while maximizing the price and quantity
of goods sold. The consumers, workers and producers who depend on local grocery stores for proximal food, employment and
markets for their products, have little or no say in the goods or
services offered.

They can only vote, as is often said, with their dollar. Because the owners/shareholders' motive is profit rather than
healthy affordable groceries, when the profit margin falls, they
may disinvest, close the doors and sell the business in order to
invest in something profitable, or in another geographic region,
leaving the community without a grocery store.[13]

Shareholder and community interests in such cases are diver-
gent rather than mutual. In contrast, a food co-op is owned by
the same community members who depend on the business for
meeting their needs. In most food co-ops, surplus is returned to
members in the form of a discount at the register or year-end patronage distribution based on purchases made from the business.
While some are explicitly incorporated as "consumer co-operatives," membership is generally open to all, including individuals
who supply the business or are employed by it, and many employees serve on food co-op boards of directors. A number of
food co-op start-ups in New England have adopted
"multistakeholder" structures that include formal consumer and
employee representation in governance (similar to Mondragón's

Eroski supermarkets),[14] recognizing their mutual interest in the success of the business. This democratic control enables representation of myriad interests beyond profit. For Crowell, that's one of the "beauties of the food co-op model":

> They could be generating so much profit for investors. Instead, they're rolling it back to their own buyers, their own consumer members, or they're rolling it into better pay for workers, more security for workers. Or, they're paying "ridiculous" amounts for local produce. None of that makes sense if your primary goal is profit-seeking. If your goal is meeting needs, it makes perfect sense.

The business of generating profit is often accomplished at the expense of the environment, consumers, producers and the employees of the firm. Not only is this relationship between the needs of users and owners antagonistic, Crowell and countless others[15] suggest that it is unsustainable:

> It's unsustainable to run an enterprise with the purpose of maximizing profit. Profit, which co-ops traditionally call "surplus," is excess wealth. That excess wealth comes from somewhere. The idea that profit just came out of nowhere is part of the problem. Somebody paid for that profit, right? Whether it's the earth, through the way we use oil, or the way we use trees and fish stocks or people, the way we outsource, underpay staff, or hire temps instead of permanent workers. That's where that profit actually comes from. More and more I see that as *the* cause of the economic crisis that we're in right now. Logically, it's only through boom-and-bust cycles that you can generate the excess profit that you're looking for. Crisis and conflict—those are prime opportunities for profit.

Rather than focus on maximization of profit, co-operatives put the needs of primary stakeholders—consumers, producers, and/or workers in the community—at the center of their mission, ownership and governance.[16] As members, the users of the enterprise are the same people who benefit from it. Again, their mutual interest lies in the sustainability of the enterprise.

Worker Co-operatives & the Co-operative Difference

In order to maximize profit, employers at a capitalist firm minimize costs including the cost of wages and benefits to workers. Capitalist employers thus have a "logical" interest in getting the most out of workers for the lowest price. This "logic" is actually the profit motive wedged between users and owners, in this case between the employer who owns the business and employees who rely on it for work. In big-business manufacturing this antagonism is sometimes managed through union negotiations. In contrast to the profit logic, worker co-operatives put the needs of workers, who have a vested interest in their continued employment and thus the sustainability of their co-operative, at the center of the business.

During the '70s through the '90s in the US (and many industrialized countries), large-scale capital diversification generated substantial profit for shareholders. Large companies took the profit made from manufacturing production and invested it in other kinds of businesses. For example, instead of (re)investing it in the infrastructure, research and development of the manufacturing plants, US Steel used the profits made in steel manufacturing to purchase Marathon Oil. In the case of US Steel (turned USX) and countless other industries, this capital disinvestment in manufacturing caused plant closures and massive layoffs. In the painful economic restructuring often called deindustrialization, the U.S. saw the "manufacturing belt" become the "rust belt." Tens of thousands of workers lost family-wage union jobs and abandoned rusty cities while investors looked for the next prime opportunity for profit. We've come to believe that these profitable boom-and-bust cycles are inevitable because we mistakenly believe we live in a strictly capitalist economy. However, co-operative enterprises challenge that belief. Had those companies been worker co-operatives, workers would have had a say and been able to represent their interest in the sustainability of their jobs. They might have invested some of that surplus into research and development, equipment, education and training. That's exactly what worker-members of the Mondragon Co-operative Corporation (MCC) have done and are doing.

During a number of Spanish recessions over the last thirty years when unemployment in Spain was on the rise, employment in the Mondragon co-operative complex remained steady or grew.

> The largest corporation in the Basque region, MCC is also one of Spain's top ten biggest corporations (in terms of sales or employment). Far better than merely surviving since its founding in 1956, MCC has grown dramatically. Along the way, it added a co-operative bank, Caja Laboral (holding almost $25bn in deposits in 2010). And MCC has expanded internationally, now operating over 77 businesses outside Spain. MCC has proven itself able to grow and prosper *as an alternative to* and competitor of capitalist organizations of enterprise.   *Richard Wolff, Professor of Economics*[17][18]

Co-operators warn that Mondragon is no "utopia" but for Wolff, "given the performance of Spanish capitalism these days—25 percent unemployment, a broken banking system, and government-imposed austerity (as if there were no alternative to that either)—MCC seems a welcome oasis in a capitalist desert."[19]

Argentinean workers faced a crisis of capitalism that would have led to massive de-industrialization as well. However, in the wake of Argentina's economic meltdown, co-operative and other non-capitalist economic models took over where the capitalist ones failed.[20] Industrial Argentina was touted by some economists as an "economic miracle" during the '90s but, while profits for some were soaring, crisis was brewing. By 2001 it erupted into a total meltdown of the Argentine political economic system. Argentines were faced with massive manufacturing plant closures, unemployment and capital flight. Middle-class Argentines were literally locked out of their bank accounts. They poured into the streets of major cities banging pots and pans demanding "que se vayan todos!" (They all must go!)[21]

Amid the chaos, workers took over their closed factories, resumed production and continued to fight legal battles to retain the rights to their "occupied" factories long after the protests in the streets had cleared. This movement is ongoing. As of 2013, there were 311 recovered enterprises organized as worker co-ops employing 13,000 workers.[22]

A stable job, affordable goods and financial services are important to most anyone who works for a living, buys groceries and pays rent or a mortgage to keep a roof over their heads. Most businesses that we rely on to provide these services, capitalist and co-operative alike, employ people like ourselves who work hard providing these necessities for themselves and others. So, financial solvency is as important to the people relying on co-operatives as it is to people relying on a capitalist business for their goods, services and livelihoods.

This brings us back to the question of the co-operative difference. If, rather than profit, the purpose of co-operatives is contributing to the human fulfillment of its members by satisfying particular needs and desires, then what are the values and principles guiding the structures, policies and decision-making in co-operatives?

The Co-operative Values and Principles

The cool thing about the Co-operative Values and Principles is that they were developed by co-operators themselves. As Crowell points out, they "didn't drop out of the sky from some philanthropist or omnipotent leader, they grew up in the context of the movement." They certainly didn't drop out of a textbook on economics. The Principles and Values come out of a legacy of centuries of co-operative experience across sectors and industries, addressing the unique challenges, opportunities and goals of working co-operatively. They are integral to the economics of co-operative enterprises, guiding every mechanism of a co-operative from structure to operation—from voting to investment, pay scales and management. However, the vast majority of economists don't "get it" because they can't even see it![23]

We outlined the Principles and Values in Chapter One but given their importance, let's take another look. According to the International Co-operative Alliance, co-operatives are based on the ethical *values:*

- self-help
- self-responsibility
- democracy
- equality
- equity
- solidarity

In the tradition of their founders, co-operative members believe in the personal *values*

- honesty
- openness
- social responsibility
- caring for others

Most economists and other regular people don't understand co-operatives because they are economic enterprises based on *values* that most people deem *non-economic* and even anti-economic. When we think of economic "values," we usually think of costs of production, efficiency and profit. Democracy? Equality? Honesty? How could these be *economic* values? Yet co-operatives are economic enterprises *based* on these values and they are essential for co-operatives to continue their economic production and distribution of goods and services in a co-operative manner.

OK. So co-ops are based on these values but how do they put them into practice? The Co-operative Principles are helpful guidelines for putting co-operative Values into practice. Tom Webb, faculty member at St. Mary's University Masters Program in Co-operative and Credit Union Management (the only such degree in North America), has twenty-five years of experience as both manager and member of several co-operative enterprises. He reminds us that the Values and Principles are essential for co-operative success; they are interconnected and best understood in relation to each other. Equality, honesty, independence, self-responsibility and the other Values are essential to the character of a co-operative business and its capacity to survive. Without them member-owned democratically controlled enterprises tend to fall apart or demutualize (remove co-operative ownership).

The Co-operative Difference and Shared Co-operative Advantage at a Glance

Here's a point-by-point contrast with capitalist enterprises:

Characteristic	Capitalist Enterprise	Co-operative Enterprise
Organizational Structure	Privately owned, often autocratic	Member-owned and Democratic
Values	Profit and *maybe* some other values decided upon by owner(s) or board of directors	Self-help, Self-responsibility, Democracy, Equality, Equity and Solidarity, Honesty, Openness, Social responsibility, caring for others and maybe some other values agreed upon by members
Principles	Profit and *maybe* some other principles decided upon by owner(s) or board of directors	1) Voluntary and Open Membership 2) Democratic Member Control 3) Economic Participation 4) Autonomy and Independence 5) Education and Training 6) Co-operation Among Co-operatives 7) Concern for Community
Purpose for Existence	Generating profit for owner(s) or shareholders	Fulfillment of its members by satisfying particular needs and desires

Co-operatives are member-owned, democratically-controlled enterprises based on Co-operative Values and guided by Co-operative Principles. They differ from capitalist businesses in 1) organizational structure; 2) values upon which they are based; 3) guiding principles and; 4) their very purpose for existing!

Whether it is a consumer, worker or producer co-operative, Co-operative Values and Principles provide a framework for the ethical negotiation of decisions co-operatives have to make. The membership and its interpretation of the Principles thus constitute (or should constitute) uniquely co-operative management styles, measures of efficiency and methods for development.[24] They protect the Autonomy and Independence of co-operative enterprises and their members' Democratic and Economic Participation.

Mondragon attributes much of their success to adherence and identification with the Co-operative Principles and Values.[25] Mondragon interprets the Co-operative Principles uniquely and has added three principles that reflect their overriding commitment to labor and building sustainable worker co-operatives:

1. Open admission
2. Democratic organization
3. The sovereignty of labor
4. Instrumental and subordinate nature of capital
5. Participatory management
6. Payment solidarity
7. Inter-cooperation (co-operation with other co-operatives in all ways and at all levels)
8. Social transformation
9. Universality
10. Education[26]

Just reading these principles on the Mondragon website gives us a chill. Sovereignty of labor! Subordinate character of capital! Whoever heard of such things? These principles convey the message that something very different is going on here. This is a

revolutionary business model. Some of the Mondragon principles are so revolutionary, or so specific to Mondragon, that
they may need some explanation. Here are some definitions from
the web site:

- *Sovereignty of labor* is upheld because labor is understood by
  Mondragon co-operatives as the main factor in the transformation of "nature, society and human beings themselves."
  Thus there is a strong emphasis on job creation. The wealth
  generated in the co-ops is distributed according to the labor
  provided in two forms—what they call "advanced payment"
  and "co-operative dividends."

- *Instrumental and subordinate nature of capital* means that
  Mondragon recognizes the importance of capital for development and deems its saving worthy of remuneration in accordance to the effort involved rather than profit. Capital is in the
  service of people (especially labor) rather than profit and ac-
  cordingly is managed in a participatory manner with standards
  for transparency and information sharing.

- *Payment solidarity* means that within a Mondragon co-op
  the ratio of highest to lowest paid is 4:1 on average. Also
  Mondragon co-operators maintain their pay levels in line with
  those of workers in the same industry and region, so that they
  don't create a "labor aristocracy" of Mondragon co-operators.
  In addition to contributing to regional solidarity, controlling
  pay levels means that more surplus is available for the collective
  project of creating more co-ops and building a co-operative
  economy.

- *Social transformation* refers to the Mondragon process of development, growing ever more co-operatives to provide more
  jobs through the reinvestment of surplus; support for community development, to which ten percent of net surplus is devoted; providing a social security system for all members; and
  economic and social co-operation with other institutions.

- *Universality* means solidarity with the international co-operative movement and with all those who work for economic
  democracy and support peace, justice and development. Practicing universality involves Mondragon's active participation in

the international forums and associations of the "social economy" and in education and training activities to disseminate co-operative culture locally and worldwide.[27]

True to their principles of social transformation and universality, Mondragon teamed up with the United Steel Workers Union. Together with the Ohio Employee Ownership Center they developed a new union co-op model to facilitate co-operation between unions and worker co-ops and possibly develop new co-ops in the future.

Managing a business with the Co-operative Principles and Values can be challenging. However, drifting away from them can undermine co-operative success. It takes time to have meetings, involve membership and make informed decisions based on people's values and concerns. These activities demand energy, time and financial resources. Thus abiding by the Principles and Values is sometimes seen as "getting in the way" of business. Co-ops struggle to balance the Principles with norms of efficiency that drive a typical business. It may take time and resources to be guided by Principles and Values, but as Mondragon's success demonstrates, they are among co-operatives' greatest assets. Co-ops tend to last longer, have more customer loyalty, higher standards of production and have more equitable distribution of surplus than conventional businesses.

In conclusion

The "co-operative difference" that is shared across all industries and sectors is the Identity based in Values and Principles. The economic value of that Identity is often misunderstood but it can be seen at work in the accounting, management, challenges and opportunities of individual co-operative firms across consumer and worker-co-op sectors.

Despite the substantial impact of co-operatives, and the vast differences between co-operatives and capitalist firms, the Co-operative Identity rooted in Values and Principles is ignored, misunderstood and/or invisible to mainstream economists and business schools worldwide.[28] Co-operatives have also been largely invisible to a general public that confuses credit unions with banks and producer co-operatives with publicly held corporations. Together consumer, producer and worker co-ops comprise a substantial fraction of the world economy. One billion members of co-operatives are providing 100 million jobs worldwide. Even the U.S.—a pillar of capitalist profit and culture—is home to some 30,000 co-operatives operating in 73,000 places of business, managing $3 trillion in assets, $500 billion in revenue and $25 billion in wages.[29]

Considering their economic impact and the vast difference between co-operative and capitalist enterprises, how could it be that co-operatives are so widely invisible and/or misunderstood? Why do we mistake producer co-operatives for corporations and credit unions for capitalist banks?

One reason is that the very foundations upon which co-operative businesses are built and thrive—the Co-operative Principles and Values—are deemed *non-economic*! Thus their *economic* value is invisible. The co-operative difference is banished from American high schools and universities where students learn that economics is about self-interested individuals maximizing profit in a competitive world.

Co-operatives don't exist in the capitalist economy that we learn about in school, on T.V. and in the newspaper. This invisibility has huge implications for the present and future success of co-operatives across sectors and industries. We believe it has huge consequences for people everywhere. How can we (re)produce something that we can't even see?

The good news is co-operatives have gained substantial visibility in recent years. The United Nations International Year of Co-operatives was a great boon to co-operatives and we hope this book will contribute to increased understanding and success of the co-operative movement.

In the next chapter we explore the phenomena of economic invisibility and its detrimental effects on the co-operative movement. We turn to strategy in Chapter Seven where we share the experience of VAWC facing the challenge of invisibility and harnessing opportunities of inter-cooperation.

V

Rendering the Co-operative
Difference Invisible

THE VAST DIFFERENCES BETWEEN CAPITALIST AND CO-OPERATIVE
enterprises and the substantial economic impact of all co-operative enterprises in the U.S. and beyond were laid out in the previous chapter. So, if the co-operative difference is so great, why
isn't it a part of everyday conversations about the economy?

In this chapter we argue that a broad-scale misunderstanding
that sees the economy as strictly capitalist has made co-operatives and "the co-operative difference" invisible. Together with
other kinds of economic diversity, the co-operative difference is
undervalued and misunderstood by the general public as well as
most economists, management and business educators.

The consequences of this invisibility for co-operatives and
the co-operative movement are far-reaching. They range from a
lack of informed choices on the part of consumers and entrepreneurs to a lack of co-operative management skills; a lack of investment in co-operative economic development and a plethora
of missed opportunities due to isolation of the three cooperative
sectors. Chapter Six details these obstacles one by one but first
we explore the art of rendering economic diversity invisible.

The Art of Rendering the Real Invisible

The vitality of cooperative and other alternative economic activity is one of the best kept secrets in the economic world. Below is an iceberg image, developed by J.K. Gibson-Graham[30] and their collaborators, that illustrates this secret:

The Diverse Economy

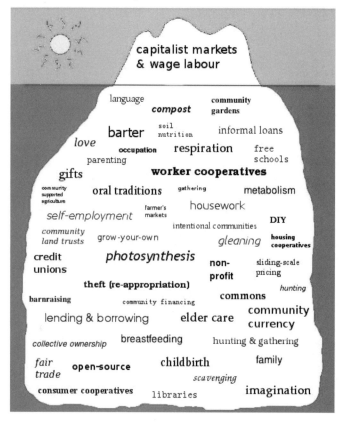

The Iceberg from the Community Economies Collective (2001). Drawn by Ken Byrne.

This image illustrates the selectivity of the capitalist storyline. The usual definition and imagination of the economy includes only those processes—waged labor production in a capitalist firm for a market—above the water line while a myriad of other kinds of economic activity remain invisible below the water line. Economies or systems of production and distribution of goods and services might be better understood as a web of interrelationships and interactions that satisfy all sorts of needs and desires. They are both human and nonhuman, and they happen under all sorts of economic arrangements (above and below the waterline). Among the goods and services that satisfy our needs and wants, some are paid for and others are given freely or stolen. The labor providing those goods and services is also variously gifted, paid for or sometimes stolen.[31] Most of us work for a wage in exchange for our labor time. However, we also give our labor as volunteers, and some people are forced to work in brothels or prisons, without "freedom of contract." Moreover, many people provide labor of care for elderly relatives, neighbors and children (their own and others) without a dime of monetary compensation.

In the U.S. and worldwide, more than **fifty percent** of the production and distribution of goods and services is **noncapitalist** (that is not motivated by profit).[32] Despite their obvious economic importance, these activities and the values involved are rendered invisible by the usual economic storyline. For example, the provision of goods and services within the household is invisible to economic measures because unless a good or service is exchanged in the market (as in a nursing home or daycare facility), its value doesn't "count" in economic terms.[33] As a result most people, especially in the U.S, believe that we live in a thoroughly "capitalist society."

The story we learn

Ethan Miller of the Community Economies Collective gives us a stark commentary:

> The dominant story defines The Economy as "The Market System," regulated by the law of supply and demand. The basic building-blocks of this economy are the rational, self-interested individuals and groups who seek to satisfy their supposedly-

endless needs for growth and accumulation (profit-making) in a world of scarce resources. Competition is the name of the game. Economics is about understanding this competition and all that it entails: money, markets, prices, stocks and bonds, supplies and demands, employment, investment, profit, the world of companies, capital, and finance.

Economic space that is not occupied by the Capitalist Market, we are told, is occupied by the State. The State acts as both an accomplice to The Economy's power and growth and as a fail-safe mechanism for when The Economy falters. It creates and upholds the legal frameworks that allow the Capitalist Economy to thrive and it also "fills in the gaps" by supplying the essential goods and services that this economy cannot (or will not). The tension plays out endlessly: how much, or how little, regulation should the State impose on the Market?

State socialism, often posed as "the" alternative to the Capitalist Economy, solves this problem by *taking over* the State and absorbing the Market into its bureaucratic clutches. Where there used to be Market and State, now there is just *State*—as far as the eye can see.

No matter how you cut it, the Market and the State define all possible "economic" space in this story. Other kinds of activities that meet human needs—growing food, giving birth, bartering, caring for elders, gift-giving, etc.—are not seen as economic, but rather *social* activities, "recreations" or "hobbies" that are marginal at best to the *real* economy. The *real* economy is where *real*—capital—is generated, distributed, and accumulated. The *real* economy (now that State Communism is "dead") is named "Capitalism," a giant system like the weather—beyond our control and understood by only the most elite "experts." The rest of us just hope for sunny days and carry umbrellas.[34]   *Ethan Miller, 2005*

The idea that the economy is one big system solely driven by profit and self-interest shapes what we see and what we *believe* possible. It not only wipes the co-operative difference off the economic map, it also erases all the unpaid labor of care for children and elderly, most of which happens *outside* the "labor market," and other volunteer labor, gifts, barter and subsistence economies that sustain people the world over! This story is not only dead wrong, it's destructive. It is a big obstacle to cultivating all kinds of economic options including co-operative economies.

It is not just ordinary people who are fooled by this elaborate distortion. Departments of economics at universities in the U.S. and most countries worldwide are dominated by capitalist economics (neoliberal and classical alike)[35] and its assumptions that blind economists to the cooperative difference and all kinds of economic diversity. As a result it doesn't occur to most economists and many other highly-educated people that co-operative economics have real-world relevance.

This distorted understanding of the economy is shared by people holding very different perspectives. Many on the right look to the capitalist economy as the chariot of democracy bringing development and opportunity to the poor and uneducated.[36] They believe in the idea that success in a capitalist world requires hard work and ingenuity. Poverty is attributed to a lack of investment and development or to laziness and ineptitude. This perspective sees the capitalist system as a "meritocracy" where success is expected and deserved by the hardest workers and most innovative entrepreneurs. Those who fail to move ahead in such a system are considered lazy or lacking in some other way.

In contrast, many on the left are unsatisfied with and even angry about the capitalist economy because it is a crisis-ridden, environmentally-destructive, undemocratic system that creates and perpetuates vast inequality.[37] Some people feel trapped in this system that they didn't create and have little say in changing. This perspective often blames the capitalist system itself for poverty, inequality and environmental troubles. Capitalism is viewed as a dominant unstoppable force over which we have little or no control.

As different as these perspectives may be, they share the same mistaken assumption that, for better or worse, the economy is a singular over-arching "system" called capitalism. Invested in a fantasy of hope or inevitable destruction, these opposite perspectives share a limited understanding of what *is* and thus what *is* economically possible.

Missing and dismissing the co-operative advantage

Unlike economic activities such as unpaid household and labor of care, subsistence food production, barter and gift economies, most co-operatives produce goods or provide services for sale in some kind of market where money is exchanged. They can thus be measured and "counted" like traditional enterprises. In terms of employment, the combined impact of co-operatives of all sectors and industries, rivals that of multinational corporations! However, from such a measuring perspective, the values upon which co-operatives are based remain as invisible as the values that motivate people to provide goods and services, often free of charge, to neighbors, children and elderly people outside the context of enterprise. Self-help? Self-responsibility? Democracy? Equality? Equity and Solidarity? Honesty? Openness? Social responsibility and caring for others? "Experts" can't "measure" these values and as a result, they remain submerged below the waterline of visibility. They are undervalued and ignored.

A first step in recognizing and benefiting from "the co-operative difference" **is to let go of the idea that economies and markets are strictly sustained and motivated by profit and self-interest.** Once we let go of that idea, we can expand our institutional, political and personal imaginations beyond strictly capitalist enterprise and development.

A second step towards communities benefiting from the power and potential of co-operative models (and facing the inevitable obstacles and imperfections within them) is having the ability to learn about them in schools through formal education. The earlier co-operative activities are presented, the more likely they will be learned, used and improved upon. Unfortunately, co-operatives have been largely misunderstood and ignored by educational institutions and academics across disciplines.

Dismissal by formal education

Considering their substantial economic impact, the notable absence of co-operatives from formal educational institutions is surprising and disturbing. Like the popular news media, schools of economics and business management assume, at least since the fall of the Berlin Wall, that there is no alternative to capitalism. Economics textbooks discuss the transition to capitalism in Eastern Europe but otherwise present nothing other than investor-led capitalism.

A handful of economists have studied this issue. Surveys of introductory textbooks in economics and business management in the US, Canada and Europe show that the mere mention of co-operatives in textbooks is rare. When co-operatives do get a cursory mention, the information presented is often incorrect!

Panu Kalmi notes that both the quantity and quality of information on co-operatives in European economics textbooks has declined steadily since 1930 and sharply after WWII. The reason for this, he says is *not* because they have declined in membership, retail market share, or financial deposits. On the contrary, evidence suggests the economic impact of co-operatives has steadily grown. He says the reason for their disappearance from economics textbooks seems to be a shift in the discipline of economics from being locally-sensitive and institutional to emphasizing **top down solutions to economic problems.**[38]

Rodrick Hill documents the widespread absence of co-operatives from economic textbooks used in the US and Canada.[39] He notes that co-operative enterprises could and should appear in a variety of places in introductory texts especially in the basic description of forms that enterprises can take. Yet in the most widely used texts, co-operatives are conspicuously absent. A leading American textbook (also widely used in Canada) sets the stage of business in the U.S: [40]

> Business firms in the United States take one of three forms: proprietorships, partnerships or corporation. (Stiglitz 1993, 543).

No mention of co-operatives!

Hill argues that co-operatives should be mentioned in textbooks first of all because *they exist* and are even dominant in some sectors such as agriculture. Moreover, students should have the opportunity to learn about them because co-operatives raise basic questions about authority and democracy in economic enterprises.

> By their general neglect of democratic forms of economic institutions, such as co-operatives, the introductory textbooks fail to describe adequately actually existing institutions, ignore questions of economic democracy, and miss an opportunity to offer some interesting lessons in the basic principles of economic organizations and their development. (Hill 2000, 293)

Co-operatives are also ignored and misunderstood by business schools and management programs. John Chamard published a study of the most popularly taught business and management textbooks. In short, he says, the treatment of co-operatives in Canadian and American introductory business textbooks also ranges from nonexistent to hostile.[41]

Dismissal by a capitalist mindset focused on size, privilege and power

Worker co-operatives are also dismissed by people, especially on the left who don't see them as a *viable and powerful* model. Over the last few years, the three of us have given many presentations on worker co-operatives after which we often find this stream of thinking and a strong emotional resistance to the politics of possibility we are presenting. We have come to expect common, sometimes hostile reactions that suggest worker co-operatives are too small in size to affect the *real* problem which is global capitalism and that they are a privilege of the white upper-middle class. Together, these perspectives add up to the critique that worker co-operatives aren't big enough, democratic enough or radical *enough* deserve attention.

> *For years, we have been told a story about "The Economy"—the Capitalist Economy, to be precise—that has made us believe in its overwhelming power and inevitability. This story has hidden from us our power, potential, and value as creative human beings.*   Ethan Miller (2005)

Thus worker co-ops are dismissed because they are few in number and tend to be small in size. This dismissal often comes from an *anti*-capitalist perspective. It suggests that worker co-operatives may be progressive for their members but they're vulnerable and too small to affect the global capitalist system.[42]

But why discount the experience of an enterprise and its members for being small?

Mondragon was small. Tiny, in fact. In 1956, Mondragon as we know it was non-existent. If it weren't for people believing in integrated co-op development and planning for the long term, it would probably still be small. The Mondragon Co-operatives started with one small co-op of five of Don Jose Maria's students. Don Jose Maria Arizmediarrietta didn't discount the effort and possibility of his students because they were few in number. He empowered them with an education in principles of co-operation. They didn't build "utopia" but in just sixty years they transformed the Basque region into a world-class hub of co-operative manufacturing. The power of one small co-operative business and a co-operative bank has created hundreds of community-owned enterprises and thousands of worker-owned jobs.

A worker co-op doesn't have to be big to have a powerful impact on its members and its community. We are, however, inspired by the broad-scale success of worker co-operatives in the Basque Region of Spain and Northern Italy. These examples fly in the face of the criticism that worker co-operatives are necessarily vulnerable, inward-looking and small. Moreover, by pooling resources among co-ops—just as members pool resources to form and operate individual co-ops—they can address important issues like education, expansion and development of new co-ops. VAWC and the Neighboring Food Co-operative Association are excellent examples of co-ops marshaling scarce resources into a system directed by co-ops to achieve goals otherwise unattainable by individual co-ops. We are inspired by one billion co-operative members worldwide whose co-ops are providing one hundred million jobs.[43] Imagine what might be possible if, like VAWC and NFCA, all of those co-ops directed surplus toward development!

Another common criticism is that worker co-operatives are a privilege of the white upper-middle class and they don't address the problems of racism and inequality. On the contrary, we believe that co-operatives have the capacity to address racism and inequality at their core. Systemic racism and inequality, not to mention the structures of poverty they produce, exemplify the need for alternatives and the need for education about the alternatives—for all people.

Jessica Gordon Nembhard reminds us that African Americans have a long and strong history of co-operative ownership. Yet she says that history has been largely hidden by racism and white supremacists.[44] The solution is not to further suppress the African American history and present engagement with co-operative enterprise and dismiss the model. On the contrary, economic empowerment through co-operative enterprise provides a path to resist further explotitation by capitalist institutions. Co-operatives should be held up as real examples of self-empowerment in the past, present and future for all communities especially those struggling against poverty and racism.

One example that addresses these concerns is the Federation of Southern Co-operatives (FSC). FSC is primarily African-American in its membership, but it also includes White, Chicano and Native American members working to empower themselves to produce a livable income and retain ownership of black-owned land. The FSC represents no fewer than 25,000 low income families organized into over one hundred co-operatives in rural communities across the U.S. South.[45]

Another example is one of the largest worker co-operatives in the U. S. Co-operative Home Care Associates in the South Bronx is a worker co-operative owned mostly by people of color. Its membership of nearly 2000 workers is mostly of African American and Latin American decent.[46]

Co-operatives are not immune to the problems and consequences of poverty and racism but they are not and do not have to be the sole privilege of white people, any more than they are or have to be that of black people. Co-operatives aren't perfect. Members report experiencing sexism, ageism and racism *within* their worker, consumer and producer co-operatives. The co-operative difference, however, means that they can bring these issues to the table and address them on the basis of equality with other members. Employing the Co-op Principles and Values is a mechanism for holding members accountable to Open and Voluntary Membership.

Dismissive perspectives of the left have little effect on the daily operations and experience of worker co-operatives that persist with or without its approval. However, they do constrain dialogue on worker co-operatives as a viable model. As researchers investigating worker co-ops and presenting the model, we have often felt personally disheartened and shut down by an angry audience member who insists that worker co-ops don't address the *real* problem; that they are too small and inconsequential to matter. By implication, of course, our work is insignificant—why would we want to waste our time? These reactions come from well-intentioned academic professionals and activists who strive for social change but whose perspectives, we believe, get stuck in a cycle of complaint rather than dialogue about and development of real possibilities.

Erbin Crowell, suggests that the dismissal and subsequent ignorance of the co-operative model is partly cultural. He suggests that there is a stream of thinking that is stuck in a paternalistic, philanthropist-led model of social change. He says, *the co-operative model is bottom up; theirs is a paternalistic and top down.*

Conclusion

This chapter argued that the dominant story and belief that we live in a strictly capitalist economy hides a world of economic diversity and potential for enacting economies in line with values other than profit. The myth of an economy governed solely by self-interested competition and profit is perpetuated by educational institutions. Co-operatives and the "co-operative difference" are misunderstood and ignored by economists, business and management educators. Co-operatives are also dismissed because they are viewed by many on the left as inherently weak and tainted by privilege. Thus a lack of education and a capitalist mind-set renders the power of the co-operative difference invisible. We believe the invisibility of co-operatives and the co-operative difference has had far-reaching consequences. We explore the depth of these consequences in the next chapter.

VI

The Consequences
of Invisibility

THE CHALLENGES FACING WORKER CO-OPERATIVES and the entire co-operative movement are substantial and deeply entrenched. In this chapter we elaborate four specific ways in which the invisibility of the co-operative difference obstructs co-operative economies from flourishing:

1. Lack of informed choice
2. Lack of co-operative expertise, governance and/or management skills
3. Lack of financial investment and understanding of co-operative development
4. Isolation of Co-ops by sector

Exploring these in further depth might inform solutions; with that in mind, we consider them below.

I. *Lack of informed choice = fewer patrons and fewer co-opreneurs*

We graduate or drop out of highs schools and colleges into the world believing that investor-led firms are the only kind of economic enterprise. We enact this belief in our personal and professional lives, in our roles as governmental, legal, political, media and educational workers; and as parents, church members, consumers and investors. Some people start businesses. However few businesses—whether they be in the trades, services or retail—begin as worker co-ops because entrepreneurs don't think of them as an option.

> *People don't think of a worker or consumer co-op as a natural choice. You have to think too hard for it. When something becomes integrated it's a no brainer, you have choices, it might not be your automatic response but it's more logical.*
> Suzette Snow Cobb, Manager Greenfields Market,
> Franklin Community Co-operative

The lack of education about co-operatives reduces the possibility of people making informed choices. If potential customers knew about the co-operative difference, they might choose to patronize a co-op over a capitalist business. However, most of us don't recognize the co-operative difference even when we see it. People who might be interested don't seek out or become members (much less start up) co-operative enterprises to fulfill basic needs (like employment, groceries and financial services) because they don't see how they are different from other businesses. Investor-led firms are thus the "norm" partly because educational, legal, political, economic/social institutions assume they are "normal" and make them appear as if they are the only enterprise option.

Over 120 million Americans are members of co-operatives.[47] Can you imagine how many would be conscious and active members if they lived in a world in which co-operatives were fully visible?

II. *Lack of co-operative and collective management skills*

The purposes and principles of the co-operative structure require management tools and skills that differ greatly from those used in capitalist firms. Worker-members face industry and location-specific-challenges on a daily basis. They also face unique challenges involved with democratic worker-membership for which they have to develop sound decision-making processes, communication skills and mechanisms for accountability. Examples of both kinds of pressure are evident in the story of Common Wealth Printing (see pages 81–89). Common Wealth faced obstacles related to changing technology and markets as well as internal dynamics related to decision-making, management and financing growth versus paying a living wage.

Worker co-ops have confronted the lack of collective management and communication skills both on the job and during the hiring process. In Chapters Two and Three we discussed some helpful management and communication strategies based on the experience of worker co-operatives in our region which have between three and fifteen members, most operating with collective structures. The challenge of effective co-operative or collective management may be even more complicated and acute in larger worker co-operatives.

Erbin Crowell describes some of the differences between being a manager at a traditional firm versus being a manager at a worker co-operative based on his thirteen-year experience at Equal Exchange, a worker co-operative with more than 120 members, based in West Bridgewater, Massachusetts:

> Being in a worker co-op doesn't take away any of the business challenges or interpersonal challenges that might come up but it totally changes the focus of the business. When you're a manager in a worker co-op, at least in my experience, your problem is never motivating employees. It's guiding their energy. It's trying to help them, help facilitate things that they

want to do so they're contributing to the direction the organization needs to go in together. That's a totally different problem than you run into in the mainstream business world. There, your job is more about coercion; it's more about getting people to come to work. In a worker co-op you have the advantage that your core stakeholder—the employees—have a vested interest in the economic health of the business and not tear it down whereas in mainstream business one of your key inefficiencies is employee theft, employee slacking and conflict.

Another big difference that requires a radically different outlook from standard business training is the challenge of coming up with financial reporting that accounts for the core purposes of the co-operative rather than just profits and losses. Crowell explains:

> The standard balance sheet shows your profit and loss—that's the goal—as long as the profit and loss looks good, you're good. But one of Equal Exchange's core goals was to overpay producers. Yes, *overpay*! We created a supplemental report, under the balance sheet that said, oh by the way, we paid this much above market to the farmers, we provided this much in credit, we paid this much to our workers in patronage... All of that doesn't show up in a typical balance sheet.

Learning from the experiences of former worker co-operatives points to the need to overcome isolation among co-operatives and develop mechanisms of mutual support, finance and education. Financial reporting is just one among challenges co-operatives encounter. Access to financial resources, conflict, governance, management hierarchies, burnout and lack of participation can be especially challenging for worker co-operatives. When these issues are entrenched, they may become acute during times of growth and contraction. Developing governance structures that can accommodate growth as well as autonomy and democratic values, is a key challenge but becoming too internally focused can also be problematic. The difficulties involved with growth have led to the dissolution of some co-operative businesses. For examples, Kim Coontz points to the demutualization of two formerly successful worker co-ops: Burley Design, a 28 year-old bike manufacturing co-op was sold to a private entrepreneur when it was under financial pressure and Good Vibrations, a sex-toy business, "demutualized at the peak of business success."[48]

There is a lack of sound co-operative management training for worker, consumer and producer co-operatives across industries. Crowell suggests that many co-ops get caught in the trap of judging themselves according to how the mainstream capitalist economy works. As the current Executive Director of the Neighboring Food Co-op Association he describes the challenge we see in the financial reporting of many co-operative enterprises:

> ... it's essentially the same financial reporting that any business does and that's wrong. That is the wrong report because mainstream accounting privileges profit over everything else. But that's not what a co-op is for. A co-op is for service. So part of the question is **how do you create financial accounting that looks out for the financial health of the business while also valuing the social impacts that are the core purpose of the co-op?**

Where can a food co-op manager go to explore the question that Crowell poses?

Co-ops may perform the same service or produce the same good as a capitalist firm but democratic control presents complex challenges and opportunities that differ greatly from capitalist firms. Learning to balance the mission of the co-operative, the needs and desires of members, employees and patrons with the financial viability of the enterprise is especially challenging when most of the tools available to co-op managers are capitalist in design. Most co-operative managers have to learn the complexities of balancing co-operative structure, governance, mission and principles of co-operation on the job. Suzette Snow Cobb, co-General Manager of Franklin Community Co-op offered a glimpse of 'Member Economic Participation'—one of the Principles of Co-operation in practice at the food co-op where she works:

There are definitely **different levels of participation.** In terms of **economic participation,** all members put in their **equity money** and certainly shop at the co-op but their involvement in **understanding the structure of the co-op** and understanding where they might take time and participate in other ways varies ... 46 to 47 percent of our sales go to members ... and roughly 200 of 2100 members volunteer work hours; some help stock or bag, for an additional discount every month. Another small percentage of members don't work as volunteers but actively participate in annual meetings, forums or board meetings. They would all probably identify as being more involved. [Emphasis ours]

Typical business (and business training) isn't concerned with democratic participation, co-operative ownership or serving members. Since most management tools are capitalist rather than co-operative in design, managers navigate these unique dynamics of member participation with considerable difficulty.

Where can a successful (or struggling), large scale, consumer, producer or worker co-operative look to find management capable of dealing with problems specifically co-operative in nature? They can look to a pool of candidates with a co-operative spirit but little experience in management or to a much larger pool of candidates with the best training in business management. The problem, of course, is that the training available for business managers is oriented to capitalist rather than co-operative structures. According to Edgar Parnell:

> Senior managers of large-scale cooperatives, directly recruited from investor-owned businesses rarely have access to any appropriate development or training; as a consequence they are often left to discover for themselves how they should function within a cooperative organization. Many never learn what it means to properly manage a co-operative undertaking, often with disastrous consequences.[49]

Highly trained managers tend to bring the organizational rules and patterns they learned in capitalist businesses and business school to their co-operative workplaces. Wholesale misunderstanding by management can result in traditional capitalist antagonism between members and management, mission drift, and (in the worse cases) lead to the demutualization of the company. It doesn't happen often but there have been several cases in which profit maximizing CEOs convinced members and co-op boards to sell the co-op to private interest. Musselburgh and Fisherrow Co-operative Society Limited demutualized controversially in 2007 after 145 years of co-operation![50]

Joseph Stiglitz, a famous American economist whose introductory textbooks (ironically) ignore co-operatives seems to understand the need for uniquely co-operative management training and the affects that a lack of such training could have. According to Stiglitz:

> Simply to transplant the organizational patterns and rules of operation designed for the capitalist corporation into a co-op is to undermine the latter's identity and condemn it to eventual disappearance.[51]

Fortunately, there is a move by co-operative educators to shift the paradigm of business and management training toward co-operative models. John Chamard, Tom Webb and colleagues at the University of St. Mary's in Nova Scotia founded a Master's degree in Management of Co-operatives and Credit Unions to address the need for sound training in management, marketing and finance specifically for co-operatives. The only one of its kind in North America, this program was created for co-op managers like Snow-Cobb (class of 2013) and Crowell (class of 2011). The program is a part-time, low residency masters program open to co-op members and managers whose co-operative workplaces support their participation in it.

> Throughout the curriculum, each management issue and function is explored within the context of the unique co-operative business environment created by the purpose, values and principles of co-operation. The program is based on the premise that co-operation among co-operatives is not only

"nice" but is essential to ensuring that globalization does not leave co-operative businesses on the periphery of the economy.[52]

The University of Massachusetts Co-operative Enterprise Collaborative (UMCEC) is another bright light in the dark educational landscape of economics. It began in 2009 as a collaboration between VAWC, Neighboring Food Co-op Association, professors and students in the Economics Department. They co-developed a curriculum and certificate program in Applied Research in Co-operative Economics that offers courses in the economics of co-operative enterprise and links students with regional co-operatives for mutually beneficial labor and research internships. This is the only educational program co-developed by co-operatives in the U.S. and it flies in the face of a discipline that has long ignored co-operatives.

What a difference ten or twenty such programs could make!

III. *Lack of investment and understanding of co-operative development*

As economic models that are radically different from capitalist ones, co-operative development strategies are also radically different from capitalist development. Here again invisibility plays a big role and defines the work of the cooperative movement. There are at least three aspects to consider here—especially for worker co-ops the smallest co-op sector:

- The role of government and consultants
- Understanding and utilizing surplus
- Motives for expansion and development

Invisibility and the Role of Government

One consequence of the lack of education and training available in our universities is that business managers, policy makers, government and non-profit developers graduate **largely uneducated** about co-operatives, their history and the co-operative difference. Even those who might be interested in (and working on) co-op development have few tools with which to approach it.[53] People who staff government agencies and businesses engaged in regional and national economic development are wholly unaware and undereducated about the co-operative difference. Let's look at what happens.

Governments are, arguably, concerned with economic development for the purpose of human well being. However, decisionmakers in many countries including the U.S. are trained to focus almost exclusively on the tip of the economic iceberg. As a result, development agencies and organizations at the city, state and federal levels remain largely unaware of co-operatives, especially worker co-operatives, so their efforts and strategies focus on capitalist development. For John Curl, this legislative oversight—evident at least since New Deal legislation—is no coincidence:

> Urban and industrial worker cooperatives were **planned out** of the U.S. economy, rural and farmer cooperatives were **planned into** the economy by the New Deal. The contrast is stark. In the rural case, there was a general national consensus that rural America could prosper only if the government promoted cooperatives. And so it happened. The opposite took place in urban and industrial areas, the stronghold of the wage system. The New Deal stopped their promotion of cooperatives at city limits. They were trying to save and revitalize industrial capitalism, not replace it, and that required not doing anything to threaten the labor pool.[54]

While governments offer tax subsidies and infrastructural support to attract private capital investment, tax benefits and incorporation statutes for worker co-operatives remain non-existent or obscure.[55] For example, Massachusetts has a clear statute for Employee Co-operative Corporations (MA General Law 157A) that most states do not have. MA General Law 157A, part of MA General Law 157 about co-ops of many types, was replicated by Connecticut, New York, Vermont, Maine, Oregon and Washington. However thanks to a lack of training, even in those states with clear worker co-op legislation, legal counsel and development consultants have advised worker co-op start-ups to incorporate with the bylaws of agricultural producer co-operatives or other corporate structures.

> *So, all along we worked on the bylaws that were for farmers—the way they were set up—and not for an installation company like us. But hey, we needed something because there was not much. CDI [Co-operative Development Institute] did their best. They were working with local farmers... so it was an easy template to use but as we found out years later this [laughing] doesn't apply to us.*
>
> Phillipe Rigollaud, (PV)[2]

In such a climate, it's surprising that we have co-ops at all! According to Crowell,

> If you examine areas in the world where cooperatives are a significant, permanent sector of the economy, such as the Emilia Romagna region of Italy, you will see that the government there has organized the economic playing field to make that possible, with advantages granted to cooperatives in recognition of their promotion of social justice and prosperity.

In Italy, the contrast is stunning. Co-operatives there are more visible, prolific and integrated than in most countries. In Emilia Romagna of Northern Italy, 8000 co-operative enterprises account for forty percent of the region's GDP. Co-operatives generate over sixty percent of the town of Imola's GDP and over half its 100,000 residents are members of co-ops.[56] This is partly due to a long history of strong co-operative identity, especially in Northern Italy, that includes clear legislative recognition of co-operatives.[57] In 1992, the Italian government passed a law, drafted by co-ops, that requires co-operatives to contribute three percent of their surplus to development funds managed by various co-operative federations.[58]

From this we can see the need for a co-operative movement that is strong locally, regionally, and nationally. Worker co-ops in the Pioneer Valley recognized this and have been building local, regional and national alliances. As we will see later, VAWC has taken to heart the example of the Italian co-operative movement. They saw Italy's three percent and raised it by two! VAWC member co-operatives now contribute five percent of their annual surplus to co-operative development.

Understanding "surplus" in a worker co-operative

In the context of a worker co-operative, the difference between the price of a good (or service) sold and the costs of production is **surplus** rather than profit.[59]

One of the beautiful things about worker co-operatives is that workers democratically redistribute the surplus they generate as *they* decide. That's one reason we want more co-ops as surplus remains in the community, rooting jobs and wealth. **However**, it's also a big reason they often don't expand and multiply. Rather than being accumulated by non-workers as profit (as with investors in capitalist businesses), in a worker co-op surplus is distributed equitably. Worker-members frequently redistribute the surplus to themselves, to their communities and to sustaining their business. This redistribution of surplus then appears as a disincentive to growth because current worker-members don't necessarily stand to benefit financially from the addition of new workers.

Let's clarify this a little more: In a capitalist enterprise, profits are accumulated by an owner, owners or shareholders who decide what they want to do with it. The owner of a small business, for example, may accumulate a relatively small profit. It might be just enough to buy a house or accumulate a college fund for her kids. However, if the small business owner were to develop another small business of equal size and success, s/he could double the profit. Therein lies the profit motive for growth.

The same small business structured as a worker co-operative would not have the profit incentive for growth because additional surplus produced by additional workers in a new location may, though not always, be redistributed equally among new members. In this case wealth is distributed rather than accumulated. Thus expansion could mean more risk and work without the incentive of profit. But the story doesn't end there. For worker and cross sector co-operative development, overcoming this obstacle simply requires specifically co-operative approaches.

Co-operative motives for expansion and development

Capitalist and co-operative businesses share some incentives and disincentives for expansion. Regardless of its organizational structure (co-operative or capitalist) a business could benefit from expansion by taking advantage of economies of scale; or it could suffer from expanding too quickly. Again, capitalist enterprises have one motive for expansion that co-operatives do not have: the profit motive. This motive is immediately self-serving to owners, managers, and investors. Worker co-operatives often aim to increase surplus and members' share of surplus distribution, however, they do not have the profit motive strictly speaking so co-operators may have to see themselves as part of a larger social and economic venture to grasp that co-operative expansion may be self-serving. Mondragon and the Arizmendi Association, which we discuss below, have achieved this.

Let's look again at the hiring of new workers. In contrast to a capitalist business, surplus is not accumulated by one or more owners or non-working shareholders. Worker co-operatives usually redistribute surplus to the workers who produce it. While there may be other incentives[60] for growth, individual worker-members may have little to gain financially by adding additional worker-members because additional surplus is distributed to the workers who generate it.[61]

Example: A worker-owned fast food restaurant with productivity and surplus equal to the productivity and profit of a successful capitalist one, does not have the same "profit motive" for expansion because the surplus isn't accumulated by non-workers. A worker co-op could add new locations and more workers but the new profits (or surplus) generated may be distributed among the workers. A new venture could add significantly to the surplus (often called profit margin) of the whole business which would benefit all worker-members. However, the group of worker-owners do not benefit like a single owner would, especially if the new venture is less profitable than the first enterprise, because increased surplus is distributed among workers rather than concentrated for the benefit of one owner.[62] Any decline in the profitability of the entire venture drags down patronage for the individual workers whereas a private owner would still benefit from an expansion less profitable than the core business because he/she would have more workers producing more surplus. Thus expansion or franchising of a worker co-operative is less likely than the expansion or franchising of capitalist model operating in the same industry.[63]

So let's look at how co-operatives have achieved growth.

Co-operators in places all over the world have developed strategies to expand the number of worker co-ops *both in spite of and because of the core practice of democratically redistributing surplus.* The Mondragon Co-operative Corporation is a key example of a co-op-led development strategy. Foreseeing the problem of financing, the founding father of Mondragon encouraged community members to invest their small savings in a co-operative bank in order to finance development. They created the "Caja Laboral Popular"—the people's bank—with the slogan "Savings or Suitcases" referring to the fact that jobless Basques were fleeing the region in search of work. Some sixty years later, retirement savings and surpluses from co-ops of substantial size and quantity are invested in the co-operative bank which is still charged with financing and developing new co-operatives. The result: hundreds of community-owned enterprises and more than 80,000 worker-owned jobs.

Mondragon Co-operatives' self-funding development strategies have inspired a number of models for co-op development in the U.S. VAWC, which we discuss at greater length in the next chapter, borrowed some of these social inventions. The Evergreen Co-operatives, a large co-operative development initiative in Cleveland, Ohio was also inspired by the Mondragon Co-operatives.[64] Another example is the Arizmendi Association of Co-operatives in the Bay Area of Northern California which is named after Mondragon's founder.

The Arizmendi Association's model addresses challenges involved with co-operative development including those faced by startups of traditional business like financing, business planning and training. It also addresses the disincentive implied by the redistribution of gains. The idea behind the model is to **empower worker co-operatives *themselves* to fund the development of new worker co-ops.**

In 1995, the organizers of the Arizmendi Association approached a successful Berkeley worker co-operative called the Cheese Board Collective,[65] with the vision of helping to create "the largest possible number of decently-compensated work opportunities in democratically-operated businesses that function as part of an interdependent economic framework."[66] They wanted to create an association of worker co-operatives dedicated to developing new co-operatives. The Cheese Board became a founding member of the Association. They lent training, organizational structure, recipes, start-up funds, and even their reputable name to the project.[67] Arizmendi staff members became experts of the Cheese Board Collective's business model and operations to create new independent worker-owned bakeries that would provide new worker-owned jobs. With these tools and a vision for replication, the Arizmendi Association opened the first independently-owned co-operative Arizmendi Bakery in 1997. Arizmendi Fourth Street, in San Rafael became the Association's second member.

The Arizmendi Association has repeated this process five times. When the new worker-owned businesses become profitable they fund future development through membership in the Association. The six independent co-operative bakeries of the Association, including the Cheese Board Collective, sustain some 140 worker-owned community rooted jobs that pay about twice as much as a typical bakery when the business reaches maturity. The jobs created by Arizmendi development are highly prized: the Valencia Street location had 260 applications for fifteen positions in 2010!

Each Arizmendi co-operative bakery and Cheese Board, the mother ship are members of the Association. They pay dues and contribute expertise to the development of the next co-operative. The dues structure is agreed upon by members. Dues contributed by a new startup are based upon a percentage of surplus. This means that start-ups pay very little until they begin generating surplus (which usually takes three years). As the businesses become successful, their contribution grows and so does the Association's capacity to develop new start-ups. Membership in the Association is voluntary but the use of the Arizmendi name and recipes is contractual. If one of the co-operatives leaves the Association, they can no longer use the Arizmendi name.

Arizmendi is a great example of what is possible with a sound understanding of the unique opportunities and challenges of worker co-op development. The organizers of the Association recognized the difficulties of starting a business which they addressed by becoming experts in one business and franchising the model. They also recognized the disincentive to grow so they built an incentive into a self-funding model for replication!

Co-operators often use surplus to achieve goals that don't necessarily generate revenue and act against personal financial interest to allocate resources to their business and community. They use surplus as a mechanism to improve their company, community and environment and to fulfill the mission of the co-operative—often before themselves as individuals—thus building inter-generational assets for the future. For example, in 1999 Collective Copies opened another location and renovated a retail space that drew down patronage to individual members. Similarly, PT360, a physical therapy worker co-op in Vermont, has used surplus to cover training costs, purchase equipment and drive expansion from one to three locations in the past few years. Simple Diaper & Linen is also working on expansion projects. Existing members recently hired a new member rather than retaining patronage for themselves.

IV. *Isolation of Co-ops by Sector*

Worker, consumer and producer co-operatives evolved from a shared history of people uniting to meet social and economic needs collaboratively. Early co-operative organizers like the Rochdale Pioneers imagined fully co-operative economies in which people had access to work and affordable goods through democratically-controlled enterprises. However this shared history and shared Co-operative Identity rooted in Values and Principles has been buried by capitalist ideology, the dominant story of the economy as we usually imagine it, and by a misplaced fear of communism.

Common ownership of enterprise contrasts sharply with a private, investor-led capitalist enterprise model. At the height of the cold war and Red Scare, many co-operative enterprises were politically inclined to distance themselves from anything that seemed opposed to capitalist ideology.[68] The Co-operative Principles and Values were seen less as a guide and more as a liability. Political pressure thus led many large scale co-operatives to shy away from a strong co-operative identity rooted in Co-op Prin-

ciples and Values in an effort to appear more like a private investor-led enterprise. Of course, there was little educational effort
to countervail this misunderstanding or its affects.

One result of co-operatives appearing (and even behaving)
like capitalist businesses was that their shared identity became
buried. Some co-operative businesses drifted away from a close
engagement with the Principles and lost sight of the opportunities they offer. The power of the Principles, especially the Fifth
and Sixth Principles, went largely untapped. In the worst cases,
drifting from a shared Co-operative Identity resulted in
demutualization (failure of the enterprise or conversion to a traditional capitalist business), but the broader consequence has
been sectoral isolation and a lot of lost opportunity.

Co-operatives across sectors and industries are generating
substantial revenue and surpluses. Co-operative capital could be
a major resource for the development of more co-operatives.
And in some places it is. Sadly, however, the capital generated by
co-operatives is often invested in the private sector through traditional banks and investment houses that administer the co-ops'
retirement vehicles.

Co-ops are stronger when they support each other. Inter-cooperation helps co-ops compete more effectively with capitalist
businesses in global markets. Mondragon and Emilia Romagna
remind us of the power of inter-cooperation for building co-operative economies.

The isolation of co-operatives by sector may be one of the
most tragic consequences of invisibility of the "co-operative difference." The Sixth Co-operative Principle "Co-operation Among
Co-operatives" is a business strategy for co-operatives to gain
strength through interconnection. The de-emphasis of shared Co-
operative Identity makes engaging with this principle difficult. If
inter-cooperation isn't a goal of the enterprise, it doesn't just happen on its own. So, many co-operatives miss out on opportunities
such as joint marketing across industries and sectors, interco-op

purchasing and co-operative investment and financing.

With little understanding and education about the Co-operative Values and Principles—especially the Sixth Principle—members and managers can't see shared values and characteristics with co-operatives of other sectors. They get silo-ed off from one another with few resources shared among them.

Wrap up and onward

In this chapter we explored four consequences of economic invisibility of the Co-operative Principles and Values: 1) a lack of informed choice; 2) a lack of co-operative management skills; 3) a lack of investment in and understanding of co-operative development strategies and 4) the isolation of co-operatives by sector. As a result, co-operatives across sectors have few tools and limited resources with which to address specific challenges in their enterprise, industry and sector; they miss out on co-operative advantages and remain relatively isolated in a sea of capitalist expansion.

In the next chapter we shift our focus to VAWC as a model for co-operative-led development that addresses these consequences of invisibility directly. In Chapter Eight we conclude with a vision of an integrated co-operative economy in Western New England, highlighting cross-sector collaboration and shared resource and development pools.

VII

VAWC: Meeting the Challenges and Seizing the Opportunities

WE OUTLINED THE CO-OPERATIVE DIFFERENCE in previous chapters, and showed how it is rendered invisible by formal education, popular media and a capitalist mindset. We argued that large-scale invisibility of economic diversity has wiped co-operatives (and the co-operative difference) off the economic map which has widespread consequences for developing co-operative economies. In this chapter we turn to the Valley Alliance of Worker Co-operatives (VAWC).

VAWC is an example of a co-operative-led development model that is addressing the problems laid out in previous chapters: 1) They are not blinded by a capitalist mindset; VAWC is busy making the existence, power and viability of worker and cross sector co-operatives visible in the market and in formal educational institutions; they are informing consumers through promotion and educating students and the public about co-operatives as a clear and viable model; 2) they are cultivating skills necessary for current and future co-operators and co-opreneurs to succeed; 3) they understand and are investing in co-op development based on the experience of worker co-operation and; 4) they are an ongoing expression of the principle of Co-operation Among Co-operatives.

In this chapter, we give a brief account of VAWC's history, mission and vision and show how worker co-operatives in our region are facing challenges and harnessing co-operative opportunities together as a co-operative of co-operatives.

VAWC History

It all started at the 2005 Eastern Conference for Workplace Democracy in Manchester N.H., where members of three worker co-operatives met and found they shared a passion for co-operation and the potential for the co-operative movement in our region. During the conference, they talked into the night about their co-operatives and the potential for growth and inter-cooperation. They decided to begin meeting monthly after the conference was over in order to continue the conversations, build upon the excitement of the conference, develop a network of mutual support and explore potential of cooperation among co-ops.

It took time to establish who and what VAWC was. VAWC was organized by a group of people who wanted to learn from each other; they believed in and wanted to support and grow worker co-ops but they had no one clear vision about how to go about best doing that work. Together they explored such questions as: *Why aren't there more worker co-operatives? How can worker co-ops mobilize limited resources to develop new co-ops? How can worker co-ops contribute across sectors to be part of the wider co-operative economy? How can worker co-ops transform their unique resources, knowledge and trust into an intentional system of integrated co-op development rooted in their workplaces?* For three years they developed the relationships forged in Manchester and made new connections, building trust, a collective vision and strategies to implement it.

Deciding on a mission, goals and objectives and even who could be a "member" (and what "membership" would mean) was complicated. In the beginning, as Phillipe Rigollaud, PV

Squared's Representative and VAWC's first President, recalls, "VAWC was more like a social club" than a development organization. Not everyone who had contributed time and energy to the creation of VAWC was a member of a worker co-op and, early on, opinions varied regarding who could be a member. One position was that anyone should be able to join. Some participants who were not co-op members felt they had earned membership status and some worker co-op members felt that extending membership to supporters would keep the movement inclusive. However, others maintained that membership should be limited to worker co-operatives. For them, the examples of co-op led development in Italy's Emilia Romagna and Spain's Mondragon and Konfekoop co-operatives demonstrated that cooperators directing and funding development themselves was exciting, powerful and necessary to ensure participation from worker co-ops. The question of defining membership first arose with the idea of creating a map of VAWC: Who would be on the map?

After much debate, the VAWC map was drawn in 2006. It included worker co-operatives only and a consensus slowly emerged among cooperators that worker co-ops would be the sole members of the Alliance. It was a difficult decision to make but they felt that it was important because they saw it as the best way to follow Co-operative Principles and replicate successful international examples. Keeping VAWC's direction and funding in the hands of worker co-op members safeguarded the democratic structure and the autonomy of members. It also ensured that co-ops would literally have buy-in on the goals of creating long-term support programs specific to co-op member needs and addressing larger issues of the movement. Over the course of many meetings and several years, worker-members outlined the core goals of VAWC as member support, education, cross sector collaboration and development of worker co-operatives.

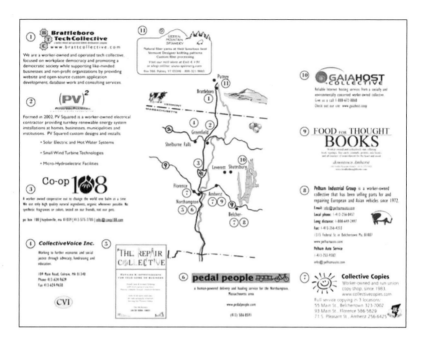

In 2008, as VAWC was immersed in conversations that would eventually lead to a formal structure, mission and membership, Erbin Crowell, former long-term member of Equal Exchange, came to the Valley and proposed using his masters thesis to explore possibilities in VAWC for co-op led development. That winter, he went overseas to study cooperative economies in Italy and at about the same time, VAWC Member Rep Adam Trott, a member of Collective Copies went to the Basque region of Spain to study Mondragon. They returned with new-found strategies and inspiration.

> *My visit to Italy was a revelation in terms of how I viewed the potential for co-operative development in my own country and region... In many ways, it was a confirmation of some of the ideas of what a cooperative economy could look like when co-ops reach critical mass in a region.*
>
> Erbin Crowell 2010[69]

I remember writing this down in every workshop of every day: innovation, inter-cooperation and maintaining the co-operative culture were the themes.

Adam Trott about his Mondragon experience in 2009

Upon returning to the States, Crowell and Trott shared their excitement with each other and with members of the Alliance. They compared notes and found that while the two co-operative complexes were very different, they shared characteristics that offered important lessons for co-operative development work in the U.S. Crowell's thesis, a report to VAWC that incorporated his conversations with Trott, has helped shape the evolution of VAWC in many ways.[70] They believed that the two co-operative complexes shared 1) a clear co-operative identity aligned with Principles and Values; 2) an emphasis on inter-cooperation among co-operatives both within and across sectors; 3) civic and legislative engagement and; 4) development that is funded and guided by co-operatives themselves.[71]

During an epic tour, affectionately called the "VAWC Road Show," Crowell and Trott visited the monthly meetings of eleven worker co-operatives in Southern Vermont and Western Massachusetts to discuss their research and how the co-operatives of the region might fund and direct a staff position.[72] They were surprised by widespread interest in a project to develop a staff position and excited by the degree to which worker-members willingly offered input.

The Alliance had yet to incorporate formally as a co-operative of co-operatives but some co-ops had been paying dues voluntarily since 2006. With three years of accumulated dues and a matching grant from the Co-operative Fund of New England (CFNE), VAWC was able to launch a pilot project to demonstrate the potential of a worker co-op-funded staff position charged with the task of building member relations, launching a marketing initiative, developing relationships with allies and developing a proposal for a long term position.

The Staff Pilot Project accomplished its goals by establishing a member agreement, joint marketing campaign and outlining a long term co-op funded staff position to follow CFNE's "step down" grant. The staff position was a major step towards co-operatively-led support and development in Western New England. Erbin Crowell held the first staff developer position for the Staff Pilot Project followed by current Staff Adam Trott.

These days VAWC representatives still have fun before, after (and sometimes even during!) meetings, but VAWC has become something more serious than "a social club." In 2010 VAWC Member Co-ops approved their Representatives to sign the first Membership Agreement that established its identity rooted in the ICA Co-operative Principles and Values. This agreement consolidated the Alliance according to a shared vision and principles and brought a formerly inchoate group of co-operative businesses into alignment with a much broader movement. They formalized their legal structure in 2011 by incorporating under Massachusetts General Law 157 as a co-operative owned by its member worker co-operatives. VAWC membership is exclusive to worker co-ops that provide funding, direction and a five percent surplus contribution to the VAWC Interco-operative Development Fund.

It isn't always easy. Some co-operatives in the region never participated or joined VAWC. Food For Thought Books had community events the same night as VAWC's monthly meetings (so they only attended a few) and they never joined despite their alignment with VAWC's mission.[73] Some co-ops were members on an informal basis during organizing stages and dropped out when the legal format took form. Representatives from Pelham Auto and Brattleboro Tech Collective were steady participants of VAWC but a lack of consensus regarding formal membership of their co-operatives meant their co-operatives never became dues paying members when membership and dues structures were formalized. In accordance with the First and Second Principles, VAWC has voluntary and open membership so worker co-operatives can drop out or (re)join any time.

VAWC Member Co-ops all have the same voting power—one member one vote—however, there is a difference in size (in monetary and membership terms). Therefore contributions of dues and surplus vary, with larger co-operatives covering a greater percentage of operating costs than do the smaller co-operatives. Member Co-ops also differ in terms years of experience, knowledge and tenure with VAWC. These differences combined could create a power dynamic tending toward informal hierarchy. So, Member Representatives work to strike a balance between utilizing the knowledge and surplus of founding member co-ops with the interests of newer members. This has required challenging dialog across co-ops of different sizes and ages to fulfil VAWC's mission.

Funding staff time with member dues was a great accomplishment with significant potential for the future. However, current resources are only enough to pay Staff part time, therefore much of VAWC's labor is still volunteer. Burnout among committed volunteers can be a problem and as in any group, there have been internal conflicts. So, the evolution and activities of VAWC are a testament to the passion and commitment of co-operators as well as the power of the nascent infrastructure they are creating.

Mission and Vision

VAWC is dedicated to building a sustainable local economy by facilitating the growth and development of worker co-operatives in Western Massachusetts and Southern Vermont. To realize this, they:

> I. Provide support for members. This includes maintaining and sharing information relevant to worker co-operatives, providing technical and organizational assistance, offering joint marketing and promotional services, developing group benefits, improving access to financial resources, strengthening ties between worker co-operatives, and developing relationships with other segments of the cooperative/labor community.

II. Develop new worker co-operatives and offer mentoring and skill-sharing to developing worker co-operatives.

III. Promote worker co-operatives in our region. This includes educating and developing community awareness of worker co-operatives as sources of meaningful employment and economic empowerment, providers of quality goods and services, and viable alternatives to conventionally owned and managed businesses.

Harnessing the Power of the Co-operative Difference

VAWC's Membership Agreement bases the identity of the Alliance and its members on the ICA's definition and identity of a co-operative rooted in Principles and Values. The Member Agreement is a living document; priorities and direction of the co-operative can change according to the needs of the membership. Priorities are drawn and decisions made democratically by voting members.

Structure & Identity

Worker co-operatives and our movement are made stronger through shared identity, statutes and structural provisions that preserve our individual autonomy while clearly identifying our organizations as co-operatives united in the common cause of developing a co-operative economy. The basis for membership for worker co-ops in VAWC is the Co-operative Identity as defined by the International Co-operative Alliance.

VAWC Membership Agreement

By identifying with the ICA definition rooted in Co-operative Principles and Values, VAWC has made the "co-operative difference" more visible to themselves and to others. They're aware that they are part of a regional, national and global movement and take advantage of Co-op Principles as a strategic guide for their structure and activities.

The Values and Principles provide coordinates for building co-operative economies. Let's look at how VAWC has interpreted the Principles:

Co-operative Principle	VAWC Model
1) Voluntary membership	VAWC membership is voluntary and open to all worker co-operatives in the region that pay dues, attend meetings and contribute surplus.
2) Democratic Control	Control of decisions and direction of VAWC is consensus-based in the hands of Members Co-ops.
3) Economic Participation	VAWC Member Co-ops pay dues and contribute surplus to co-operative development.
4) Autonomy and Independence	VAWC is autonomous and independently controlled by its members. Members may benefit from the Alliance but the Alliance has no power over individual worker-members or their co-ops, nor do outside organizations have control over VAWC or its Member Co-ops.
5) Education and Training	VAWC provides mentoring and training to new co-operatives and distributes VAWC Owners' Manuals to co-operatives. VAWC meetings are a valuable educational venue in which members can learn from each other's experiences, their mistakes and best practices. VAWC is also active in educating students and consumers in our region through publications, workshops and presentations. They co-developed a co-operative curriculum and internship program with the Dept of Economics at UMass that places students with regional co-operatives for mutually beneficial internships.
6) Co-operation Among Cooperatives	VAWC is an expression of this principle. It is a venue in which worker co-operatives can explore opportunities for co-operation with each other as well as opportunities across sectors. VAWC is a Federation Partner of the U.S. Federation of Worker Co-ops and they inter-cooperate with regional food co-ops, NFCA and credit unions. They co-founded the Valley Co-operative Business Association.
7) Concern for Community	VAWC's dedication to worker co-operation is in the service of its community of members as well as the communities in which they are nestled. In 2010 VAWC received the Austin Miller Award of the River Valley Market (a food co-op in Northampton, MA) for excellence in the principle of "Concern for Community." Their emphasis on development reflects a desire to expand co-operative opportunities to more people.

The principles of Democratic Member Control and Member Economic Participation provide clear boundaries and responsibility regarding who participates and directs co-operative entities. Thus VAWC has placed decisions regarding services provided, the implementation of educational programs and priorities for directing resources in the hands of Member Co-ops themselves. Similarly, the principle Co-operation among Co-operatives provides a strategic format for the survival and growth of VAWC, its Member Co-ops and the movement as a whole. Because it is directed by co-ops, VAWC's energy is focused on co-operative needs, and the development of co-ops within a system of support with the provision of on-going, long term support and advisement funded by dependable sources.

Making Worker Co-operatives Visible as a Powerful and Viable Alternative

In Chapter Five we discussed how a capitalist mindset and formal education that ignores co-operatives renders them and the co-operative difference invisible and we showed how even the left dismisses worker co-operatives as small and inconsequential. *VAWC is addressing the problem of a capitalist mindset head-on* by making the existence, power and viability of worker and cross sector co-operatives visible in the market and through formal educational institutions.

Individually, VAWC enterprises appear small, perhaps inconsequential to anyone but their members. However, their collective strength and success confronts dismissive attitudes based upon perceived weakness or vulnerability. VAWC makes the impact of worker co-operatives visible in our region by collecting financial data and demonstrating the collective economic impact of its Member Co-ops. The data shows that combined gross revenue of VAWC Member Co-ops exceeds seven million dollars; they employ approximately 70 people, 65 of whom are worker-members and; significantly, they increased revenue over the past four years despite an economic downturn.

The Power of Visibility

In Chapter Six we explored four particular consequences of invisibility:

1) Lack of informed choice = fewer patrons and fewer co-opreneurs

2) Lack of co-operative expertise, governance and/or management skills

3) Lack of investment and understanding of co-operative development and

4) Isolation of co-ops by sector

Here we take a look at how VAWC's strategies address this framework of problems and seem to be revealing and harnessing new opportunities.

1) Informing consumers and future co-operators

VAWC's activities in marketing and education inform consumers, the general public, students and co-op members about the co-operative difference so they can make educated economic decisions.

Marketing: VAWC informs the choices of potential consumers and spurs the imagination of consumers through joint marketing campaigns. They do this for the worker co-op sector in our region by collectively purchasing radio ad time and through a *"Working for a Co-operative Economy"* ad campaign in local food co-op newsletters. By targeting the members of food co-operatives this campaign makes visible their identity as part of a greater movement of co-operatives as do the articles they publish in other cross-sector newsletters, local papers and international journals.

Education: Not only is VAWC making their collective impact more visible through joint marketing and promotion, a third of VAWC's mission is dedicated education. VAWC has participated in educational efforts since its founding, participating in public events and conferences, and delivering guest lectures in universities, colleges and high schools. They have sponsored research on worker co-operatives and supported other educational efforts including this book. In 2009 they began working with faculty in the Economics Department at the University of Massachusetts to develop a co-operative curriculum and certificate program. They co-founded the University of Massachusetts Co-operative Enterprise Collaborative (UMCEC)[74] which also includes the participation of the Neighboring Food Co-op Association. UMCEC developed curriculum for courses in the economics of co-operative enterprise and created a Certificate in Applied Research in Co-operative Enterprise. The first of its kind in the U.S., this program provides courses in the economics of co-operative enterprises and places students with regional co-operatives for mutually beneficial internships.

UMCEC enriches a discipline that, with few exceptions, has largely ignored the co-operative sector of the economy.[75] Feedback from students who took the "Economics of Co-operative Enterprise" course developed by UMCEC suggests that they are hungry for alternatives that work. Enrollment doubled the second term the course was offered and has continued every semester since.

As of 2014, over two hundred students have taken the course, with 25 currently enrolled. Three undergraduates have worked with VAWC directly, and several have worked with other co-ops. Two undergraduates who wrote articles for *The Grass Roots Economic Organizing Newsletter* and were inspired to enroll as a team in a graduate program to study co-operative economics.

2) Developing co-operative expertise, governance and management skills

> *I wish sometimes that there was already a Mondragon in the U.S. I think it would make life easier for the rest of us. You know... they went through the struggle before we're going into it. Our trouble is trying to reinvent the wheel here all the time. Maybe that's why the co-op movement, the collective movement is not as big as we hope.*
>
> Phillipe Rigollaud, (PV)[2]

Monthly meetings are a venue in which Member Co-op Representatives can learn from each other's experience, mistakes and best practices so they don't have to—as Phillipe Rigollaud says—keep reinventing the wheel. They support each other during difficult times and share experience with internal conflict, accountability, communication, scheduling, growth, financing, hiring, firing, consensus and other governance issues. The four longest-lived Member co-ops of VAWC have more than 100 years of combined experience to share with newer members and start ups. VAWC provides mentoring and training to new co-operatives including the six conversions they have supported. They have developed a manual for co-operative governance, boilerplate bylaws for start-ups and have developed a fund for co-operative start-up and expansion of existing co-ops.

3) Understanding and investing in co-operative development

VAWC is addressing the lack of financial investment by investing directly in development, education and support. As stated earlier VAWC is funded by and accountable to its members. They do not seek federal or private grants for their core funding and are free to puruse their own priorities. A matching grant provided by the Co-operative Fund of New England to fund the Staff Pilot Project was deliberately designed with a "step-down" structure with the aim that the position would be funded by the co-operatives themselves. VAWC dues are based on gross revenues of Member Co-ops. They are currently set at one eighth of one percent of gross revenue, which follows the example set in Italy where member co-operatives contribute one quarter of one percent of gross revenues for dues.

Emilia Romagna and Mondragon demonstrate the importance of marshaling surplus, mobilizing shared resources and a clear co-operative identity grounded on Co-op Values and Principles. As mentioned previously, VAWC borrowed a funding mechanism from Italy in which co-ops themselves wrote into law that, to be a co-op, an enterprise had to contribute three percent of surplus to development. VAWC founded the Inter-cooperative Development Fund into which members contribute five percent of their surplus for the purpose of developing new and expanding existing co-operatives. The Inter-cooperative Development Fund is housed in the Co-operative Fund of New England but managed by the Member Co-ops themselves. VAWC staff was on the founding board of the Co-operative Capital Fund, a high-risk equity-like fund, also with the Co-operative Fund of New England, which addresses need for accessible funds for worker co-op start-ups through a direct loan or collateral pool.

The success of VAWC's development model is tangible even at this early stage. Since 2010 staff and members have supported the conversion of six businesses from traditional capitalist models to worker co-operatives. VAWC assisted Valley Green Feast Collective (2009), Brattleboro Holistic Health Center (2011), Simple Diaper and Linen (2012), Broadfork Permaculture Co-operative (2013) Stone Soup Farm (2013) and Real Pickles (2014) with supporting documents, governance, structure and bylaws and many of them borrowed from CFNE. As new co-ops gain strength, the support of new members shifts from incorporation to strategizing about marketing, networking and expansion.

Despite the excitement of new co-operatives, development takes time so it's important to keep a long-term vision. Mondragon began with just one worker co-operative started by five men educated in the principles of co-operation. Growth there was slow but in just sixty years they've developed an industrial co-operative economy employing more than 80,000 workers. VAWC has made great strides in pooling the financial resources of worker co-operatives, but creating a development and support co-operative doesn't happen overnight. When they began meeting in 2005, there were eleven worker co-operatives in our region, five of which co-founded VAWC. There are now fourteen, nine of which are members. VAWC was recognized by the Eastern Conference for Workplace Democracy with its Award for Co-operative Advocacy and Development at the summer conference, 2013.

4) *Developing a network of co-operation among co-operatives*

The Valley Alliance of Worker Co-operatives is rooted in the ideals of co-operation, mutuality and solidarity. VAWC is itself an expression of co-operative principles—a "co-op of co-ops"—that have come together as a means of strengthening the efforts of our individual co-ops to develop their businesses, serve their members, and contribute to the wider co-operative economy. Our core goal is to provide ourselves with the resources and support we need to advance co-operatives, empower our members, and benefit more people in our communities.[76]

VAWC's founding was a collaboration among worker co-operatives. In the early days there were few outlets for cross-sector collaboration, however, developing a shared identity among worker co-operatives based upon the Co-operative Principles and Values has cultivated a shared identity across worker, consumer and producer sectors. Joint marketing in food co-operative newsletters was among VAWC's first steps in partnering across sectors. Interco-operation has opened up other "co-opportunities" such as providing additional markets for worker co-op products and services. River Valley Market, a consumer food co-op in Northampton, hired PV Squared to install solar panels on their building and; Co-op 108 markets their body oils in regional food co-ops. PV Squared connected their credit union with VAWC businesses and included gift certificates for local co-ops in their gift packages for new clients. Brattleboro Holistic Health Center gave VAWC member co-operatives discounts on massages during the holiday season. VAWC meetings are often held at area co-operatives including some NFCA food co-ops and in 2014 VAWC Membership elected Suzette Snow-Cobb — a manager at Franklin Community Co-operative — as a Stakeholder Director on VAWC's Board.

In 2011, VAWC co-founded Valley Co-operative Business Association (VCBA) with representatives from Franklin Community Co-op, NFCA and the UMass Five College Credit Union. The mission of the Association is to represent, assist and promote the co-operative movement; encourage collaboration; coordinate strategies and policies; establish and manage relations with government; prepare legal issues regarding co-operatives; and coordinate regional and national relations for member co-operatives in order to connect regional agendas and one day have impact on a national scale.[77] Considering the traditional isolation of co-operative sectors, for us, VCBA is one of the most exciting recent and ongoing activities of VAWC. We discuss VCBA at greater length in the next chapter.

In summary, by agreeing to make financial commitments and legally formalize their organization, VAWC has empowered its membership with additional strength through interdependence and made their power more visible by demonstrating their collective economic impact. Together, VAWC members can take advantage of opportunities in collective advertising, purchasing, inter-cooperation, marketing and increased purchasing power.

They also have the ability to pool and direct co-operative funds for expansion and development. A shared Co-operative Identity has not only opened up opportunities within the worker co-op sector, it has also opened up possibilities across sectors. It's not utopia and it doesn't happen overnight but these activities are the seeds of an integrated co-operative economy.

Conclusion

In this chapter we described how VAWC is meeting the challenges and seizing the opportunities of co-operative economic development. We gave a brief history, outlined their mission and vision, and showed how the Co-operative Principles and Values have shaped their structure, governance and activities. We also explored how VAWC is addressing the problem of a capitalist mindset and the four consequences of invisibility through promotion, education, investment and inter-cooperation. We are inspired by how much VAWC has accomplished in such a short time but hear member representatives' warnings that ongoing accomplishments are hard won: It's a process.

In spite and because of the challenges involved with building new roads to co-operation, in the next chapter we share a VAWC inspired vision for building an integrated co-operative economy in our region. We introduce three of the founding members of the Valley Co-operative Business Association and one non-member participant in its early conversations. We share some of their activities and take a minute to imagine the potential of further integrated co-operation across sectors.

VIII

Envisioning a Regional Co-operative Economy

We envision a co-operative economy where one can live an entirely co-operative day; an economy built on workers' self-determination and freedom of action and association; an economy of breadth and depth that puts working people in control of their economic destiny while serving their communities in accordance with the Co-operative Values and Principles. (VAWC's vision, www.valleyworker.org)

The existence of a plethora of co-operatives in any region is exciting but it does not make a co-operative economy. The degree to which co-ops identify with Principles and Values varies and access to co-op jobs, products and services is still limited. Co-ops address problems of access, growth and development with great difficulty alone but together they can make big changes in their own businesses and communities.

Together co-ops can:
- Take advantage of the co-operative difference
- Build on "co-opportunities"
- Demonstrate economic and environmental impact
- Engage legislators and municipalities on policy
- Create integrated co-operative economies

In Chapter Seven we explored the VAWC model and some of its activities. In this Chapter we consider how VAWC and its regional co-op partners are working together to bring shared visions of sustainable co-operative economies into being.

Imagine Ed's Co-operative Day

Ed's daughter woke him up early. He shuffled to the kitchen to make coffee. His coffee beans originated in Guatemala. They were produced by a co-operative of farmers who sold the beans to a worker co-operative at a pre-determined fair-trade price (aimed at supporting farmer sustainability) that processed them for the U.S. market. Ed's banana also originated in Central America. Thankfully, it was produced by a co-operative of farmers, imported by the same worker co-operative that roasted and marketed his coffee and sold it to his local food co-op where he purchased it a couple of days ago.[78] His bread (produced by a worker co-operative in the next town) the butter he spread on it (produced by a farmers' co-operative in the region) and his orange juice (from a farmers' co-op in Florida) were also purchased at the food co-op. All of these products were linked to his food co-op by a co-operatively owned distributor that transports goods to over forty regional food co-ops.

His daughter's baby food was processed and delivered by a worker co-operative—an offshoot of the worker co-operative that launders and delivers fresh cloth and compostable diapers.[79] The neighborhood has an appliance and yard service co-operative so he doesn't have to purchase all that equipment on his own and the garbage and compost is picked up by a worker co-operative, too.

Upon arriving to work, Ed walks through the door like he owns the place, because he does.[80] He's a worker-member of a co-operative bakery. He and his co-members make a decent living so he can pay his home mortgage (a loan from a credit union); he can be a member of the food co-op, have the occasional lunch out at a worker co-op restaurant next door, and pay a little bit more for coffee produced and processed by co-operatives. His retirement savings is kept in an inter-cooperative capital fund and; health insurance is also provided by a co-operative, purchased collectively with other worker co-op businesses.

What would it take to bring Ed's co-operative day into being?

From Vision to Reality

In the Connecticut River Valley some components of Ed's day are already in place. Co-operatively-produced goods like coffee, teas, oils, nuts and bananas, bread, dairy products and juices are available at food co-operatives. However many people don't know that, say, Cabot Creamery, Florida's Natural or Welch's are co-operatives. Co-operative financial services provided by credit unions are also widely available. We have a high concentration of worker co-operatives here. As illustrated by the worker co-op profiles, they provide many goods and services from auto repair, trash and recycling hauling, diaper services, alternative health care, food and vegetable home delivery, copy services and publishing to installation of photovoltaic panels, co-operatively produced yarns and body oils. However they are still few in number compared to conventionally-owned options. The number of worker co-op jobs and access to co-operative goods and services is still very limited. We don't yet have co-operative options for healthcare, retirement or education in our region. So there are many questions and challenges to address:

• How could worker co-op jobs and co-operative goods and services be accessible to a greater population?

• How could the co-operative movement be a vehicle for raising wages and providing meaningful work especially for those of us without jobs or earning low incomes?

• What would it take for such a movement to meet healthcare, retirement and educational needs co-operatively?

• How can co-ops reach this vision of a co-operative day together?

• How can they pool resources to achieve common goals?

• What activities do co-ops need to participate in to be part of the working solution to their challenges?

• And, what kind of educational programs would support co-operatives?

Living an entirely co-operative day is a reality for many in the Basque Region of Spain thanks to the Mondragon Co-operative Corporation which employs 84,000 people 82 percent of whom are members.[81] They have access to co-operative health care, retirement and education. Co-operative capital not only provides retirement for workers, it can be drawn on to fund expansion and development of the co-operatives thus providing job security for workers despite Spain's economic downturn.[82] These kinds of services are made possible in part through secondary co-operatives—co-ops of co-ops, also called 'meso-level' co-ops—that work together toward development and expansion of individual co-ops and the system as a whole.

In New England there are an estimated 1400 co-operatives with membership of five million. They employ 22,000 people in all sectors and industries including credit unions, food co-operatives, farm and marketing co-ops, energy co-ops worker co-ops and others.[83] But these co-operatives are not integrated like those of Italy and Spain. They don't necessarily identify with the Co-operative Principles and Values or work together and support one another.

The smaller Connecticut River Valley region of Western Massachusetts, Southern Vermont and Northern Connecticut is home to a high concentration of co-operatives across co-operative sectors. We mentioned some of these in Chapter One. They are too many to name but the list includes farmer members of agricultural producer co-operatives like Our Family Farms and Cabot Creamery; consumer co-operatives such as Co-op Power,

River Valley Market, Franklin Community Co-operative, Brattleboro Food Co-op, Putney Food Co-op and Leverett Food Co-op; credit unions like UMass Five College, Freedom and Polish Credit Unions; and worker co-operatives including the ones highlighted in this book. Many of these co-operatives maintain a strong, clear co-op identify and some have begun working together within and across co-operative sectors to advance the region's co-operative economy. Significantly, there are *three* secondary co-operatives in our region: VAWC, the Neighboring Food Co-operative Association (NFCA) and the Valley Co-operative Business Association (VCBA). The Valley is also home to eight student-run businesses at the University of Massachusetts, Amherst; the University of Massachusetts Co-operative Enterprise Collaborative and the Co-operative Fund of New England.

The Valley Co-operative Business Association (VCBA) emerged from conversations about how co-operatives within and across sectors could work together and what they could do together to benefit themselves and their communities. It gained momentum from the UN's declaration of 2012 as the International Year of Co-operatives:

> The Valley Co-operative Business Association was established by a group of food co-ops, worker co-ops and a credit union to make our co-ops more visible, to advance our region's co-operative economy and to make the benefits of co-operation more available in our community.[84]

VCBA is a co-operative of co-ops made up of members from the producer, worker and consumer co-op sectors. It is a secondary co-operative not unlike like those founded in Italy's Emilia Romagna, set up to share resources, development and educational mechanisms. VCBA Member Co-ops are exploring strategies that build on and expand the strengths of co-ops and their associations.

Before further description of VCBA and its potential, we take a closer look three of its founding members: UMass Five College Federal Credit Union, Franklin Community Co-operative and the Neighboring Food Co-op Association (NFCA). You'll come across a lot of numbers in this section. Bear with us. We include them to demonstrate economic impact and to help grasp the current and potential magnitude of those involved with VCBA.

UMass Five College Federal Credit Union[85]

All credit unions differ drastically from capitalist banks.[86] However not all credit unions recognize (and harness) the power of the co-operative difference. UMass Five College Credit Union is one that does and it built on its co-op identity by being one of the founding members of VCBA.

Like most co-operatives and co-op associations, UMass Five began as a conversation. Then, in 1967, a handful of UMass employees each contributed five dollars to launch a small credit union to meet the immediate needs of members and their families. In 1971 they opened membership to students and employees of the five colleges, including Amherst, Hampshire, Mount Holyoke and Smith Colleges, and it has been growing ever since. In 2011, UMass Five had 27,000 members and $350 million in assets. UMass Five places the Co-operative Principles and Values at the forefront of their operations. Membership increased by five percent between 2010-11 so, it seems this values-based approached is serving members well.

As a non-profit 501(c)1 cooperative, the mission of UMass Five is to "always put the interests of membership first and make a positive difference in their financial lives." Their vision is to maintain strong credit union heritage and to practice and promote co-operative values in everything they do. They are committed to having a direct, positive impact and influence on members' financial well-being while growing the member base by maintaining strong partnerships with sponsor organizations and providing a workplace culture that encourages professional growth, empowerment, and teamwork. This vision is pursued while steadfastly maintaining financial stability and adhering to regulatory requirements.[87]

UMass Five interprets the Co-operative Principles uniquely but engagement with them highlights characteristics they share with co-operatives across sectors. They are listed in full on UMass Five's website but here we zoom in on the principle that is particularly relevant to the current discussion: Co-operation among Co-operatives.

> UMass Five works closely with River Valley Market and Leverett Food Co-op to build and maintain good connections between those that support food co-operatives and those that support credit unions. By offering membership to members of these organizations, we are able to raise awareness of these co-operatives for our members while also increasing our visibility with their members. We are also members of the National Cooperative Business Association (NCBA) and the Credit Union National Association (CUNA), and have close relationships with the National Cooperative Grocers Association (NCGA), the Cooperative Development Institute (CDI), and area cooperatives.

The structure and activities of UMass Five are influenced by the same principles as consumer, worker and producer co-ops of various industries. This shared identity facilitates inter-cooperation among co-operatives and among co-op associations. That's how Jon Reske, Vice President of Marketing and Sean Capaloff-Jones, Manager of Member Outreach, got into conversation with VAWC, NFCA and Franklin County Community Co-operative staff about creating a cross-sector association for co-operative businesses of all stripes in our region.

The Franklin Community Co-operative[88]

The Franklin Community Co-op (FCC) is a food co-operative and leading example of the power of co-operation in our region, expanding opportunities through the creation of secondary co-operatives made up of co-operatives. FCC co-founded the Neighboring Food Co-op Association in 2007 and the Valley Co-operative Business Association in 2011.

FCC's story began in the 1970's when community members formed a buying club to access unprocessed pesticide-free foods. Its first iteration was the Montague Food Co-op, which opened its doors in Turners Falls, MA in 1977, run completely with volunteer labor. With the help of a VISTA[89] program, they hired a manager and incorporated as Franklin Community Co-op. After much debate, members decided in 1987 to move operations to a new location in Greenfield, MA. Members donated hundreds of hours of labor to make the move possible and their work paid off. The co-op's sales increased seventy percent almost immediately after opening its doors in Greenfield.

The Greenfield location thrived and surveys revealed that members were interested in an even larger store with a wider product line. The co-op purchased a large empty building on Main Street that had recently been vacated by J.C. Penney. Community support for the co-op's expansion was widespread as people recognized the value of having a thriving business in place of an empty storefront on Main Street. The co-op opened for business on Main Street in November 1993, under the operating name Green Fields Market with a bakery and deli as welcome new additions. Membership and sales continued to grow and FCC built on its success. Considering membership west of its center in Greenfield, in 2007, FCC purchased McCusker's Market in Shelburne Falls to become a co-op with two stores serving some 2100 members and their communities.

Like its predecessors in the late nineteenth century, early members of the Montague Food Co-op joined forces to access healthy, unadulterated, affordable food. The Franklin Community Co-op continues this mission and, in the process, generates some $8.5 million in revenue and substantial surplus for members and greater community. Surplus to members is returned through a discount at the register (two percent for non-working members, ten percent for working members) and to the local community in support of healthy living and promotion of co-ops. In 2009, they used surplus to sponsor the production of "Food for Change," a documentary about Franklin Community Co-op and other food co-operatives around the country.[90] They also supported the production of this book.

FCC directs resources to diminishing their ecological footprint via composting, energy and water conservation initiatives such as night covers for refrigeration equipment, eliminating unnecessary lights, and installing low flush toilets, bike racks and solar panels by PV Squared, one of the worker co-operatives highlighted in this book. It was also the first consumer co-operative in our region to host interns from UMCEC's internship program.

Their aim to be "an outstanding example of the Co-operative Values and Principles" is evident in these educational initiatives as well as in their inter-cooperative activities. Not only is FCC a founding member of the Neighboring Food Co-op Association and the Valley Co-operative Business Association, as a member of the National Grocers Association they participate, with 143 other co-ops in the national "Go Co-op" initiative that informs consumers of the presence and impact of co-op products.

Suzette Snow-Cobb, current Marketing and Membership Manager, has been behind these inter-cooperative and educational initiatives from conversational beginnings to formal development. According to Snow-Cobb, the only way to survive and thrive is through collaboration. She's been an advocate for inter-cooperation in countless meetings among co-operatives, as well as in classrooms, on the radio and at co-operative conferences nationwide. Like Crowell and Trott, her experience comes from working in the co-operative itself (she's worked in various positions at FCC since 1998) as well as from study and international examples. She says the more she learns through work experience and study, including her Masters in Co-operative and Credit Union Management at St. Mary's University that took her to Italy in 2012, the more she's encouraged to keep breaking down barriers between co-op sectors. She was recently elected to VAWC's board as Stake-holder Director, to further the goal of inter-cooperation by providing invaluable cross-sector insight and perspectives.

The Neighboring Food Co-op Association

The Neighboring Food Co-op Association is another founding member of the Valley Co-operative Business Association.

> The Neighboring Food Co-op Association (NFCA) is a co-operative network of over 30 food co-ops and start-up initiatives that are working together toward a shared vision of a thriving regional economy, rooted in a healthy, just and sustainable food system and a vibrant community of co-operative enterprise.[91]

NFCA members are "member-owned, democratically governed community grocery stores ranging in size from large, multiple storefront retailers with thousands of members to smaller markets with just a few hundred."[92] While most of the co-ops have been in operation since the 1970s and '80s, several began in the 1930s and '40s! They are rooted in a history of members working together to access healthy organic products and promote fair trade as well as supporting early development of farmer co-operatives like Deep Root Organic and pioneers in the fair trade industry like Equal Exchange. Around the same time VAWC began organizing, NFCA grew out of a meeting convened by the Brattleboro Food Co-op in Vermont in 2004.

Co-op board members and managers from some twenty food co-ops of Western New England gathered to discuss shared experiences and possibilities for the future. In light of economic, cultural and political trends in the region, the group explored such questions as:

- What might our region's economy look like in 2020?
- How could food co-ops work together with like-minded organizations and networks to create more resilient communities as we look toward a post-petroleum economy?
- How could we avoid duplication of effort in order to support other initiatives, focus on our core strengths and advance a shared vision for the future?[93]

After the 2004 meeting, food co-operatives in the region continued scenario planning and began linking up with food-systems leaders who recognized that food co-operatives had a values level connection with development goals because they were proactive about sourcing local food in their stores and having positive relationships with farms. With the support of resources and staff time from the National Co-operative Grocers Association and the Co-operative Fund of New England, they formed a steering committee to keep the momentum and conversations going.

In Spring 2007 representatives from thirteen food co-operatives of the Connecticut River Valley braved a snow storm to spend the day together in Middlebury Vermont. They drew up the "Middlebury Manifesto," a declaration of their values and commitment to work together. This declaration established the Neighboring Food Co-operatives as an alliance that would become the NFCA. It bonded them toward common goals including:

- reorientation of the economy "from one dedicated to maximizing individual wealth to one calculated to advance the common good,"

• promotion of "regional autonomy in food production and other goods essential to human existence" and

• providing "occasions for collective action to build a co-operative economy in our geographic region."[94]

In order to know where they wanted to be in 2020, the food co-ops needed to know where they were. In 2007, they hired Doug Hoffer to lead an independent study on the impact of food co-operatives of the association.[95] The data produced by that study was a major step toward understanding and demonstrating the collective impact of the food co-operatives. The image was compelling: seventeen co-ops surveyed had a combined membership of 64,000 and aggregate annual sales exceeding $161 million. They supported local economies and provided more stable employment than typical grocery stores:[96]

• Member co-ops purchased more than $33 million in local products in 2007, including $10 million in fresh farm products, $18 million in locally-processed foods and $5 million in other products.[97]

• The 17 co-ops surveyed paid $28.6 million in employee wages, and the average wage was 18% higher than the average for food and beverage stores in the same states.

• Co-ops had lower staff turnover (36%) when compared to supermarkets (59%) and more staff employed full-time (62% compared to 43% in supermarkets).

• Taken together, member food co-ops in Vermont were among the top 25 employers in the state.

• Co-ops supported government and infrastructure with $7.3 million in sales, excise, and other taxes, $434,000 by employees, and $500,000 in property taxes.[98]

In 2010, the NFCA steering committee hired Erbin Crowell, then employed by VAWC and CFNE, as its first executive director. Among his first tasks was to formally incorporate the asso-

ciation, and he made the case for its founding as a second level
co-operative with food co-ops as its members. By 2011, NFCA
member co-ops had a combined membership of 80,000. They
employed 1450 people and generated annual revenue of $200
million.[99] The economic might of these thirty plus co-operatives
is on par with large-scale capitalist grocery chains! This collective strength can empower the NFCA to make big changes in the
food system.

In addition to working collaboratively with other food co-op
associations such as the National Co-operative Grocers Association, NFCA is committed to developing cross-sector relationships in order to bring a strong, resilient economy based in a
healthy food system into being. Cross sector partnerships include
those with Deep Root Organic Co-op,[100] Organic Valley,[101]
Cabot Creamery[102] and Equal Exchange,[103] in addition to VAWC
and UMass Five.

The power of knowing their economic impact and collaborating with co-operatives, farmers and like-minded enterprises
enables NFCA to envision and enact big changes in the regional
economy. Let's take a look at some of their activities.

*1) Using shared buying power and information to change the
food system*

Large scale capitalist grocery stores have certainly used information and buying power to change the food system for
profit.[104] Considering their numbers (illustrated above), co-operatives present a viable and powerful alternative to that model.
They have the power to make food-system changes in the service
of sustainable communities and support farmers rather than
profit for distant shareholders.

NFCA is working with farmers to increase distribution of locally and co-operatively produced food. They conducted feasibility studies among Member Co-ops to identify products that
could be produced or processed locally rather than sourced from

afar. They have prioritized purchasing products from other co-operatives whereever possible. Top products include grains such as oats and bulk foods, beans, peas and frozen vegetables. In 2009, they partnered with Deep Root Organic Co-op to source vegetables for the "Farm to Freezer" pilot project to fill a niche in local frozen vegetables. For three consecutive years they have made locally-produced frozen peas, broccoli and corn available in food co-operative freezers in Western New England.

2) Strengthening co-operatives through inter-cooperation within and across sectors

The NFCA leverages its collective assets and knowledge to strengthen its own members and assist in the development of new food co-operatives but their activities and mandate reach beyond the consumer sector to strengthen co-operatives across sectors. NFCA's identification with the Co-operative Principles—especially the Sixth Principle, Co-operation Among Co-operatives—and their cross-sector partnerships have opened up ideas and conversations that no one would have expected seven years ago.

The NFCA makes the case for cross sector collaboration through its "Go Co-op" initiative, which educates consumers about the impact of co-operatives across the food system and economy, and encourages them to purchase products supplied by other co-ops. They strengthen producer and worker co-ops and credit unions through educational activities, joint presentations at conferences, and participation in the UMass Co-operative Enterprise Collaborative at the University of Massachusetts, Amherst, where NFCA Executive Director Crowell teaches "Introduction to the Co-operative Movement. They participated in and led events for the 2012 International Year of the Co-operatives that sparked important conversations thoughout the co-op economy. They are building on this momentum, and transitioning from the "Year of Co-operatives" to the "International Decade of Co-operatives."

3) Healthy Food Access Project

In partnership with the Co-operative Fund of New England, NFCA has been working to increase access to healthy, local foods among economically marginalized people and communities in New England. The Healthy Food Access Project facilitates information sharing about programs aimed at improving food access and seeks to raise the profile of food co-ops as a solution to the challenge of healthy food access in the region.[105] They surveyed 29 co-ops about their access programs for getting healthy and local foods to under-served populations, documented strategies including costs and benefits in order to compile a tool kit for co-op programs that encourage healthy food access for all.

Programs vary considerably among member co-ops. For example, "Food For All" at City Market/Onion River in Burlington provides discounts for people on disability or using EBT, WIC. The "Community Card Program" at Berkshire Co-op Market distributes gift cards to community organizations for social service recipients in Great Barrington; the "Co-op Basics" program of the Franklin Community Co-op reduces surplus margins on some sixty staple foods to make them affordable for all and; Putney Food Co-op partners with local school districts to provide cooking classes and healthy snacks at a discount. By increasing documentation and flow of information about these programs, food co-ops can learn from each other, create new programs and improve existing activities.

Bringing it Together

The economic impact of worker co-operatives compared to cross-sector co-operatives in our region is relatively small. For example, compare VAWC's seven million dollars in collective annual revenue to NFCA's $200 million or UMASS Five's $350 million in assets. However, worker co-operatives are among the most powerful examples of what people can do in the co-operative context. With declining real wages and high unemployment, worker co-operatives are crucial to the development of a co-operative economy. Considering their number and size relative to the other co-operative sectors we might consider them a missing link.

An increase in the number of worker co-operatives would not only benefit communities with sustainable jobs, it could benefit members of co-operatives in other sectors. For example, food co-op membership might increase with a greater number of worker co-ops providing living-wage jobs and consumers might buy more organic, local and fair trade products if they weren't cutting corners to make ends meet.

In Chapter Seven we discussed the activities and history of VAWC. As a co-founder of the VCBA, VAWC Member Co-ops communicated their advantage and vision to the whole movement. VAWC has supported the conversion of six worker co-operatives since 2009. Imagine what might happen if co-op development were on the agenda of increasingly strong associations of co-operatives across sectors!

To put this into perspective, let's look at one of several producer co-operatives that participate in VCBA's shared Co-op Month advertisement: Cabot Creamery.[106]

Cabot Creamery, which is part of the 1,800-member dairy co-operative Agri-Mark, has been a proponent of cross-sector collaboration in our region and beyond. A producer co-operative owned by dairy farmer members across New England and upstate New York, Cabot values its identity as a co-operative distinct from investor held corporations. Cabot has supported the development of regional dairy co-ops such as Our Family Farms (Pioneer Valley Milk Marketing Co-op). Like NFCA, VAWC, Franklin Community Co-op and UMass Five, they honor their roots in the Rochdale Co-operative Principles.[107] They value community, equality, democracy and local ownership and aim to incorporate the Co-operative Principles in every aspect of operation. They have co-operative partners throughout the country with which they share these Co-op Principles and

> *Working together with other dairymen we have the ability to hire a staff and provide services that allow us to market high quality value added products... It's something that we couldn't do alone. It has to be done in the co-operative space.*
>
> Rob Foster, dairy farmer and
> Co-operative Director of Cabot Creamery

Values including NFCA and members of the VCBA.

The Cabot story began in 1919 when farmers from the Cabot area joined forces in order to turn their excess milk into butter and market it throughout New England. Ninety-four farmers joined at the cost of five dollars per cow and a cord of wood to fuel the boiler. They purchased the village creamery (built in 1893) and began producing butter under the Rosedale brand name. "Over the next two decades, as the nation's population flocked to urban areas, Cabot's farmer-owners thrived by shipping their milk and butter south. While the national economy shifted away from agriculture, the Vermont economy was still largely based on dairy farming."[108] In 1930 when cows outnumbered people in Vermont, the company hired its first cheese-maker and began to produce cheddar for market and by 1960 membership had grown to 600. In 1989 Cabot took first place in the cheddar category at the US Championship Cheese Contest in Green Bay, Wisconsin. In 1992 the Cabot's farmer-owners merged with 1800 farm families of Agri-mark, a southern New England co-op dating back to 1918.

Cabot is not a member of the VCBA, however, along with a number of other regional co-operatives they have participated in the shared Co-op Month advertisements for three years running. —And considering the history of isolation between co-operative sectors, having agricultural producer co-operatives in conversation with worker and consumer co-operatives in VCBA is exciting. According to USDA statistics, marketing and input supply co-operatives account for about a third of total farm sector revenue and input purchases in the U.S.[109] By participating in conversations with founding members of VCBA during the international year of co-operatives, did Organic Valley, Our Family Farms and Cabot Creamery plant a powerful seed that could expand beyond collective advertisements?

UMass Five, NFCA, Franklin Community Co-op, VAWC, and producer co-ops like Cabot Creamery, Organic Valley and Our Family Farms are examples of the rich co-operative resources in Western New England that identify with the Co-operative Principles and Values. These enterprises and associations participate in very different co-operative sectors (producer, consumer, and worker) and industries (financial, food/grocery, printing, distribution, etc.) so they have much to offer one another and they are reaching out. As collaboration between agricultural co-operatives and development opportunities expand, we imagine integrated networks of co-operative production, supply and consumption.

Are these co-ops perfect? No, of course not. They experience internal struggles and financial pressures. They aren't immune to the political strife and interpersonal conflict that happens in all sorts of human organizations. However, they are working together, cultivating trust and building on common values and principles to produce opportunities for themselves and others. Conversations have turned into organizations, ideas into goals and dreams to missions.

The Valley Co-operative Business Association

VCBA began when John Reske from UMass Five, Suzette Snow-Cobb from Franklin Community Co-op, Erbin Crowell, from NFCA and Adam Trott from VAWC got together to talk about what it would look like if co-ops in the Valley began working together across sectors. They believed the best way to promote the co-op model was to put it into practice and incorporated VCBA as a cross sector co-operative in Massachusetts, forming a federation of co-operatives.

VCBA Member Co-ops are asking themselves:

- How can we build on the success of current co-ops and identify new opportunities for co-operative enterprise?

- How can we best promote co-ops' sustainably rooting capital and employment in our communities?

- How can we pool resources to support existing co-operatives and build new ones?

Since October, 2012 co-operatives across sectors have participated in shared advertising for Co-op Month and 2014 this full page ad ran in the Valley Advocate, *the* Daily Hampshire Gazette *and the* Greenfield Recorder.

They have begun pooling resources to support co-operatives and promote the model in a number of ways including policy, education, promotion, interco-op purchasing and advertising, shared services and resources. For example, NFCA members offer a discount to co-operatives advertising in their newsletters and VAWC advertises almost exclusively in the newsletters of food co-operatives in the region to reach a market that is already familiar with Co-operative Principles and Values. They pool resources for the annual cross-sector ad you saw on the previous page as well as for expensive radio time that might otherwise be inaccessible to individual Member Co-ops.

Co-ops can expand markets for each other in interesting ways beyond advertising. For example, the NFCA has been a valuable connection for getting worker co-op products like Co-op 108's body oils and salves into its extensive network of co-op stores. Collective Copies initiated this trend early on with its co-op retail centers that started with coffee from Equal Exchange in 2006 and expanded to other goods like Fedco Seeds, canning equipment from Mondragon, yarn from Green Mountain Spinnery, and oils and salves from Co-op 108. As mentioned in the previous chapter, PV Squared initiated interco-op marketing recently by including gift certificates and coupons for regional co-operatives in the gift packages they give to new clients. Brattleboro Holistic Health Center gave discounts to VAWC member co-ops during the holidays. These practices solidify identity among a network of co-operatives, distinguish co-operatives from capitalist enterprises in similar industries and build on the strength of co-operatives working together.

VCBA participants have planted seeds of inter-cooperation poised to bear substantial fruit in the future. As the Association grows and formalizes they may be able to purchase inputs or even health insurance collectively someday. They could pool surplus, like VAWC does, to develop businesses that fill niche markets and address common needs. The NFCA represents a market that rivals large-scale capitalist super market chains. Their feasibility studies are a great example of how co-ops can work together to pinpoint development co-opportunities like grain production and frozen vegetables, providing niches that could be filled by worker and producer co-operatives.

VAWC Member Co-ops bring themselves to the table of co-operative development by contributing five percent of their surplus to the VAWC Interco-operative Development Fund designated for expanding existing and developing new co-operatives. Imagine if one tenth of the 1400 co-operatives in New England joined this cross-sector effort! That would be a powerful force for co-operative development.

By working together, co-op associations also have a greater influence on educational institutions that could provide the research and training they need. For example the University of Massachusetts Co-operative Enterprise Collaborative's program in Applied Economic Research of Co-operatives not only educates students about the co-operative model it has provided several co-ops with useful data on the economic and environmental impact of their businesses in the community. One study analyzed the carbon footprint of area worker co-operatives compared to similar capitalist businesses while another explored strategies to improve low-income access to healthy food and food co-operative membership.

Co-ops benefit from the experience and lessons of past associations because the lessons of failed co-ops and associations don't necessarily dissolve even if the enterprise disappears. For example, Common Wealth Printing's union helped facilitate the startup of Collective Copies and as a member of Collective Copies, Steve Strimer (former member of Common Wealth Printing) was able to bring his experience to VAWC. Steve points to a thirty-year-old notebook with minutes from meetings of co-operatives during the 1980s. It reads: "bring co-ops together, shared marketing, shared purchasing, new co-ops." That was in 1980! At the time Collective Copies didn't exist and Steve was working at Common Wealth Printing which, as noted in their profile, closed its doors in 2004.

The activities of VAWC, NFCA and VCBA are shaped and directed by the goals and objectives of the co-operatives themselves. Together, members determine the goals and benefits their secondary co-ops are working toward: broad-reaching development strategies, marketing the co-op identity and educating about the advantages of the co-op model, creating co-op curriculum, affecting economic policy and building regional economic development models.

> *The sky is the limit, really. Systems are in place that bring co-operatives together among and across sectors. They approach issues that individual co-ops won't or can't deal with alone. They're expanding a major strength of the co-operative model: the ability to marshal scarce resources to for the benefit of members and their communities.*
>
> Adam Trott, VAWC Staff

Conclusion

Seeing what just a few co-ops and co-op associations can do together inspires us to imagine what might happen if more co-ops invested resources and participation in co-op led development and support. To conclude this chapter we would like invite co-op members and co-op boards in the Valley, across New England, indeed across the U.S., to get together, eat some food and talk about how they might work together, how they are or could be investing co-op capital and resources into the co-operative economy and how members and their communities might benefit from working with other co-operatives.

There are approximately 209 credit unions in Massachusetts, 25 in Vermont, 21 in New Hampshire and 120 in Connecticut.[110] What might happen if members from all of these credit unions pushed their respective credit unions to participate in cross-sector, value-motivated conversations and development efforts like the Valley Co-operative Business Association? Imagine if they joined VAWC in directing surplus to the purpose of developing worker and other co-operative businesses and if all worker co-ops in the United States joined those of Italy and did the same. When co-ops themselves 'step-up' and participate in development as in Emilia Romagna in Italy and Mondragon in Spain, profound change occurs. How can co-ops do the same here?

An integrated co-operative economy begins like most co-op businesses do—with a conversation. Individual co-ops such as Collective Copies, Franklin Community Co-op and UMass Five began with conversations and have grown into powerful economic engines and community institutions. VAWC began with a conversation, as did the NFCA and VCBA. Mutually beneficial relationships, formal organizations, structures and commitments have grown from conversations transforming the idea of a sustainable co-operative economy into strategic practices of association, collaborative opportunities and co-operative development.

Our hope for this chapter and this book is to spark similar conversations in board rooms, member meetings and at kitchen tables. How can *your* co-op work with other co-ops to face obstacles and harness opportunities together?

Part Three Notes

Chapter IV

[1] By "difference in industry" we mean the good or service provided. Co-operatives of the same sector could be involved in vastly different industries, such as printing, auto repair or health services. For example, VAWC Member Co-ops differ in the goods and services they provide (they differ in industry) but they are all co-ops of the same sector (worker co-operative sector).

[2] See http://www.ica.coop/coop/principles.html (accessed 3/15/14).

[3] Unless otherwise noted, all quotes from Erbin Crowell are taken from an in-depth interview we had with him in 2009. At the time he was the staff developer for VAWC and was instrumental in solidifying its structure and current financing. He is now exectutive director of the Neighboring Food Co-operative Association.

[4] According to Ajowa Nzinga Ifateyo (2012) there are some 328 million direct shareholders in capitalist enterprises compared to one billion members of co-operative enterprises worldwide. See *Grassroots Economic Organizing (GEO) Newsletter*, Volume 2, Issue 12. http://www.geo.coop/story/power-cooperation.

[5] Ifateyo, AN. 2012, "Power of Co-operation." Grassroots Economic Organizing (GEO) Newsletter. Vol. 2, Issue 12. http://www.geo.coop/story/power-cooperation (accessed 10/19/13).

[6] Ketilson, HL., and Birchall, J. 2009. "The Resilience of the Cooperative Business Model in Times of Crisis." International Labor Organization, Geneva.

[7] Ibid.

[8] Some larger second tier credit unions were harmed. Credit unions are usually too small in size to support some of the financial services their members require, so they set up a network of 23 "corporate" credit unions in order to provide their members with additional services made possible by an economy of scale. These 23 corporate credit unions are in turn members of their own corporate credit union, US Central Federal. While the smaller "natural person" credit unions (those whose membership is made up of people rather than other credit unions) hadn't invested in risky mortgage backed securities (AKA bad loans cut up in pieces and sold to bankers) and were thus not directly affected by the large scale defaults and ensuing crisis; the US Federal corporate credit union *had* invested in them and was thus in jeopardy when the crisis hit. As of 2009 the federal plan to shore up the

losses affected some "natural person" credit unions. The loss, however, would be distributed among some 7900 member credit unions. According to FDIC and NCUA statistics, in 2008, commercial bank failure rates were almost triple that of credit unions (0.60% to 0.23%), and that increased to almost five times the credit union rate in 2010 (1.86% to 0.40%)." Matt Cropp gives a snapshot of these statistics on his finance blog (11/22/11): http://www.dailyfinance.com/2011/11/22/in-pictures-banks-vs-credit-unions-in-the-financia/ (accessed 6/26/12).

[9] See http://www.bankersacademy.com/pdf/ Impact_of_Financial_Crisis_on_CUs.pdf (accessed 6/28/12)

[10] Beware: politicians say they're willing to stand up to big banks that put profit before people. *All* private banks put profit before people. The law mandates that they maximize profit for shareholders.

[11] The pressure to maximize profit often leads banks into risky investments. Sometimes those investments can produce a favorable return on customers' deposits—a high interest rate on savings for example—but the risks taken by bankers can also produce disastrous results. We saw such a disaster in 2008 when the capitalist banking system nearly collapsed under the pressure to produce a profit. The demand for profit led financial professionals from the highest levels of management to the lowest mortgage broker into risky, destructive practices. The consequences of this irresponsibility ultimately became the burden of the greater public. In order to save "the system" we had to bail out the banks.

[12] In the Valley we have: the Franklin County Community Co-operative; River Valley Market; Leverett Food Co-op, Old Creamery Co-op, the Brattleboro Food Co-operative and several others. There are approximately thirty food co-operatives in Western New England that are members of the Neighboring Food Co-operative Association (NFCA). A full list of those co-ops can be found on NFCA's website: www.nfca.coop.

[13] There are non-cooperative exceptions to the strictly capitalist grocery store model. Some locally-owned small-town grocers, for example, are committed to their communities in the goods and services they provide. They do this, however, *despite their business model not because of it.* Whole Foods is an example of a large-scale semi-alternative capitalist business that has found it profitable to incorporate a mission and values into its business model. Part of their success can be attributed to a broad-scale desire on the part of consumers to integrate their values with consumption. Food co-ops take this desire one step further by rooting capital and control in the community rather than to profit interests of distant shareholders.

[14] For more on Mondragon's Eroski supermarket's see Thompson, D. 2001. "Mondragon Ersoki as a Mass Retailer"

[15] "The capitalist economic model and all of its contradictions is the subject of much critique and analysis in popular and academic publications. For an

in-depth critical academic analysis of capitalism, see Havey D. 2010. *The Enigma of Capital and the Crisis of Capitalism.* Oxford University Press. New York and Smith, N. 1984. *Uneven Development: Nature, Capital and the Production of Space.* University of Georgia Press (3rd ed 2008), Athens. See also, Teller-Elsberg, J., Folbre, N. and Heintz, J. 2006. *A Field Guide to the US Economy.* The New Press, New York. Georgia and; McKibbin, B. *Deep Economy: Economics as if the World Mattered,* One World Pubications, Oxford.

[16] In the case of hybrid co-operative structures, membership is made up of multiple stakeholders (which could include any combination of worker, consumer and producer stakeholders) in whose interest the enterprise would operate.

[17] See Wolff, R. 2012. "Yes there is an alternative to capitalist: Mondragon shows the way." *The Guardian.* http://www.guardian.co.uk/commentisfree/2012/jun/24/alternative-capitalism-mondragon (accessed 6/26/12)

[18] Ibid. 2012. We changed the text slightly in this quote, using the more common abbreviation "MCC" rather that "MC" that Wolff used in the original.

[19] Ibid 2012. http://www.guardian.co.uk/commentisfree/2012/jun/24/alternative-capitalism-mondragon (accessed 6/26/12).

[20] During Argentina's economic crisis, people developed broad-scale barter networks, alternative currencies, co-operatives and all kinds of volunteer, buying clubs and neighborhood networks to satisfy their economic and social needs.

[21] Avi Lewis and Naomi Klein point out in "The Take," "que se vayan todos!"—"they all must go!" was a rejection of the total system: political leaders, the International Monetary Fund and multinational corporations alike.

[22] For more details see "Take"by Avi Lewis and Naomi Klein; Lavaca Collective. 2007. *Sin Patron.* Haymarket Books, Chicago and; Magnani, E. 2009. *Silent Change.* Herrick Translation. Editorial Teseo, Buenos Aires.

[23] The late Elinor Ostrom and her collaborators, are a notable exception. As mentioned earlier, they won a Nobel Prize in Economics in 2009 for their work on cooperation and collective action.

[24] The work of Sonja Novkovic and Tom Webb of St. Mary's University in Canada indicates that the Co-operative Principles and Values offer important guidance for the managerial function of individual co-operative firms, survival strategies of inter-cooperation, as well as a capacity to encourage entrepreneurship. For example see: Novkovic S. 2008. "Defining the Co-operative Difference." *Journal of Socio-Economics.* Vol. 37 (pp 2168-2177).

[25] In a series available on SolidarityEconomy.net, "A Deeper Look at the Mondragon Principles" John McNamara explores Mondragon's Principles

and Values in action. See: http://www.solidarityeconomy.net/
index.php?s=mcnamara (accessed 2/16/13)

[26] http://www.mondragon-corporation.com/ENG/Co-operativism/Co-operative-Experience/Co-operative-Culture.aspx/ (accessed 10/20/13)

[27] Ibid.

[28] Northern Italy and the Basque Region of Spain, where co-operative
economics, management and enterprises are visible at all levels of education,
are two notable exceptions to this rule.

[29] Deller, S., Hoyt, and Hueth, B. 2009. "Research on the Economic Impact of
Co-operatives," University of Wisconsin Center for Co-operatives.

Chapter Five

[30] J.K. Gibson-Graham is the pen name of two economic geographers, Julie
Graham and Katherine Gibson who have spent most of their working lives
studying economic diversity. Their pen name sounds like one person (this
was a fun and tricky way to foil academic hierarchy) but they were two
women who collaborated cross-continentally for many years. Julie Graham
was a professor at UMass who lived in Western Mass before her death in
2010 and Katherine Gibson is a professor at Western Sydney University in
Australia. Their work and the work of the Community Economies Collective
documents economic diversity and shows how "the economy" as we tend to
think of it is partly a big, misconstrued idea. You can learn more about
Gibson-Graham's work and collaboration as well as a series of projects and
publications that it has inspired on the website of the Community Economies Collective: http://www.communityeconomies.org/Home

[31] The foundation of capitalist economies in the Americas was built by labor
stolen from American Indians, Africans and Europeans in the form of
slavery and indentured servitude. Slavery is illegal in most countries but
persists in a variety of forms in many places even in the US. See Curl, J.
2009. *For All the People: Uncovering the Hidden History of Cooperation,
Cooperative Movements and Communalism in America.* PM Press, Oakland.

[32] For more information on non-capitalist production of goods and services
see: Waring, M. 1990. *If Women Counted: A New Feminist Economics.*
Harper Collins, San Fransisco; Ironmonger, D. 1996. "Counting Outputs,
Capital Inputs and Caring Labor: Estimating Gross Household Product."
Feminist Economics Vol 2 Issue 3; Daly, G. 1991. "The discursive
construction of economic space: Logics of organization and disorganization."
Economy and Society 20 (1):79-102 and; Gibson-Graham, J.K. *The End of
Capitalism (ad we knew it).* University of Minnesota Press, Minneapolis.

[33] Marilyn Waring gives a clear description of "what counts" according to the
United Nations System of National Accounts (UNSNA). The UNSNA is the
system that measures economic activity in terms of GDP and GNP which was
developed during WWII to measure a country's capacity to win the war. Only

the goods and services that go through the market are measured as part of the GDP—a supposed measure of the health of an economy. See: Waring, M. 1990. *If Women Counted: A New Feminist Economics*. Harper Collins, San Fransisco.

[34] See: Miller E. 2005. "Solidarity Economics: Strategies for Building Solidarity Economies from the Bottom Up and the Inside Out." *Grass Roots Economic Organizing (GEO) Newsletter*. June: http://www.geo.coop/archives/SolidarityEconomicsEthanMiller.htm. See also: http://www.communityeconomies.org/people/Ethan-Miller.

[35] Neoliberalism is a political orientation that combines liberal perspectives and economic theories to construct policy aimed to drive capitalist economic growth. Neoliberal policies favor deregulation, privitization and free trade.

[36] We are referring broadly to academic and popular economic views that support free trade policy based on the idea that even though it may be painful (thanks to economic restructuring and layoffs), ultimately, supporting capitalist economic development and competition will raise all boats. The root of this idea can be traced to a nineteenth-century economist David Ricardo. It has much influence on the political economic landscape. Institutions that support varying strains of this perspective (often called "neoliberal") are the International Monetary Fund, the World Trade Organization and the World Bank. For a quick review of the debate between neoliberal perspectives and protectionism (which is typically viewed as the opposite) from a neoliberal perspective, see: Roberts, R.2006. *The Choice: A Fable of Free Trade and Protectionism*. Prentice Hall, Saddle River NJ.

[37] We are referring to the diverse concerns raised by workers and activists all over the world. A recent example of these concerns is the ongoing Occupy Wall Street movement, the protests of which reached a visible peek in the U.S. during the fall of 2011 in NYC's Zuccotti Park. The popular slogan "we are the 99%" brought attention to great disparities in the distribution of wealth. In the U.S. the upper 1% of the income share was almost 25% of the total.

[38] See Kalmi, P. 2007. "The Disappearance of Cooperatives from Economics Textbooks." *Cambridge Journal of Economics*. Vol. 31 pp 625–47.

[39] See Hill, R.2000. "The Case of the Missing Organizations: Co-operatives and Textbooks." *The Journal of Economic Education*. Vol. 31, 3 281–295 and; Hill, R. and Myatt, T. 2010. *The Economics Anti-Textbook: A Critical Thinkers Guide to Microeconomics*. Books, London.

[40] Hill (2000), Chamard (2004) and Kalmi (2007) note that economics departments across the world have been heavily influenced by the U.S. brand of economic thinking.

[41] John Chamard is a professor at St. Mary's University and co-founder of their Masters Management in Co-operatives and Credit Unions, a low residency program that focuses exclusively on the unique history, challenges

and opportunities of co-operative enterprise and is directed to actively working co-operative managers or worker-members. See Chamard, J. 2004. "Co-operatives and Credit Unions in Economics and Business Texts: Changing the Paradigm." *Journal of Co-operative Management*. Vol.1: 34–40.

[42] See Healy, S. 2009. "Alternative Economies." In Thrift N and Kitchen R (eds) *The International Encyclopedia of Human Geography* 338–344. Elsevier, Oxford.

[43] See http://usa2012.coop/about-co-ops/cooperatives-around-world(accessed 10/20/13).

[44] See Gordon Nembhard, J. 2004. "Cooperative Ownership in the Struggle for African American Economic Empowerment." *Humanity and Society*. 28, 3 and; Nembhard, JG. 2014. *Collective Courage: A History of African American Co-operative Economic Thought and Practice*. Pennsylvania State University Press.

[45] See http://www.federationssoutherncoop.com/.

[46] See http://www.chcany.org.

Chapter VI

[47] See Ifateyo, A.N. 2012. "The Power of Cooperation." *Grass Roots Economic Organizing (GEO) Newsletter*. http://www.geo.coop/story/power-cooperation(accessed 10/12/13).

[48] See http://www.usworker.coop/system/files/ USFWC_News_Nov2009.pdf(accessed 10/08/12) and; Shoeing, J. 2010. "The Rise and Fall of Burley Design Cooperative." *Oregon Historical Quarterly*. 111, 3.

[49] See Parnel, E. 2000. "Reinventing Co-operation: The Challenge of the 21st Century" Report to the International Co-operative Alliance.

[50] The longevity of co-operatives is more remarkable than the demise of individual enterprises. However, the stories of demutualized co-operatives offer valuable lessons for present and future co-operators worldwide. For more about demutualization see: Galor Z.2008. "The Demutualization of Cooperatives: Reasons and Perspectives." http:/ www.coopgalor.com/doc DemutualizationCooperatives21.5.08.pdf (accessed 10/20/13) and Parnell, E. 2009 "UK Consumer Co-operation, Recession and Rebirth." International Co-operative Alliance Research Conference September 2-4. http:// www.co-oppundit.org/files/icareserch09_new.pdf (accessed 10/20/13).

[51] Quoted by Zagmani and Zagmani (2010), p. 30.

[52] See: http://www.smu.ca/academic/sobey/mm/about.html.

[53] Co-operative development organizations do fantastic work but they also make avoidable mistakes due to the scarcity of co-operative education. For example, PV Squared's early bylaws were drawn with consultants from CDI

who mistakenly offered the bylaws of an agricultural producer co-op as a template.

[54] Johnson, M. and Curl, J. 2012. "Lessons for Building a Co-operative Movement." Grass Roots Economic Organizing (GEO) Newsletter. 2, 13. http://www.geo.coop/story/lessons-building-co-operative-movement (accessed 10/20/13)

[55] Governments at a variety of levels compete with each other to make their region (city, state or country) an attractive option for capital investment. Two cities of the same or different countries could be in competition to attract a single corporation. Federal and state entities could also have competing interests. For example the interests of the United States Agency for International Development may be in conflict with city governments trying to protect local jobs. Tax-funded infrastructural development and training, and tax subsidies for new business are justified in the name of job creation but cities and towns rarely break even in terms of actual income and taxes paid by workers in new jobs. Critics often call this development approach "corporate welfare" suggesting that corporate welfare costs exceed social welfare expenditures.

[56] Restakis, J. 2010. *Humanizing the Economy: Co-operatives in the Age of Capital.* Society Publishers, Gabriola Island. (p. 57).

[57] See Ibid. and Zagmani, S. and Zagmani, V. 2010, *Co-operative Enterprise Facing the Challenge of Globalization.* Elgar Publishing Ltd. Cheltnnham, UK and; Logue 2006. "Economics, Cooperation, and Employee Ownership: The Emilia Romagna Model." Ohio Employee Ownership Center. Kent, Ohio. http://www.community-wealth.org/articles/outside-us.html

[58] According to Logue (2006), the 1847 Basevi Law outlines constitutional recognition of co-operatives. It encourages self-capitalization through tax incentives and mandates that in the event of dissolution, co-operative reserves be distributed to another co-operative or co-op federation (rather than to membership). The 1992 law amends it to require that all co-operatives contribute three percent of surplus to co-operative development funds run by various co-operative federations—a generalization of the Lega Coop's ongoing practice.

[59] Many co-operative businesses actually use the word profit to describe surplus but, again, we find this confused terminology unfortunate.

[60] These could be increasing market share, and the benefits of economies of scale like a discounted price for inputs purchased in larger quantities.

[61] Or they are directed to some other purpose that fulfills the mission of the business.

[62] Conversely, all of the risk of the new venture falls to a single-owner who must absorb the loss by themselves whereas the group of worker-members spread the loss over a larger group. Both models contain reasons for risk aversion.

[63] This example is oversimplified. There are many reasons a co-operative might choose to expand even when doing so may not financially benefit members. For example, Equal Exchange has a substantial motive for expansion since expanding its market and market share enables it to better fulfill its mission.

[64] For more information about Evergreen Co-operatives see: http://evergreencooperatives.com/about/evergreen-story/and; Alperovitz, G. and Howard, T. 2010. "The Cleveland Model."In The Nation 1 http://www.thenation.com/article/cleveland-model (accessed 10/20/13).

[65] The Cheese Board Collective began as a small conventionally-owned cheese store in Berkeley CA in 1967. In 1971 the two original owners sold the business to six employees and stayed on themselves as worker members of the newly converted egalitarian worker owned business. By 1995, when they were approached by Arizmendi organizers, the Cheese Board Collective had grown substantially into a bakery and café and semi-autonomous pizza shop down the street. Consensus based and collectively managed, the business generated a steady surplus and worker pay and benefits were more than double industry average. Cheese board members wanted to expand the number of good, worker-owned jobs like theirs but they weren't interested in having a larger collective of their own. Rather than expanding their own business, they decided to incubate and fund the development of new worker-owned collectives.

[66] Marraffino, J. 2009. "The Replication of Arizmendi Bakery: A Model of the Democratic Worker Co-operative Movement." *Grass Roots Economic Organizing (GEO) Newsletter*. 2, 3. http://www.geo.coop/node/365 (accessed 10/20/13).

[67] A number of worker co-operatives, including the Swallow Café Collective and the Juice Bar Collective, were started in association with The Cheese Board Collective. The Arizmendi Association took these efforts to a new level by building the mission of development into the new co-operatives they helped develop.

[68] "Greed is good."A quote from Michael Douglas' character the 1987 film "Wallstreet" by Oliver Stone exemplifies what we mean by capitalist ideology.

Chapter VII

[69] Crowell, E. 2010. "The Valley Alliance of Worker Co-operatives: Exploring the Potential of Co-op Led Development." Masters Thesis, can be found via VAWC's website and see: http://valleyworker.org/slide%20show%20try/crowell.vawcreport.final_.st_.mary_.pdf (accessed 10/20/13).

[70] Ibid.

[71] Ibid.

[72] The number of worker co-operatives in our region has grown. There are now sixteen worker co-operatives, the newest four started up between 2010 and 2013 with VAWC support and mentoring.

[73] Food for Thought members were excited about VAWC and they supported its mission in notable ways including hosting a fundraiser for this book. Food for Thought Books received VAWC's support during a difficult period, however, they never became members before closing their doors permanently in 2014.

[74] See: www.umasscec.edu

[75] For more about the conspicuous absence of co-operatives from economics textbooks (which we imagine has participated in the absence of co-operative development) see Kalmi (2007), Chamard (2004) and Hill (2000) and Chapter Five of this book.

[76] See http://valleyworker.org/about-vawc/ (accessed 10/20/13).

[77] See http://vcba2012.coop/ (accessed 10/20/13).

Chapter VIII

[78] Farmers' and worker co-operatives are not perfect but this co-operative supply chain is a far cry from the one dominated by the United Fruit Company (now Chiquita brand) in the 1950's that used profits generated by Central American producers to fund a CIA coup and sparked a thirty six year civil war in Guatemala. Equal Exchange and their farmer co-op partners use surplus to fund things like training programs for women in Guatemala, ecotourism in Nicaragua and new classrooms in El Salvador. For more information on their projects, see: http://www.equalexchange.coop/farmer-partners (accessed 4/23/13).

[79] It is important to recognize that co-operative production and distribution of goods and services happens in all kinds of monetized and non-monetized ways. Many households participate in co-operative production and exchange, barter and other methods of satisfying needs that our focus on enterprise in this book does not address. For example, goods and services within and among households are often produced and distributed invisibly, either non-monetized within and/or bartered among households. For more on co-operative production in the sphere of "reproduction" see: Morrow, O. 2014. "Urban Homesteading: gender and self-provisioning in the city." Ph.D. Dissertation. Graduate School of Geography, Clark University.

[80] Props here to Black Star Co-op in Austin Texas, a consumer-owned worker managed brewery that uses this as their slogan: "walk in like you own the place, because you do."

[81] See Mondragon's 2011 Annual Report: http://www.mondragon-corporation.com LinkClick.aspx?fileticket=cTBqsjF7Q18%3d&tabid=331 (accessed 4/19/13).

[82] For more details on Mondragon and Co-operatives in Italy, see: Restakis, J. 2010. *Humanizing the Economy: Co-operatives in the Age of Capital.* Society Publishers, Gabriola Island, BC and; Zagmani, S., and Zagmani, V. *Co-operative Enterprise Facing the Challenge of Globalization.* Elgar Publishing Ltd. Cheltnnham, UK.

[83] See http://nfca.coop/co-opeconomy and; Deller, S., Hoyt, A., and Hueth, B. 2009. "Research on the Economic Impact of Co-operatives" University of Wisconsin Center for Co-operatives at http://reic.uwcc.wisc.edu/sites/all/REIC_FINAL.pdf (accessed 4/24/13).

[84] See http://vcba2012.coop/?page_id=28

[85] History and quotes in this section come from UMass Five College Credit Union Website See: https://www.UMass Five.coop/our_history_mission_and_vision.html (accessed 2/25/13).

[86] For a more detailed exploration of how credit unions differ from banks please see Chapter Four of this book.

[87] See https://www.UMass Five.coop our_history_mission_and_vision.html (accessed 10/30/2013).

[88] History and quotes from this section are derived from an interview with Suzette Snow-Cobb as well as the Franklin Community Co-op website: http://www.greenfieldsmarket.coop/

[89] The Volunteers in Service to America, a well known volunteer program in the U.S., was founded in 1965 to fight poverty in America. For more information, see: http://www.nationalservice.gov/programs/americorps/americorps-vista

[90] For further details see: http://foodforchange.coop/

[91] See http://nfca.coop/ (accessed 3/7/13).

[92] Crowell, E. 2010. "The Neighboring Food Co-op Association: Collaboration for a Thriving Regional Economy." *The Natural Farmer* Issue on Organic Farming and Co-ops. See http://nfca.coop/sites/default/files nfca.natural_farmer.2010.flyer.pdf (accessed 3/4/13).

[93] Ibid.

[94] Ibid.

[95] This study was mostly financed by food co-operatives in Hanover N.H., Brattleboro and Burlington VT.

[96] IMPLAN software estimated the "multiplier effects" of the seventeen co-operatives surveyed, taking into account factors such as the circulation of wages, taxes and local purchases in the regional economy. The study estimated a total of $279 million in direct and indirect economic impact, a total of 2,263 jobs generated as well as $13.7 million in tax revenue for host states. Since the study was conducted, individual co-ops and the NFCA as a

whole continued to grow. By 2009 the NFCA had more than 20 members and "...between 2007 and the end of 2009 the 17 co-ops included in the original study grew about 8% in revenue, 4% in employees, and 17% in members." http://nfca.coop/sites/default/files/ nfca.natural_farmer.2010.flyer.pdf.

[97] This study defined "local as being sourced within the state or within 100 miles.

[99] These data and figures can be found on the NFCA website: http:// nfca.coop/sites/default/files/nfca.natural_farmer.2010.flyer.pdf and, for Hoffer's summary report see http://www.go.coop/sites/default/files/pdfs/ hoffersummary.pdf

[99] See www.nfca.coop/about (accessed 2/22/2013)

[100] A producer co-operative of 20 member farms in Northern VT and Southern Quebec.

[101] An organic dairy co-operative with 1834 farmer members.

[102] Another dairy co-operative with 1200+ family farm owners (described in fuller detail below).

[103] An internationally operating worker co-op with 100+ members based in Bridgewater MA.

[104] For example, they direct consumption through "membership" without consumer representation in the absence of values and principles beyond profit.

[105] See http://nfca.coop/healthyfoodaccess

[106] The history and quotes from this section are taken from Cabot Creamery's website. See http://www.cabotcheese.coop/pages/about_us/; and http://www.cabotcheese.coop/pages/about_us/history.php (accessed 3/1/13)

[107] See Chapter One for a more in-depth discussion of the Rochdale Co-operative Principles.

[108] See http://www.cabotcheese.coop/pages/about_us/history.php

[109] See U.S. Department of Agriculture. 2006. "Farmer Cooperative Statistics." Service Report 67. http://reic.uwcc.wisc.edu/agricultural/ (accessed 5/ 18/13).

[110] See http//www.creditunionsonline.com for a list of credit unions by state.

Bibliography

Alperovitz, G. 2005. *America Beyond Capitalism: Reclaiming Our Wealth, Our Liberty and Our Democracy.* Hoboken, NJ: Wiley & Sons

Alperovitz, G., T. Williamson, and T. Howard. 2010. "The Cleveland Model: Thoroughly Green and Worker-owned Co-ops Are a Vibrant Response to Economic Distress." *The Nation* March 1, online: http://www.thenation.com/ article/cleveland-model#axzz2bm1nYeZi

Benello, C.G. 1992. *From the Ground Up: Essays on Grassroots and Workplace Democracy*, ed. H.C. Boyte, and L. Krimerman. Boston, MA: South End Press

Birchall, J., and H.L. Ketilson. 2009. "Responses to the Global Economic Crisis: Resilience of the Co-operative Business Model in Times of Crisis." Sustainable Enterprise Programme, Geneva: International Labour Organization

Byrne, K., and S. Healy. 2006. "Cooperative Subjects: Toward a Post-Fantasmatic Enjoyment of the Economy." *Rethinking Marxism* (2): 241-271

Chamard, J. 2004. "Co-operatives and Credit Unions in Economics and Business Texts: Changing the Paradigm." *International Journal of Co-operative Management* 1(2): 34-40

Clamp, C.A., and A. Innocentus. 2010. "Social Entrepreneurship in the Mondragon Cooperative Corporation and the Challenges of Successful Replication." *Journal of Entrepreneurship* September, 19: 149-177

Community Economies Collective. 2001. "Imagining and Enacting Noncapitalist Futures." *Socialist Review* 28 (4): 93-135

Coontz, K. 2009. "Western Worker Co-ops Share Experiences and Expertise." *Networks News Update from Co-operation Works!* December pp 10-11, online: http://www.cooperationworks.coop/sites/default/files/NetWorksDecember2009_1.pdf

Crowell, E. 2010. "The Valley Alliance of Worker Co-operatives: Exploring the Potential of Co-op Led Development." University of Saint Mary's Masters Thesis online: http://valleyworker.org/slide%20show%20try/crowell.vawcreport.final_.st_.mary_.pdf

Crowell E., and A. Trott. 2009. "The Valley Alliance of Worker Co-operatives: Exploring the Potential of Co-op directed Development" *United States Federation of Worker Co-operatives News* July

Curl, J. 2009. *For All the People: Uncovering the Hidden History of Cooperation, Cooperative Movements and Communalism in America.* Oakland, CA: PM Press

Center for American Women in Politics. 2011. "Gender Differences in Voter Turnout: Factsheet." Rutgers University, online: http://www.cawp.rutgers.edu/fast_facts/voters/documents/genderdiff. pdf

Daly, G. 1991. "The Discursive Construction of Economic Space: Logics of Organization and Disorganization." *Economy and Society* 20 (1):79-102

Deller, S., A. Hoyt, and B. Hueth. 2009. "Research on the Economic Impact of Co-operatives." University of Wisconsin Center for Co-operatives, online: http://reic.uwcc.wisc.edu/sites/all/REIC_FINAL.pdf

Dow, G. 2003. *Governing the Firm: Workers' Control in Theory and Practice.* Cambridge, UK: Cambridge University Press

Ellerman, D. 1990. *The Democratic Worker-owned Firm.* Winchendon, MA: Unwin Hyman Inc

Ellerman, D. 2005. "Translatio Versus Concessio: Retrieving the Debate about Contracts of Alienation with an Application to Today's Employment Contract." *Politics and Society* 33(3): 449-480

Ellerman, D. 2007. "On the Role of Capital in "Capitalist" and in Labor-Managed Firms." *Review of Radical Political Economics* 39(1): 5-26

Galor, Zvi. 2008. "Demutualization of Co-operatives: Reasons and Perspectives." Online: http://www.coopgalor.com/doc/DemutualizationCooperatives21.5.08.pdf

Gibson-Graham, J.K. 1996. *The End of Capitalism (As We Knew It)*. Minneapolis, MN: University of Minnesota Press

Gibson-Graham, J.K. 2006. *A Postcapitalist Politics*. Minneapolis, MN: University of Minnesota Press

Gibson-Graham, J.K., J. Cameron, and S. Healy. 2013. *Take Back the Economy: An Ethical Guide for Transforming Our Communities*. Minneapolis MN: University of Minnesota Press

Gordon Nembhard, J. 2004. "Non-Traditional Analyses of Cooperative Economic Impacts: Preliminary Indicators and a Case Study." *Review of International Co-operation* 97(1):6–21

Gordon Nembhard, J. 2004. "Cooperative Ownership in the Struggle for African American Economic Empowerment." *Humanity and Society* 28(3): 298-321

Gordon Nembhard, J. 2014. *Collective Courage: A History of African American Cooperative Economic Thought and Practice*. Philadelphia, PA: Pennsylvania State University Press

Green Mountain Spinnery and M. Stone. 2009. *99 Yarns and Counting*. Woodstock, VT: Countryman Press

Harvey, D. 1990. "Between Space and Time: Reflections on the Geographical Imagination." *Annals of the Association of American Geographers.* 80(3): 418–434

Harvey, D. 1998. "The Body as an Accumulation Strategy." *Transactions of the Institute of British Geographers* 16: 401–421

Harvey, D. 2005. *A Brief History of Neoliberalism.* New York, NY: Oxford University Press

Healy, S. 2010. "Traversing Fantasies, Activating Desires: Economic Geography, Activist Research, and Psychoanalytic Methodology." *Professional Geographer* 62(4): 496-506

Healy, S. 2009. "Alternative Economies." In *International Encyclopedia of Human Geography,* ed. N. Thrift and R. Kitchen, 338-344. Oxford, UK: Elsevier

Hill, R., and T. Myatt. 2010. *The Economics Anti-Textbook: A Critical Thinkers Guide to Microeconomics.* London, UK: Zed Books

Hill, R. 2000. "The Case of the Missing Organizations: Co-operatives and the Textbooks." *Journal of Economic Education* (3): 281-295

Holmstrom, M. 1985. "How the Managed Manage the Managers: Workers Coo-Ops in Italy." *Anthropology Today* 1(6): 7-13

Hoover, M. 2008. "Another Workplace Is Possible: Co-ops and Workplace Democracy." In *Solidarity Economy: Building Alternatives for People and Planet,* ed. J. Allard, C. Davidson and J. Matthaei, 239-253. Chicago, IL: ChangeMaker Publications

Howard, T. 2010. "The Cleveland Model." *The Nation* March 1, online: http://www.thenation.com/article/cleveland-model

Ironmonger, D.1996. "Counting Outputs, Capital Inputs and Caring Labor: Estimating Gross Household Product." *Feminist Economics* 2(3): 37-64

Kalmi, P. 2007. "The Disappearance of Cooperatives from Economics Textbooks." *Cambridge Journal of Economics* 31(4): 625-647

Ketilson, L.H., M. Gertler, M. Fulton, R. Dobson, and L. Polsom. 1998. "The Social and Economic Importance of the Co-operative Sector in Saskatchewan." Center for the Study of Co-operatives, University of Saskatchewan, online: http://usaskstudies.coop/?page_id=984#Co-operatives_-_Saskatchewan

Kremer, M. 1997. "Why are Worker Cooperatives So Rare?" NBER Working Paper Series, National Bureau of Economic Research, Cambridge, MA

Lavaca Collective. 2007. *Sin Patron*. Chicago IL: Haymarket Books

Lindenfeld, F., and J. Rothschild-Whitt, eds. 1982. *Workplace Democracy and Social Change*. Boston, MA: Porter Sargent Publishers

Logue, J. 2006. "Economics, Cooperation and Employee Ownership: The Emilia Romagna Model." Kent University, online: http://dept.kent.edu/oeoc/oeoclibrary/emiliaromagnalong.htm

MacLeod, G. 1998. *From Mondragon to America: Experiments in Community Economic Development*. Sydney, Nova Scotia: Cape Brenton Press

Marraffino, J. 2009. "The Replication of Arizmendi Bakery: A Model of the Democratic Worker Cooperative Movement." *Grassroots Economic Organizing (GEO) Newsletter* Volume 2, Issue 3. Online: http://www.geo.coop/node/365

Mckibbin, B. 2007. *Deep Economy: The Wealth of Communities and the Durable Future.* New York, NY: St. Martins Griffin

Miller, E. 2005. "Solidarity Economics: Strategies for Building Solidarity Economies from the Bottom Up and the Inside Out." *Grass Roots Economic Organizing (GEO),* online: http://www.geo.coop/archives/ SolidarityEconomicsEthanMiller.htm

Morrison, R. 1991. *We Build this Road as We Travel.* Philadelphia, PA: New Society Press

Novkovic, S. 2008. "Defining the Co-operative Difference." *Journal of Socio-Economics* 37: 2168-77

Nzinga Ifateyo, A. 2012. "The Power of Co-operation" *Grassroots Economic Organizing (GEO) Newsletter* Volume 2, Issue 12. Online: http://www.geo.coop/story/ power-cooperation

Ostrom, E. 2000. "Collective Action and the Evolution of Social Norms" *Journal of Economic Perspectives* 14(3): 137-158

Parnel, Edgar. 1999. *Reinventing Co-operation: The challenge of the 21st Century.* Oxfordshire, UK: The Plunkett Foundation

Parnel, Edgar. 2009. "UK Consumer Co-operation: Recession and Rebirth." Online: http://www.co-oppundit.org/files/ icareserch09_new.pdf

Restakis, J. 2010. *Humanizing the Economy: Co-operatives in the Age of Capital.* Gabriola Island, BC: New Society Publishers

Roberts, R. 1994. *The Choice: A Fable of Free Trade and Protectionism.* Upper Saddle River, NJ: Prentice Hall

Ruggeri, A. 2014. "Informe del IV relevamiento de Empresas Recuperadas en la Argentina. 2014." Ciudad Autonoma de Buenos Aires, ARG: Cooperativa Chilavert Artes Graficas

Sahadi, J. 2007. "CEO Pay 364 Times More than Workers." *CNN Money* August 29, online: http://money.cnn.com/ 2007/08/28/news/economy/ceo_pay_workers/index.htm

Shoeing, J. 2010. "The Rise and Fall of Burley Design Cooperative." *Oregon Historical Quarterly* 111(3): 312

Smith, N. 1984. *Uneven Development, Nature, Capital and the Production of Space.* New York, NY: Basil Blackwell

Swyngedouw, E. 1997. "Neither Global nor Local: 'Glocalization' and the Politics of Scale." In *Spaces of Globalization: Reasserting the Power of the Local,* ed. K. Cox. 137-166. New York, NY: Guilford

Taylor, K.B. 1999. "The Quest for Universal Capitalism in the United States." In *21st Century Economics, Perspectives of Socioeconomics for a Changing World,* ed. W.E. Halal, and K.B. Taylor, 349-348. New York, NY: St. Martin's Press

Teller-Elsberg, J., N. Folbre, and J. Heintz. 2006. *A Field Guide to the US Economy.* New York, NY: The New Press

Thompson, D. 1994. *Weavers of Dreams.* Center for Cooperatives, Oakland, CA: Regents of the University of California

Thomspon, D. 2001. "Mondragon Eroski as a Mass Retailer" The Co-operative Grocer Network, November- December (097) online: http://www.cooperativegrocer.coop/articles/ 2004-01-08/mondragons-eroski-mass-retailer

Trott, A. 2008. "Growing a Transformative Businesses." In *Solidarity Economy: Building Alternatives for People and Planet,* ed. J. Allard, C. Davidson, and J. Matthaei J, 224-27. Chicago, IL: ChangeMaker Publications

Turner, B. 1999. "Collective Copies: An Exercise in Workplace Democracy." SS Division 1 Exam Spring, Stan Warner, Hampshire College

Waring, M. 1990. *If Women counted: A New Feminist Economics*. San Francisco, CA: Harper Collins

Webb, J. 2006. *Organizations, Identities and the Self*. New York, NY: Palgrave

Webb, S., and B. Webb. 1907. *History of the Trade Unionism*. New York, NY: Longmans Green and Company

Webb, S., and B. Webb. 1921. *The Consumer's Co-operative Movement*. New York, NY: Longmans Green and Company

Wolff, R. 2012. "Yes There Is an Alternative to Capitalism: Mondragon Shows the Way" *The Guardian/UK* June 25, online: thhttps://www.commondreams.org/view/2012/06/25-4

Zamagni, S., and Zamagni, V. 2010. *Co-operative Enterprise: Facing the Challenge of Globalization*. Cheltenham, UK: Elgar Publishing Ltd

Internet

Gar Alperovitz
http://www.garalperovitz.com/
http://truth-out.org/opinion/item/10424-america-beyond-
capitalism

Black Star Co-op
http://www.blackstar.coop/

Brattleboro Holistic Health Center
http://brattleboroholistichealth.com/

Cabot Creamery
http://www.cabotcheese.co-op/pages/about_us/co-
operative_roots.php 9/9/09

Collective Copies
http://www.collectivecopies.coop/

Co-op 108
http://coop108.com/

Co-operative Home Health Care Associates
http://www.chcany.org/

Credit Union National Association
http://www.cuna.org/

Credit Unions Online
http://www.creditunionsonline.com/

Evergreen Cooperatives
http://evergreencooperatives.com/

Equal Exchange
http://www.equalexchange.coop/worker-owned/

Gaia Host Collective
http://www.gaiahost.coop/

International Co-operative Alliance
www.ica.co-op

Mondragon Corporation
http://www.mondragon-corporation.com/language/en-US/
ENG.aspx

Mondragon Economic data:
http://www.mondragon-corporation.com/language/en-US/ENG/
Economic-Data/Most-relevant-data.aspx

National Association of Credit Unions
http://www.nafcu.org/

National Co-operative Business Association
http://www.nfca.coop/

Neighboring Food Co-op Association
http://nfca.coop/

Northampton Association of Education and Industry
http://www.historic-northampton.org/highlights/
educationindustry.html

Pedal People
http://www.pedalpeople.coop/

Pelham Auto
http://pelhamauto.net/

The Peoples Market
http://www.umass.edu/rso/peoples/
Pioneer Valley PhotoVoltaics
http://pvsquared.coop/

Saint Mary's University, Masters of Management: Credit
Unions and Co-operatives
http://www.smu.ca/academic/sobey/mm/about.html

SEIKATSU in Japan
http://www.seikatsuclub.co-op/english/

Simple Diaper and Linen
http://simple.coop/

Toolbox for Education and Social Action
http://toolboxfored.org/

United Steel Workers Union and Mondragon collaboration
www.usw.org
http://www.usw.org/our_union/co-ops
http://www.usw.org/media_center/releases_advisories?id=0523
(accessed 8/23/12);
http://www.oeockent.org/coopdev/the-union-cooperative-model

UMass Center for Student Business
http://www.umass.edu/rso/csb/

UMass Five College Credit Union
https://www.umassfive.coop/

UMass Co-operative Enterprise Collaborative
http://www.umasscec.org/

United Nations International Year of the Co-opperative
http://social.un.org/coopsyear/

The United States Federation of Worker Co-operatives
http://www.usworker.coop

US Federation of Southern Co-operatives
http://www.federationsoutherncoop.com/

The Valley Alliance of Worker Co-operatives
http://valleyworker.org

Valley Co-operative Business Association (VCBA)
http://vcba.coop/

Valley Green Feast
http://www.valleygreenfeast.com

Interviews

Arthur, E. Personal INTERVIEW. May 2008

Benavente, J. Personal INTERVIEW. May 2008

Brace, G. Personal INTERVIEW. May 2009

Crowell, E. Personal INTERVIEWS. November 2008, December 2008

Gardner, Bob. Personal INTERVIEW. August 2009

Gaslin, M. Personal INTERVIEW. April 2008.

Garofalo, L. Personal INTERVIEW. April 2012

Greenberg, C. Personal INTERVIW. April 2009

Deluca, E. Personal INTERVIEW. May 2011

Hahn, K. Personal INTERVIEW. May 2008, June 2008

Haines, G. Personal INTERVIEW. April 2008

Hanlon, R. Personal INTERVIEW. February 2012

Hasbrouk, L. Personal INTERVIEW. June 2009

Hebert, E. Personal INTERVIEW. March 2008

Jarrett, A. Personal INTERVIEWS. September 2008, November 2008

Leighton, J. Personal INTERVIEW. January 2010

McCleester, D. Personal INTERVIEW. January 2010

Mutz, L. Personal INTERVIEW. April 2012

Olsen, C. Personal INTERVIEW. November 2006

Pinkham, K. Personal INTERVIEWS. November 2006, March 2008

Roy, S. Personal INTERVIEW. March 2008

Sable, B. Personal INTERVIEW. September 2009

Shar, M. Personal INTERVIEW. May 2008

St. Jean, A. Personal INTERVIEW. May 2008

Snow-Cobb, S. Personal INTERVIEW. April 2008

Rigollaud, P. Personal INTERVIEW. February 2009.

Strimer, S. Personal INTERVIEWS. November 2006, February 2008, October 2008

Trott, A. Personal INTERVIEWS. November 2006, May 2008, December 2009

Wetmore C. Personal INTERVIEW. March 2008

Weil, A. Personal INTERVIEW. December 2008

Wright, N. Personal INTERVIEW. November 2006

Zucco, R. Personal ITERVIEWS. November 2006, March 2008

History of Cooperatives in the Pioneer Valley Region

By John Curl

Over 530 industrial worker cooperatives opened in 37 states of the USA and Canada in the decades following the Civil War, 1866 to 1887. At least 87 of these cooperatives were in New England, 27 of which were located in the Connecticut River Valley and Western Massachusetts. Beyond these were numerous cooperative stores and farmer cooperatives. All were part of an extensive social movement that arose spontaneously among American working people in response to the economic problems brought on by the industrial revolution. In the early 1800s the "free" population in the U.S. was predominantly made up of self-employed farm families, but by the end of the century most Americans were employees. How that saga came to pass delineates a central struggle of generations of working people on this continent that is still being played out. That story is far beyond the boundaries of this short historical sketch, yet it is in that context that we glimpse some of the history of cooperatives created by the working people of the region of the Pioneer Valley.

Indian and Settler Cooperatives

The earliest cooperatives in the Pioneer Valley region were Algonquian.[1] The Pocumtuc, Norwottuck, Nipmuc and, in the north, Penacook villages practiced a sustainable, communal and cooperative way of life along the rivers for uncounted generations, until their world was destroyed by European colonization. The first group of settlers arrived in the Springfield area in 1636. In Northampton the first settlers purchased land rights from the regional council of chiefs in 1654, with the settlers limited to certain areas, while the tribes reserved the rights of fishing, hunting and raising crops in the rest of the land.

Each settler family was allotted several acres for a home site and a plot of meadowland, with the rest of the settlement retained as a commons for grazing livestock and gathering firewood. This pattern was typical in Massachusetts: every settler community revolved around a commons, and the collective tending of this land was typically their first cooperative endeavor. As settler communities expanded, the system of common land was slowly dismantled.

New England Association

The growing towns of the Connecticut River region felt the beginning of industrialization in the early 1800s. The New England Association of Farmers, Mechanics and Other Workingmen (NEAFMOW), founded in 1831, was the most important broadly based organization of working people in America at that time. It was organized by workers fighting for a shorter work week and improved working conditions. NEAFMOW's mission was to organize all working people into one big union. Membership included farmers, mechanics, urban workers, master workmen, and factory workers.

NEAFMOW held its third annual convention in Northampton in September, 1834. At their previous conventions, they discussed "cooperative trading," and "some 40 cooperatives were reported to have been started as a result of the interest thus stimulated."[2] No further information about these cooperatives survives, but they were probably small purchasing and marketing operations for artisanal products and agricultural produce. In the following years the organization faded.

Northampton Association

In 1841 a group purchased a silk company in Northampton and transformed it into a cooperative colony: the Northampton Association of Education and Industry also known as the Florence Colony. It became one of the most successful settlements of the Associationist[3] movement, which sought a way beyond the oppressions of the emerging factory system through cooperative colonies. At least thirty-four Associationist colonies, averaging well over one hundred members apiece, sprouted across the Northern states from the Atlantic to the Mississippi in the 1840s.

Many members of the Northampton Association were well-known abolitionists. One of its members was Sojourner Truth. She was living at Northampton when she dictated the classic *The Narrative of Sojourner Truth*. Underground Railroad leader David Ruggles was a member of the Association and George Benson, brother-in-law of abolitionist William Lloyd Garrison, was one of Northampton's founders. Another prominent resident was Dolly Stetson, the president of the Brooklyn Female Anti-Slavery Society during the late 1830s.

Northampton regularly hosted anti-slavery lectures, and was renowned as a center of radical Abolitionism. Among its visitors were Frederick Douglass and Garrison. The town of Florence formed nearby, and became an important stop on the Underground Railroad. Over its four-and-a-half-year life-span, over two hundred people belonged to the community. They supported themselves with a silk farm and milling industry, and were governed by a constitution that detailed their vision of an egalitarian America. However, the Northampton Association disbanded in 1846.

Protective Unions

John Kaulback, a NEAFMOW member, organized America's first consumer cooperative movement, the Protective Unions (PU). Their first buying club began meeting weekly at a "dividing store" in Boston in 1845 to distribute products and produce. Their first purchase was "a box of soap and one-half box of tea"[4] saving members 25 percent by cutting out the middleman. At their height in the Valley, there were PU stores in Brimfield, Ware, Amherst, Cummington (two stores), Chesterfield, Northfield, Gill, Whately, Leydon, Shelburne, Hawley, Montague, and Greenfield. The PUs, like the later Sovereigns of Industry and contemporary co-op associations like VAWC, the NFCA and VCBA, did not see cooperative stores as ends in themselves, but as the beginning of more extensive economic cooperation that would eventually branch into production.

The PU bought wholesale passing on products and produce to members at near cost. Members paid an initiation fee and small monthly dues. Three-fifths of this was to be "invested in fuel and groceries, or such other objects."[5] The PU's program was to bring about "the elevation of the laboring classes" through "cooperation, mercantile and fraternal."[6] Its general fund was to be "devoted to the use of sick members," and PU members formed "visiting committees" to care for them.[7] "Divisions" were locally controlled and autonomous, but federated for wholesale buying and other mutual-aid. Unlike the Rochdale system, they sold at near cost instead of giving rebates, and originally sold only to members. Many PUs set up production and service cooperatives for their members. The Protective Union opened stores in towns throughout the Valley. At their height there were PU divisions throughout New England, New York, Michigan, Illinois, Wisconsin and Canada, with about 6,000 members. A schism developed in the organization in 1853. It broke into two competing organizations, but it was the financial panic of 1857 that destroyed both PUs. The economy plunged and their competitors hit both rival Protective Unions with ferocious economic attacks.

Wounded by price wars, blacklisted by merchants, employers, and suppliers, neither PU was able to meet members' needs, and by 1860 the Central Divisions of both were gone. However, many local groups survived and continued to thrive independently.

National Grange

Oliver Kelly founded the National Grange of the Patrons of Husbandry in 1867 as a secret fraternal order of farmers. A *grange* is a farm homestead. They based their founding statement on "co-operation in all things,"[8] and organized cooperatives to meet the needs of their hard-pressed members. With the Grange, farmer cooperation evolved from informal and local efforts to a widespread and well-organized movement. When the economy faltered in 1872 and fell the next year, membership soared. Grange business agents began organizing cooperative purchasing of farm implements and supplies at wholesale prices or at special reduced rates.

The first Grange in Massachusetts, Guiding Star Grange #1, was organized in June 1873 in Greenfield. Over the following months, seventeen more were organized in the state including, in the Valley region, Northfield, Deerfield, South Deerfield, Pittsfield, Ware, Conway, Barre, Monson, Hadley, Amherst, Cheshire, Palmer, and Brattleboro, Vermont. December, the Massachusetts State Grange was formed at a meeting in Greenfield by representatives from that first group of locals. Four women were the first officers elected, and the following year Joseph P. Felton of Greenfield was elected state master. During the period 1874–76, the Grange opened cooperative stores in the Valley region towns of Greenwich Plains, Colrain, Hatfield, Amherst, Easthampton, Westfield, and Chesterfield. In 1875 they adopted the Rochdale cooperative system (developed in England) of selling to the general community at about market rates and giving members rebates and special discounts, which prevented price wars with other businesses. During the 1870s and early 1880s, over 500 Grange cooperative stores opened in rural areas around the country.

Sovereigns of Industry

The depression that began in 1873 wrought great suffering on industrialized areas. This led Massachusetts Grange organizer, William Earle to conclude that the benefits of cooperatives should be brought to industrial workers. In 1874, he called a meeting in Springfield of sixty like-minded people (including one women and Grange founder Oliver Kelly) from eight states. At this meeting, they founded the Sovereigns of Industry (SI) to serve Northeastern industrial workers, with Earle as president. Like the Grange, it began as a secret society. Its plan was to "unite all people engaged in industrial pursuits," including wage earners and individual producers, into local councils which would set up cooperative stores, to promote "mutual fellowship and cooperative action among the producers and consumers of wealth throughout the earth."[9]

The SI set up a democratic system of local and state councils, with a national council whose main job was to educate about cooperation. Local councils were elected democratically to manage each store. The national council employed John Orvis, formerly a member of the Brook Farm community, as the SI national lecturer. SI's first store was opened in Springfield in 1874, followed by three more in other parts of that city, as well as stores in Westfield, Southbridge, Shelburne, Athol, two stores in Colrain, and another in Brattleboro. The Sovereigns went on to organize 101 councils and 46 stores in their first year, mostly throughout New England.

After only four years, the Sovereigns central organization was brought down by the economic depression of the time. Hard times brought them to life, and harder times killed them. Few working people had cash, so sales volume in most stores plummeted to next to nothing. Some stores tried a credit system, with disastrous results.

Despite the failure of the Sovereigns and the fading of the Grange, many individual cooperative stores survived, and could be found in communities all over the United States throughout the 1880s. In 1886, an observer[10] noted stores started by the Sovereigns of Industry still functioning successfully in Massachusetts in Webster, Worcester, Maynard, Lowell, Beverly, and Kingston; in Connecticut in New Britain and Birmingham (Derby), and in Maine, Lewiston and Dexter.

Independent Co-op Stores

After the Civil War a number of independent cooperative stores opened in the Valley region, including Fitchburg Cooperative Grocery (1864), Gardner Cooperative Association (1868), and Holyoke Cooperative Association (1870). The Gardner store joined the Sovereigns of Industry for a few years, outlived that organization, and was reportedly still very successful in 1913. Mount Tom Cooperative Association was successful in Holyoke between 1875 and '80. Adams Cooperative Association Meat Market started in 1886. The Polish Cooperative Bakery Association opened in Adams in 1916, and thrived for decades, until it was reorganized as joint stock company in 1948. In 1919 Finnish cooperative stores in Gardner and Fitchburg joined with co-op stores in New Ipswich and Milford, New Hampshire, and five other cities to form United Cooperative Society. Their joint operation lasted three years, after which, those four stores reverted to a smaller chain based in Fitchburg.

Cooperative Creameries

In the 1880s dairy farmers organized cooperative creameries in Amherst, Hatfield, Lee, Hinsdale, Cummington, Springfield, Conway, Egremont and Rutland. A contemporary historian[11] described the Springfield Cooperative Creamery, organized in 1882: "There are eighty-three shareholders among the farmers within nine miles of the city... About half the milk and cream is sold and the rest goes into butter. Eggs are also bought and sold... The great reason for starting the creamery was to furnish a steady market to the farmers for their milk."

Shoemaker Cooperatives

The shoe workers' union known as the Knights of St. Crispins opened a cooperative factory in North Adams in 1870. The cooperative grew out of a labor dispute over control of the shop floor. Instead of negotiating, the employer brought in contract laborers—recent Chinese immigrants from San Francisco—to replace the striking workers. According to a contemporary account, "The strike at North Adams... on the introduction of Chinese labor, led to the establishment of a cooperative shoe factory. A report says: 'The men speak with pride of their new feelings of self-reliance and freedom, as well as the quality of their work.'"[12] Thirty of the Crispin shoemakers (a mix of New England Protestants, Irish, and French Canadians) rented a nearby warehouse and opened the North Adams Cooperative Shoe Company, with Isaac Tyler as director. For a while they struggled to stay afloat, members drawing wages only sufficient to pay their basic needs. They got through that hard period, and the factory was still successful in 1875 but it disappears from the historical record the following year.

The Spencer Cooperative Boot and Shoe Co. was founded in 1886 by members of the Knights of Labor. A worker described the Spencer Cooperative Boot and Shoe Company:

> Although only fifteen workmen are employed, the monthly product is about $2,500. The work being on a finer quality of shoes than elsewhere in Spencer...All employees and stockholders must be Knights of Labor...Each workman will receive profits according to his wages...The agents visit the Knights of Labor assemblies and in many cases induce the members to call at the local stores for the shoes with a label of the cooperative company and thus create a market. Where cooperative stores sell boots and shoes, as at the Industrial of New Bedford, Mass., the Knights of Labor Cooperative Shoe Store of Clinton, Mass., and the Cooperative Shoe Store of New Market, N.H., a market for the products of the factories is secured. The agents sell somewhat outside of New England, in New York and adjacent states.[13]

However, they struggled to compete with large factories, complaining, "large concerns are able to furnish a shoe inferior to the K of L shoe for less money and ours are crowded out."[14] In December, 1887, an article in the *Boston Labor Leader* said that the Spencer cooperators "do not expect that their brothers will pay a larger price for their goods, but they do ask that when they make a superior article for the same price it should be bought by all workingmen."[15] They attached a yellow KOL label to their shoes so they could be recognized, and sold them in three cooperative stores in New England towns.

The Knights of Labor opened another cooperative shoe factory in Westborough in 1886. Other Massachusetts cooperative shoe manufacturing companies were opened in Worcester in 1867, Natick (1869), Boston (1871), five in Lynn between 1871 and '72 and another in '86, four in Stoneham (1873, '75, '82, and '83), Truro (1873), two in Marlborough in 1876, Hudson (1884), East Weymouth (1885), and in North Scituate, Danvers, Beverly, and Brockton in 1886. Another cooperative shoe shop was opened in New Haven in 1871.

Cooperative Granite Works

Further upriver in Vermont was the Cooperative Granite Works of South Ryegate, founded in 1885. J.D. Grant, secretary of Granite Works described their origin a year after its founding:

> A number of stonecutters were thrown out of employment in consequence of having organized a branch of the Granite Cutters' National Union here, and not only were they denied employment by the two firms in the granite business here at that time, but were blacklisted... A large proportion of the men were householders and had families living here, and they did not wish to go away for work while there was plenty of it at their own door. And the result was the birth of this little enterprise... But this was only the beginning of tribulation, for... they hatched a scheme to have us all arrested for conspiracy...the case is in the hands of the law today, and not yet settled. Business growing...We started with no cash capital, members putting in

their shares as a rule by labor, a certain rate per month...We believe cooperation is the missing link between capital and labor, and ... the ultimate result will be success.[16]

Cooperative Granite Works originally invested control of the shop floor to one superintendent, but grew unhappy with that arrangement, and later invested that power in a 5-member board.

Other granite cooperatives in the state were opened in Quincy in 1881, and West Quincy in '85. The Springfield and Newburyport Cooperative Mining Company started in 1875.

Other Industrial Worker Cooperatives

A cooperative machine company opened in Greenfield in 1870 and a cooperative hardware factory in the same town in 1880. Further south in Weathersfield, Connecticut, a cooperative hardware manufacturer opened in 1872; in Ansonia an auger bit shop (1885), in Seymour a tailor shop (1886), in Southington, a cooperative cutlery manufacturer (1886).

Other industrial cooperatives in eastern Massachusetts in this period include cooperative newspapers (Boston 1866, Fall River 1870, Haverhill 1884); machine shop (East Boston 1865); shipyard (East Boston 1866); foundries (Boston 1866, Somerset 1867, Lynn 1872, Kingston 1876, Taunton 1877); stove companies (Taunton 1886, Silver Lake 1888); ice company (South Hingham 1872); mill (Tiverton 1874); cotton manufacturing company (Fall River 1874); elastic fabric company (Chelsea 1887); piano manufacturing (Boston 1884); laundry (Boston 1887); glass factory (Sandwich 1888); and tailors (Boston 1888).

Furniture Cooperatives

In the 1870s groups of furniture makers formed cooperative chair companies in East Templeton (1872), nearby Orange (1878) and Athol (1879). After 1865 industrialization transformed furniture making from a highly skilled handicraft to a machine trade. As mechanization became widespread in the industry, the older hand tool skills became obsolete, and less skilled workers were able to learn machine operations in a comparatively brief time. That resulted in lower wages and poor working conditions in furniture factories, as well as increasingly long annual layoffs. In 1877 wages in the industry fell ten to thirty percent and the work season was less than six months per year.

In 1872 a group of chair makers in East Templeton who had lost their jobs when a chair company went bankrupt, formed their own cooperative chair company. It got off to a prosperous start. It survived a major fire in 1880, and had fourteen members in 1886. They also hired a number of non-members as helpers, ten of whom worked in the factory in 1886. Some members contracted with the cooperative for specific operations, and had their own helpers. They were still prosperous in 1887.

The Athol Co-operative Furniture Co. was started in 1879 by a group of unemployed workers. Their first year was hard, and ended with a loss of $2,000. But they persisted, and paid themselves five to ten percent higher than the typical going wage. Surviving a fire in 1882, they were still successfully in business in 1887.

In Orange a group formed a furniture cooperative in 1878, and the following year filed their charter, with $5,000 capital. Ten percent was reserved yearly as a surplus fund, and the rest of the profits went to the workmen in proportion to their pay. The Orange co-op however dissolved after three years, over disputes over differences in pay.

Cigar Cooperatives

Tobacco growing in the river plains around Westfield resulted in a thriving cigar making industry in town. Cigar making was still a skilled handcraft in the 1870s, despite the introduction of moulds and simple machinery. However, many shops used child labor for certain operations, and wages in the industry were very low. Between 1868 and 1875 eight cooperative cigar shops opened in Westfield, and another in nearby Springfield.

The American Cigar Makers' Cooperative, located in Westfield, was the most successful, with an annual business of $125,000 in 1870. In 1872 an internal dispute in the Cigar Manufacturers' Cooperative Association over the introduction of moulds, resulted in a group of workers walking out. Almost all of the Westfield cigar cooperatives failed during the Long Depression that began in 1873, leaving only the American Cooperative still in operation in 1879.

In eastern Massachusetts two more cigar cooperatives opened in Boston in 1880 and 1888, and in another in Plymouth in 1888

Knights of Labor

The Knights of Labor (KOL) opened cooperative boot and shoe factories in Spencer and Westborough in 1886, a cooperative newspaper in Holyoke in 1883, and in Westfield a cooperative factory making hones for tools in 1885. Elsewhere in Massachusetts they opened a cooperative hat company (Haverhill 1884), an elastic fabric company (Chelsea 1887), a cooperative printing and publishing house (Boston 1886), and four shoe factories (East Weymouth, Lynn, Brockton 1885, and Beverly 1886). In Connecticut they opened a hat company (South Norwalk 1884) and a cutlery company (Southington 1886).

The Knights were the largest worker organization in the world in the 1880s, with upwards of a million members, and they led the most extensive worker cooperative movement ever organized in the United States, with a network of approximately 200 industrial cooperatives and numerous cooperative stores at its peak in 1886–88, with the goal of transforming the economic system into what they called a Cooperative Commonwealth. The destruction of the Knights and their cooperative network was triggered by their involvement in the 1886 May Day national strike for the 8-hour day. The rise and fall of the KOL is one of the great sagas in the history of the American working people.[17]

Great Depression Cooperatives

Numerous farm cooperatives continued in the Valley region in the 20th century, but the historical record is very sparse as to worker cooperatives and cooperative stores. During the Great Depression a few cooperative bakeries were reported in Massachusetts, and two cooperative knitting mills. The mills were part of one of the more interesting episodes in the New Deal. The mill owners had shut them down because of the depression, but the government rented them, helped organize laid-off workers into Self-help cooperatives, and got them running again. The first co-op mill was opened in Millville, south of Worcester, and employed over 100 workers manufacturing wearing apparel. Under the Federal Emergency Relief Agency (FERA), between 1933-'35 aid was given to many similar cooperative "production-for-use" experiments of unemployed workers taking over idle factories and producing goods, which however could not be sold on the market, but only bartered with other cooperatives or sold to the government. The two Massachusetts knitting mills appear to have been short-lived, as the business community bombarded FERA with complaints that government-assisted cooperatives created "unfair competition"[18] to private business. Production-for-use projects were discontinued after only two years "to preserve the logic of the market,"[19] and in 1935 FERA was dismantled, replaced by the Works Progress Administration (WPA) which hired the unemployed for public service projects.

Counterculture

The Valley region participated in the great wave of collective, communal and cooperative "counter-cultural" projects of the late 1960s and early '70s. Numerous communes and intentional communities thrived in that era in Western Massachusetts and southern Vermont. Oral histories of many elders still with us today hold the keys to understanding that era, and need to be recorded. One of the largest and most successful was the

Brotherhood of the Spirit, started in Leyden, and relocated to Heath, Charlemont, Warwick, Turners Falls, and Gill, and Guilford, Vermont. Others include Montague Farm and its sister commune Total Loss Farm in Guilford; Hip Brook Commune in Amherst; Sunrise Hill in Conway; Cummington Community; Leyden Society; Earthworks and Earth, Wind and Fire in Franklin; Mullein Hill in West Glover; Mt. Philo in Ferrisberg; Free Farm and Free Vermont in Putney; Free State of the Ark in Stowe; Mayday Farm in Guilford; Milkweed Hill; Redbird; Maple Hill; Rockbottom Farm in South Stratford; and Mad Brook Farm in East Charleston. Most of these lasted only a few years and were gone by the mid 1970s.

Into the 21st Century

Beyond farm co-ops, the late twentieth century was a low point in the history of cooperatives throughout America. But the economic and social conditions of the new century have resulted in a renewed wave of worker cooperatives in many areas. The Valley region is one of the most vital and dynamic areas in the country witnessing the rebirth of the socially transforming movement of worker cooperatives today.

History of Co-operatives Notes

[1] Co-operation in Algonquin society took a different form than co-operative enterprise described in this book, however, it shares principles of organization that we recognize as distinctly co-operative.

[2] Parker, F.E. 1956. *The First 125 Years: A History of Distributive and Service Cooperation in the United States, 1829-1954.* Superior: Cooperative League, Chicago, p. 3.

[3] The "Associationist" movement refers to what we might call the "cooperative" movement today.

[4] Parker, F.E. 1956. *The First 125 Years: A History of Distributive and Service Cooperation in the United States, 1829-1954.* Superior: Cooperative League, Chicago. p. 4.

[5] Knapp, J. 1973. *The Rise of American Cooperative Enterprise 1620-1920.* Danville: Interstate. p. 22.

[6] Parker, F.E. 1956. *The First 125 Years: A History of Distributive and Service Cooperation in the United States, 1829-1954.* Superior: Cooperative League, Chicago. p. 4.

[7] Knapp, J. 1973. *The Rise of American Cooperative Enterprise 1620-1920.* Danville: Interstate. p. 21.

[8] Parker, F.E. 1956. *The First 125 Years: A History of Distributive and Service Cooperation in the United States, 1829-1954.* Superior: Cooperative League, Chicago, p. 10.

[9] Commons, John R., et al. *History of Labour in the United States*, New York: Macmillan, 1918. Vol. I: 39.

[10] Bremis, E.W. 1888. "Cooperation in New England" in Adams, Herbert Baxter. *History of Cooperation in the United States*. Baltimore: John Hopkins Press. p. 53-69.

[11] Ibid. 84.

[12] Newton, R.H. 1887. *Social Studies*. New York: G. P. Putnam's Sons. p. 95.

[13] Bremis, E.W. 1888. "Cooperation in New England" in Adams, Herbert Baxter. *History of Cooperation in the United States*. Baltimore: John Hopkins Press. p. 89.

[14] Horner, C. 1978. "Producers' Co-operatives in the United States, 1865-1980." PhD Dissertation, University of Pittsburg. pp 12-128.

[15] Ibid., 160.

[16] Bremis, E.W. 1888. "Cooperation in New England" in Adams, Herbert Baxter. *History of Cooperation in the United States*. Baltimore: John Hopkins Press. pp. 81-82

[17] For more about the Knights of Labor, see my book, *For All The People*. Oakland: PM Press, 2009, 2nd ed. 2012, pp. 86-109.

[18] Rose, N.E. 1989. "Work Relief in the 1930s and the origins of the Social Security Act." *The Social Service Review*, Vol. 63, No.1. pp. 79-80.

[19] Ibid., pp. 75-84.